A
'rooper
n the
' Tins '

SERGEANTS OF ' D ' SQUADRON, 1ST LIFE GUARDS. VERCHOCQ, CHRISTMAS DAY, 1915
Back (left to right): Lloyd, Ted Pettit, Charlie Wright. *Front*: Geo. Boylan, Fender Wright, Bob Harrison, Geo. Hindy, Fred Lidster, Jim Fleming

A Trooper in the 'Tins'

Autobiography of a Lifeguardsman

by

R. A. Lloyd

Introduction by
Major the Hon. J. J. Astor, M.P.

The Naval & Military Press Ltd

in association with

The Imperial War Museum
Department of Printed Books

Published jointly by

The Naval & Military Press Ltd

Unit 10 Ridgewood Industrial Park,
Uckfield, East Sussex,
TN22 5QE England
Tel: +44 (0) 1825 749494
Fax: +44 (0) 1825 765701
www.naval-military-press.com
www.military-genealogy.com
www.militarymaproom.com

and

The Imperial War Museum, London

Department of Printed Books
www.iwm.org.uk

Printed and bound in Great Britain by
CPI Antony Rowe, Chippenham and Eastbourne

*In reprinting in facsimile from the original, any imperfections are inevitably reproduced
and the quality may fall short of modern type and cartographic standards.*

Introduction

by Major the Hon. J. J. Astor, M.P.
(late 1st Life Guards)

IN 1911 the author, who was then eighteen, enlisted in the 1st Life Guards. It had been intended that he should go from his Southern Irish school to college and eventually become a schoolmaster. Fourteen years later this early ambition was realized. In the meantime, however, he 'saw life' in such fullness as barracks, camps, and more than three years of war service presented it.

He has a sound judgment of men, a sense of fun, and a sharp, descriptive pen. Consequently this book is eminently readable. Such as may still be anxious to know what those who first went to fight it felt about the war will gain a notion from these pages truer than from many a more pretentious work.

Commissions in the war years were rarely indeed given to the regular Lifeguardsman, and Mr. Lloyd remained a Corporal of Horse. His point of view is, therefore, that of the men under whose strict, though kindly, hands the recruit was transfigured into the fully trained and efficient soldier of Mons. A smart, keen non-commissioned officer and a marksman too, he adhered to the code of good discipline as it had been committed to him. Knightsbridge and Windsor, for all the spit and polish, were no mean schools.

It is pleasant for one of his regiment who shared so many of his admirations to read his recurring appreciations of his comrades. He appraises frankly, though always with generous allowances; and he is unstinting in his tributes to such as lived and fought up to his own ideals. Even of the best of those who fell his book is no unworthy memorial.

Class-consciousness keeps seeking in its own grubbing way to discover conflicts of caste within the British Army. It obtains as little confirmation here as in any other faithful record. To Mr. Lloyd ' the good times spent in company with great fellows of all ranks who were my comrades' make up for all the stress and the several disappointments he endured.

Above all else he was a cavalryman. Herbert, tallest horse of the unit, a most engaging equine ' character,' keeps close to him through nearly all his story of the war. An incorrigible love of forage-dumps combined with a genius for breaking head-ropes was a lasting source of worry. A full ammunition-box added as make-weight to a picketing-peg proved no deterrent. Herbert would merely drag his anchor. And yet of a cold night or a hungry dawn the horse came always first in his master's thoughts.

The day may not be distant when some trumpeter will sound the last dismount. Thereafter the fighting man will rely only upon the instruments which men have fashioned—and so farewell to much of chivalry. Thus will the one-time trooper, in exchange for the mechanization we call progress, surrender the relationship of man to horse which through a millennium of wars has continued to evoke in him a deep, instinctive quality.

It is a platitude that in modern warfare the ordinary soldier knows little of the game afoot. Mr. Lloyd was conscious of its truth; but his reader may well be surprised at the number of things he saw and understood and at the keenness of the judgments he founded on them. When the motor-ambulances tore back with the victims of the first gas attack he was there to see them and their loads. He had even some acquaintance with the horse responsible for King George's accident. It was apparently given to doing ' unexpected and original things,' especially under another rider than its own. Thus has a mosaic of incidents trivial and weighty, sparkling and sombre, been patterned into one man's picture of the war.

It is nearly twenty years since at Battersea, on his way to be X-rayed, the author beheld the ' great commotion ' with which London received the news of the Armistice, and felt himself ' quite stunned ' by it. The sons of those who fought beside him may well themselves by this be in the ranks. A generation which has not been bored by too many reminiscences of garrulous survivors, or by maternal descriptions of its sires' prowess, may indeed one day discover for itself that the war provides the greatest epic in our history. If it does, and in its researches lights upon this book, it will find there living men, with the foibles, weaknesses, and strengths of their kind. They are not all above the ruses of the old soldier. They ' scrounge,' if need presses, upon the quartermaster, or even show the inspecting subaltern the same box of bombs a few times over. They dwell upon the memory of meals, as men who are really hungry will. And yet, year after year, they stand by each other and fight as well as they know how, often indeed with greater grit than hope or inspiration.

These, then, are pages which all may read with interest and enlightenment; but to those who knew the 1st Life Guards in the war they will bring back a flood of memories of men and events surely well worth preserving in a lasting form.

1 *March* 1938.

Contents

A TROOPER IN THE 'TINS'

I

I HAD always wanted to become a soldier, and a cavalry-man at that. I was not the only boy in my old school in the South of Ireland who cherished this ambition. There were four of us in my Form. Two were destined by their fathers for the church, but side-stepped destiny by enlisting in the cavalry. The third served with distinction in the ranks of the Irish Guards. All three were killed in the war.

During the Christmas holidays, 1910–11, I, having reached the age of eighteen years, decided not to go up to college and on to schoolmastering. Accordingly, on 21 February 1911, I presented myself at the Depot of the Royal Irish Regiment in Kilkenny, enlisted in the 1st Life Guards, and that same afternoon was despatched to London to join my regiment at Regent's Park Barracks.

In the year 1911 would-be Lifeguardsmen were not transported in luxury to the headquarters of their Regiments. For the sake of economy the authorities shipped all recruits from the South of Ireland on cattle-boats plying between Waterford or Cork and Milford.

After lunch with my uncle I took train to Waterford. Being a small town, I had little difficulty in locating the quay at which my boat was moored. I felt a distinct thrill at the idea of putting out into the unknown and leaving schools behind for ever. Some time in the after-noon we weighed anchor and proceeded to crawl down the River Suir and out into the St. George's Channel. Dark-ness set in early ; there was a howling gale coming up out of the West, and the sea looked decidedly ugly. Whatever hopes I may have entertained of being a good soldier, I was destined to find out within an hour that I was a miserably poor sailor. I would not have believed that one could possibly be so horribly sick as I was throughout the whole voyage. The old boat seemed to do everything except stand up on one end and spin round like a top. Every five minutes I wished her at the bottom of the sea.

The crossing lasted nine hours. There was just one other passenger, a Welsh miner of Irish parentage, who had been over to Waterford for his father's funeral. No doubt they had given the old man a royal wake and send-off. The miner was more than drunk; he was on the verge of delirium tremens. I can still see his round, crimson face and bloodshot bulging eyes, the whole surmounted by a battered bowler hat worn at a rakish angle. He was not sea-sick, but he seemed quite incapable of staying put, as the Americans say, for more than a minute or two. He kept darting round corners and up and down companion-ways, looking like a frightened animal. Every time I met him he screamed: " Good Christ a'mighty ! " and bolted off somewhere else.

On landing at Milford I saw no more of my fellow-traveller, and I was so thoroughly down and out that my only wish was to find a corner in the train to Paddington and try to get some sleep. My next recollection is of strolling out of the terminus in London at about 6 a.m. on the morning of February 22nd, and asking a policeman to direct me to Regent's Park Barracks.

Of my walk from Paddington to Albany Street that morning not a single detail remains in my memory. I just got there. A pretty sight I must have looked. I had had a foul journey, and since midday the previous day not a bite had I eaten. The Corporal of the Guard, Joe Rose, received me in the approved manner, then called an orderly and said : " Take this youngster across to the canteen and get him some grub. Then take him to see the Doctor."

The canteen was warm and inviting. A big fire blazed at one end. All the woodwork, tables, and forms were scrubbed white. A counter ran across the room, and behind it, amid beer-barrels and mountains of cut bread and cheese, stood a burly man in shirt-sleeves. He was red-faced, red-moustached, possessed a powerful voice, and had a merry twinkle in his eye. He greeted me with a roar, and in less than no time had me sitting at a table near the fire tucking into a couple of pork-chops and a steaming hot mug of cocoa. He talked as I ate and drank, and it soon came to light that we were almost next-door neighbours. His parents used to live quite close to my people at home. They had, I remembered, a magnificent fruit-garden, the freedom of which Mrs. Lahee, his mother, had conferred on me when I was small. The garden was particularly well-found in gooseberries, and many a time I had eaten my fill there. I had, too, a faint recollection of having seen Lahee home on furlough in 1902, after the Boer War.

This reunion with a neighbour in a strange land, combined with the stimulating effects of food, soon banished all weariness and strangeness from me. This was but the beginning of many pleasant moments spent in Lahee's company. He seemed always to be ready to claim me as a friend, and many a time I have heard him roar to a group of old soldiers, who always occupied the best seats round the fire, and between whom and a rookie like me there was a great gulf fixed : " This is a townie of mine. He used to know my old mother and dad."

The orderly duly made his appearance and conducted me to the Hospital on the other side of the Square, for examination by the Medical Officer, Surgeon-Lieutenant Hayes. I entered a sort of waiting-room and sat down. With his back to me, and looking through a window on the far side of the room, stood a soldier, one Harry Tapsell. His trousers had been allowed to fall down about his ankles, whilst his shirt was gathered up so that he was bare to the waist. It was not long before I noticed a very promising specimen of a boil on his seat. Suddenly through the open door came on slippered feet the Hospital Corporal, Bill Lethbridge, carrying a boiling fomentation in an enamel bowl. He advanced noiselessly and swiftly on the unsuspecting Harry and banged the fomentation on the boil. Harry gave a yell and nearly jumped through the window, but Lethbridge, evidently practised in this form of acrobatic

treatment of boils, simply held on, and proceeded calmly to
bandage his victim.

He then turned to me. " Get stripped, lad. Where d'ye
come from ? Waterford ? My missus comes from Waterford. Know any people there named Doody ? Doctor'll
see you at once." Then he vanished noiselessly as he had
come, and left me to undress. There was no room for doubt,
in this department no time was wasted on ceremony, and
the boil episode made a lasting impression on my young
mind.

I was summoned immediately, and paraded my nakedness
before the M.O. The examination was more searching
than the previous one at Kilkenny, but I came through it
without any trouble, and was then sped away back to the
guardroom. A little while later the Commanding Officer
saw me, and I was finally approved and posted to ' D '
Squadron as Trooper No. 2829.

One more visit was undertaken—to the Quartermaster's
Store. Here I did business with Wally Webber, the
Regimental Storeman. Wally was a benevolent colossus
of some twenty stone. He supplied me with ' personal
clothing and necessaries ' more than I could keep count
of. With a dexterity born of long practice he stamped all
articles, whether of cloth, leather, wood, or metal, with my
number, and flung them into a blanket for me to carry away.
When it came to fitting me with a cap he drew a complete
blank. None of those in store was large enough. " Blimey,
young 'un," he said, " ain't you got a ruddy great 'ead !
'Ere," taking off his own cap and handing it to me, " try
this one." It was a perfect fit, and Wally kindly lent it to
me till a new one could be procured. From there I was
piloted back to ' D ' Squadron, and as the troops were all
out at Richmond Park or somewhere, I was handed over
to Bob Harrison.

Bob was a Troop Sergeant then. A Yorkshireman with
some eighteen years' service, a slightly deformed shoulder
(the result of a Boer bullet), and a genial reassuring manner.
I was afterwards to learn from years of contact with him
that he was one of the best, if not the very best fellow in the
regiment. " Good ! " he said, looking at me with one eye

half shut. " Just the chap I'm looking for. Put your kit in the store-room for the time being and come and give me a hand. I have sixteen sacks of chaff to cut, and there isn't a blighter in the Squadron to do it except you and me." So saying, he picked up a heap of sixteen large empty sacks, and strolled away to a sort of barn alongside the forge. I followed. Inside was a huge store of hay and straw and in the middle of the floor stood the chaff-cutting machine. I had never seen one before, but I was destined to become well acquainted with this monstrosity as time went on.

It consisted of a large wheel, to which were attached two knives forming a diameter to the circle of the wheel. Hay and straw mixed were passed through a wooden trough up to the knives and were cut off short by them as the wheel revolved.

" You'd better turn first," said Bob, " while I feed. Then when you see how the feeding's done, I'll change places with you." I got on the handle and turned. Of all the back-breaking jobs in the world, the worst is chaff-cutting. It soon reduced me to a rag. Nine hours on the Irish Sea in February, followed by a night in a third-class railway carriage, is not the best training for such a task. However, I realised I had run up against a man in old Bob, and I was determined to appear a man in his eyes, so I went on turning till I was ready to drop. Then he relieved me and we finished in good time. From that day forward I had three staunch friends, all of whom treated me as an equal, though each was old enough to be my father—Bob Harrison, Bill Lahee, and Wally Webber.

The troops came back to Barracks about one o'clock. I watched them from ' D ' Squadron veranda. They rode in, mud-splashed, at a brisk walking pace. The horses particularly appealed to me.

The men, too, looked fine and fit in their blue jackets, riding-breeches with double red stripes, white cross-belts, Hessian boots and spurs. Soon there was a rush for the water-troughs below me, and in less than five minutes all were tied up and feeding in the stables. The Squadron Sergeant-Major, Tam Wilson, gave me a passing glance and grunted : " No. 2 Troop." I was at once given a bed in the barrack-room of the said troop; I dumped my kit thereon, and joined in the rush to dinner.

If all one reads in the Press of to-day is true, then army cookery has made giant strides towards perfection. I sincerely hope it has. It needed to. In 1911, and indeed during all my time as a soldier, it could not very well have been worse. The kitchens seemed to be all one could desire; the food as drawn from supplies was first-rate, but when it was served up in the dining-room it was generally a filthy, unappetising atrocity. Everybody grumbled every day. No steps were ever taken to mend matters. The Orderly Officer came regularly with the Orderly Sergeant-Major into the dining-room, and inquired if everything was all right. Invariably the reply to his query was, " All right, sir." After a time, when I grew less timid, I asked why this daily fib was told, and I was informed that somewhere back in 1904 or '05 one Bill Dithers had dared to answer the O.O.'s question in the negative. Subsequent investigation had proved him a liar; he was placed under arrest, and awarded fourteen days C.B. Be that as it may, I never knew of a proper complaint being lodged from the Troopers' Mess.

The regimental authorities were, of course, responsible for this miserable state of affairs. It was, however, directly due to the incompetence of the kitchen staff. The cook-house was regarded as a sort of convalescent home. If a man had been in hospital for some time, and then returned to light duty, he scarcely ever failed to become a cook. His practical knowledge did not in the least matter, neither did the nature of his illness. There was no room in the Squadron for crocks, so into the kitchen they went. Some of these fellows actually looked every bit as unwholesome as the food they turned out.

Dinner finished, the trumpet sounded ' Stables.' I had been handed over for instruction and initiation to Joe Sykes, a soldier of some five years' service and belonging to my Troop. Joe gave me some ancient trousers to work in; handed me a bag containing an assortment of brushes and mysteries, and down we went to the stable. Here he introduced me to D. 15, his own horse, known as Jimmy, and instructed me in the ritual of picking out and washing his feet.

Jimmy was a dear little chap, slightly on the small side for a Household Cavalry horse, and as black as coal. He was as gentle as a lamb in the stable, but something of a handful outside it. In 1910, Jimmy actually jumped out over the riding-school door at Windsor. It was on one of the Riding-Master's bad days, when he would dismount the ride and then chase the horses over a string of jumps, while he yelled at them and cracked his long whip. Jimmy resented this treatment, and when the opportunity came just jumped out. The door is nearly six feet high, but that is not the amazing thing about this jump. There is an arch above the door, leaving an open space of not more than four feet. Through this opening he jumped without touching a hair, landed squarely on the cobblestones outside, and walked calmly to the trough for a drink. Though a gentler animal never existed, the sight of anything jumpable set him dancing with excitement.

My 'regimental father' had two horses and two sets of saddlery to clean that afternoon, so he gave me two sweaty girths to scrub and pipeclay. This done, I'm afraid my usefulness came to an end. I just finished grooming his horse, whilst he did the rest. I was amazed at his speed, as well as at his vocabulary, which was picturesque without being voluble. He was a man of few words.

At last all was in order and passed by the Troop Sergeant. Then up we went and found heaps to do in the room. On Joe's bed reposed a rusted sword thickly coated with sweat, splashed boots and spurs, ditto rifle. He looked at me rather hopelessly and said : " What can you do ? " I asked for the rifle. I knew something about cleaning one. As he watched me doing it he said : " Look here, young 'un, you'd better be careful. You've soldiered before, and that's a thing you'd better keep dark." I smiled and assured him I had not, but I could see he did not believe me.

I liked Joe Sykes. I hope I did him credit. He was a good soldier and he did his best to make me one. He now gave me some idea of my duties next day, sorted out my kit, and showed me how to make my bed. By that time the

B

other members of the Troop came trickling upstairs in ones and twos. They were a friendly lot, and came from many parts of the world. They included Joe Sykes of London, Daddy Long of Tetbury, Will Franklin of Slough, Harry Huntly of Erith, Freddy Baxter of Cambridge, Jane Jordan of Jersey, Gus Russell of Horsham, Jock Douglas of Kirkaldy, Ted Castle of Walthamstow, Hans Blitzer of Königsberg, Bill Leggett of Sydney, N.S.W., Charlie Marsh of Newmarket, Stevens of Swindon, Woodward of Coventry, and Corporal Jesse Randall of Goodness knows where.

Tea, consisting of bread and tea, was at 4.30 p.m. Many did not bother to go for it. Evening stables sounded at 5.30 p.m. We all paraded by the squadron water-trough while orders and duties for next day were read. Then followed the job of making the horses comfortable for the night. Only horses were dealt with at evening stables. They were watered, groomed and wisped for half an hour, then bedded down, fed, and left for the night in charge of the stable guard.

All trained soldiers not actually on duty were now free to leave barracks and go where they pleased till reveille next morning. They were granted a permanent pass entitling them to wear plain clothes when going out. The Provost-Sergeant and Sergeant of the Guard scrutinized carefully all who left barracks. They sent back all who were not considered sufficiently smartly dressed. Hard hats, walking-sticks, and gloves were *de rigueur*. Only very rarely did one see anybody go out in uniform. These privileges were not abused. The men kept just as good hours as the average civilian.

My first evening in the barrack-room was much like hundreds which followed. Most of the men were for some duty or other next day. The room rang with the jingle of burnishers. Frank Rogers struck up a song. His favourite opening number was " I used to sigh for a silvery moon." The others joined in, and all the time the work went on. I myself gradually plucked up courage to put in a note here and there, while burnishing Joe Sykes' sword, and from 7 to 9 p.m. chorus after chorus set the stones of the old Barracks ringing. In the stables below us the horses kicked at their heel-posts or banged on the metal mangers with their logs.

I think these evening hours were a source of delight to us all. They certainly form one of my happiest memories, and I never see Regent's Park Barracks without thinking of them and living them all over again.

Ten o'clock saw us in bed and the room in darkness. The restless horses beneath us gradually became silent. At least one young soldier needed no rocking that night.

II

THE days which followed were full to overflowing.
During his first six months no recruit had a minute
to call his own between daylight and dusk. So
next morning I was hurled neck and crop into this non-
stop existence.

Down we went to stables at 6 a.m. Here I was let into
the mysteries of 'mucking out.' No implements were
used in this process other than a broom and our hands.
The bedding and all it contained were clasped firmly in
large armfuls against the soldier's bosom and carried out
into the open, where experts, that is to say old soldiers,
spread it out to dry, and sorted the still serviceable from
the unserviceable. The latter was piled up like a young
Matterhorn on a wheelbarrow; the old soldiers all seemed
at the same moment to recollect that they had a pressing
engagement elsewhere, and vanished to leave the youngest
recruit to trundle the mountain over the cobblestones to
the distant dunghill. Horses were then watered and fed;
breakfast followed.

At eight o'clock some half-dozen of us, backward
recruits, as we were officially termed, paraded for set-up
drill. We were simply dressed, in blue jacket and slacks,
highlows, and white pipe-clayed gloves. The process
which followed during the next hour we called 'getting
our backs off.' Heavens, how we moved! Up and down
and across on the gravel at a nominal 120 paces to the
minute, which must at times have reached the 160 mark.
By way of variation this movement occasionally gave place
to those excruciating tortures, the balance step and the slow
march. Our drill was, however, for the most part done in
quick time.

I can still see the squad, stiff-necked and awkward,
striding along like mad geese, and swinging arms shoulder

high front and rear. We enjoyed this work after the first morning or so, chiefly, I think, owing to the liking we formed for our Drill-Corporal, Bill Butson. A better man with recruits would have been hard to find. He worked us to the last gasp, but always treated us like men. He never lost his temper nor tried sarcasm at our expense.

Recruits did not go to the riding-school to learn to ride straight away. About a month elapsed before we darkened the doors of that dread establishment.

After drill on the square we spent an hour in the gymnasium. Here we came under the influence of a rare good fellow, Sergeant-Major Charlie Dawes. A splendid gymnast and instructor, he got right down to our level and made the work a pleasure. He stood out in personality and character miles above the average blustering, ignorant N.C.O., and was, as I have since discovered, years ahead of his time in his methods of dealing with recruits. If our pace on the barrack square was fast, here it was like greased lightning, but our interest was kept alive, and we would not have missed this hour for anything in the world.

The gymnastic period over, there was a short break of about twenty minutes. This had to be made sufficient time for every man in the regiment to rush to the canteen and swallow a pint of beer and a chunk of bread and cheese. To attain this end men worked in pairs. One formed up in the beer queue, the other in the bread-and-cheese line. The canteen staff of four old soldiers went at top speed, and everybody was served in time, in fact many of the ancients managed to wangle a second pint before the trumpet recalled us to work. We recruits were solemnly advised by Bill Butson to have beer for lunch. He held the view that beer contained nutritive qualities which would help to sustain us in our strenuous activities, especially as he realized how badly we fared in the dining-room. I am convinced he was perfectly right.

We now took rifles and bandoliers and betook ourselves to Sergeant-Major Algy Riches for Musketry Instruction. This item did not come within the usual recruits' syllabus. but we were due for our annual course on the ranges in April, so we were given a month's preliminary training, mostly in theory. Algy was another Charlie Dawes. He explained to us the mysteries of the rifle, gave us the run of his miniature range, and behaved all the time like an older boy at school showing his younger schoolmates how to play cricket or rugger. He was a crack shot, and his patience and quiet good humour in dealing with young scallywags were a marvel. We learned all there was to know in Algy's department with keenness. I believe he derived as much pleasure from teaching us as we did from following his instruction.

When Musketry was over for the morning, my filial duties claimed me, so I helped, or perhaps hindered, my regimental father in stables till dinner-time.

At 2 p.m. came the big stunt of the day, inspection of all recruits by the Adjutant, prior to our second daily dose of set-up drill. First came parade by squadrons. Then we were marched on to the square and formed up in our respective squads. First-class recruits wore overalls, boots and spurs, and carried rifles and swords. The second squad was similarly attired and carried rifle or sword, whilst the backward squad wore the same dress as in the morning, was all on pins and needles, and terribly conscious of its pipe-clayed gloves.

Here we were delivered to the three great powers of the parade-ground, the Adjutant, the R.S.M., and the Drill-Sergeant. The Adjutant looked us over from top to toe and missed nothing. This particular one was typical of everything that is best in a British Officer. Even we young-sters felt that he was genuinely interested in us and not merely looking for occasion to find fault. I never knew an officer who stood higher in the opinion of the rank and file, and he deserved their esteem. Close behind him came the R.S.M.

Last of all, but far from least from our personal point of view, came the Drill-Sergeant, Tom Phillips. Here was a man who in his personality combined all that was best in the old type of Drill-Sergeant with a rare intelligence and knowledge of the recruits' physical and mental make-up. He was a man of considerable education and culture. His words of command were like thunder-claps. His glance was fierce; his eye pierced everybody at once, and his temper was something to inspire fear in a rookie's heart. To us he became a god, but a god of thunder and lightning. He had no favourites, regarded all recruits as his own personal property, just as if he had purchased us in the slave-market, and worked us accordingly. He never spared himself in the process. We soon became aware of the man beneath the outer coating of Drill-Sergeant when we saw him treat our beloved Bill Butson as a brother. The Commanding Officer, the Adjutant, and the R.S.M. were all mighty powers, but the most potent force in our young lives for the next six months or so was Tom Phillips.

In a state bordering on exhaustion we returned to our rooms when drill was finished. The temptation to throw oneself on one's bed was irresistible, but it had to be put aside, as in about ten minutes' time the trumpet sounded 'School.' All recruits, and trained soldiers not in possession of a third-class educational certificate, were now mustered and marched to the Garrison School. Here the presiding authority was the Army Schoolmaster. He was a genial soul, a good schoolmaster, though much given to spinning yarns. A private door in the rear of the school led into Albany Street and almost into the 'Crown and Anchor.' He was assisted by Jimmy Stoole, a Belfast man, and between them they ran quite a pleasant and instructive institution.

School was followed by tea, tea by stables, stables by preparation for the morrow, and then came bed.

Day succeeded day with similar routine for the next two months. There was no monotony. There were, of course, good days, and bad days when everything seemed to go wrong. The great redeeming feature of our life lay in the fact that we made progress. The backward stage on the square was left behind for the second stage, still under Bill Butson. Algy Riches had taken us down to Rainham a few times to shoot on an open range. Glorious outings! Charlie Dawes put us over more and more difficult apparatus, and was going to give us lessons in fencing. I had taken my second-class certificate at School; and, most thrilling event of all, I had actually started to ride. This period was in fact one of the most enjoyable of my life, and I shall always feel indebted to the men who made it so. I had been particularly fortunate in joining at a time when the N.C.O.s of the training personnel were the very cream of the regiment.

The duty N.C.O.s, that is to say those not on the Training Staff, were, with very few exceptions, a poorish set. If one could believe all one heard the trained soldiers say about them in the barrack-room of an evening, then they must have been a tough crowd of unprincipled bounders. However, I was to learn as time went on that the old soldiers' picture was, as usual, painted in too vivid colours. The great curse of the average N.C.O. was an abysmal ignorance. Some were aware of this themselves; others were not. The former were not past praying for, but the second category contained some bright specimens.

If a man happened to acquire a bad reputation in any respect early in his career he never lived it down. He was considered fair game, and hounded to the verge of despair by third-rate N.C.O.s in their endeavours to show themselves keen and efficient. No wonder Joe Sykes kept drumming into me the importance of earning a good name as a recruit. Thanks largely to his fatherly care, which often took expression in no mild terms, I managed to steer clear of anything in the nature of trouble.

All recruits were sent every Sunday morning to the Sergeants' Mess on fatigue. They could not attend Church Parade till they had been supplied with walking-out uniform, and this did not arrive as a rule for a few weeks. So on fatigue I went, Sunday after Sunday, with the rest. The work consisted in cleaning windows, and after that peeling thousands of potatoes. The window-cleaning was pretty soul-killing, but potato-peeling I detested still more. I consoled myself with the thought that as soon as I had received my uniform, I should say good-bye to this delectable quarter on Sunday mornings, and march to Church after the band. I was sadly mistaken. My uniform duly arrived. Four or five of us had it fitted and passed the same day. Next Sunday, and for some subsequent Sundays, the others went to Church while I continued the hated fatigues. I lodged a strong protest with my regimental father, who, being a just parent, took my complaint to the correct quarter. He was gruffly informed that as a ruddy Irishman I must also be a ruddy Catholic, and therefore outside the pale when it came to a question of Church Parade. This weighty argument almost proved too much for Joe Sykes. No Englishman will stand out against such logic rooted in tradition, and Joe was an Englishman. I managed, however, to persuade the authorities, much against their will, that I was, after all, a ruddy Protestant. So the Sunday fatigues ceased and to Church I went ever after.

These Sunday morning labours were not without an occasional bit of fun. The Regent's Canal runs some twenty yards behind the Mess kitchen. Often on a fine Sunday forenoon I have seen a respectable citizen of Camden Town, bent on a couple of hours' quiet fishing, arrive and take up a position on the towing-path with his back to our windows. He would have no end of gear, rod, landing-net, bait-can, and pockets full of odds and ends. Your fisherman sets about his task with no indecent haste. Many minutes would elapse before he was at last comfortably seated and watching his float as it lay lazily on the placid surface of the water. Meanwhile, all unknown to the poor fellow, we had been awaiting this moment at the windows. Suddenly from out the blue would come a salvo of missiles and the fisherman found himself and his gear the centre of a tornado of flying potatoes. The more stout-hearted ones would curse and rave and start all over again, only to bring on a worse bombardment than before. The more timid or more sensible moved out of range at once.

The problem of learning to ride was the one which gave me, and I believe my fellow-recruits as well, most trouble and least satisfaction. To be quite candid, our six months' riding course fell far short of attaining its object and did not turn us out anything like confident horsemen. I am convinced now that the methods employed to that end were all wrong. From the moment we first entered the riding-school and the massive doors slammed behind us, the roughriders, with the very best of intentions, and following the regulations in vogue at the time, used every device they knew to transform us from lithe, supple lads into stiff, wooden dummies. Right from the beginning nothing seemed to matter except style. Every moment of every lesson it was: 'Hollow your backs! Elbows down and back and close to the sides! Thumbs pointing towards each other! Hands down! Legs back behind the girth! Stirrup-iron beneath the ball of the foot! Heels down! Sit down in the saddle!' There could be but one result. We began as statues, and I am afraid we finished up much as we began.

Now in my humble opinion the cultivation and attainment of good style is the last phase in any process of learning. Certainly it is not the first. Proficiency in essentials should be the first objective, and style then grafted on to proficiency if and when the latter is acquired. Riding is largely a matter of balance and the attuning of the rider's body to the movements of the horse. It is a question of complete harmony of rhythm between mount and rider. A stiff rider cannot lend his body to rhythm. Mastery of balance and rhythm can only be successfully achieved through absolute freedom of movement from the start. It can be done by any young man, through daily practice in the saddle over varied country and at varying pace. In a word, the cavalry recruit should spend most of his day in the saddle in the open country, and not a miserable hour daily doing straight-backed stunts in a riding-school some 30 by 20 yards in size. I think I am not far wrong when I assert that riding-schools were originally intended for the schooling of horses in finer points of training, which the French call *haute école*. Their use in training young soldiers in the art of riding is an afterthought, and largely a waste of time.

Round and round we went therefore, day after day, at a walk, at a trot, at a canter; with saddles, on blankets, bare-backed. Training in the use of arms followed—rifles, swords, lances. Then came jumps of various makes, shapes, and degrees of stiffness. At one time we would have five jumps in the confined space of the school, wattles and brushwood in the corners, and in the middle a double contraption consisting of gate and brushwood. Over we flew, very often in our progress sitting on every part of the horse from ears to tail, and now and then actually parting company with that patient creature.

The spring was advancing, and the weather growing gradually warmer. The school was like a hot-house full of steaming horses. Every day we left it with our blue jackets soaked with perspiration.

Still Old Jerky cracked his long whip and raved, threatening to put backboards on us, whatever they might be. Joe Ratcliffe wrung his hands and thanked God aloud and fervently for the Navy. As time went on we improved, but we were not happy about our equitation course.

By a great stroke of good fortune we recruits had two spells under canvas that summer. At the beginning of May we left for Pirbright, where we spent a wonderful month under the pines, among the heather, and on the ranges. Rides, drills, and gymnasium were all forgotten, far-off things. The talk of the recruits ran on bulls, inners, and magpies. The weather was magnificent. The water in the camp was not considered safe for drinking, and as range work is thirsty work, the resulting consumption of beer was little short of phenomenal. One had to drink something. Beer in those days was still beer, and I believe it did us all a great deal of good.

We returned to Regent's Park brown and fit at the beginning of June, and got down again to the old routine. The Coronation of King George V provided an interesting interlude, though as recruits we took no active part in it.

The whole regiment marched down to Pirbright early in July. The month's annual Musketry Training was a holiday for all, and a veritable godsend to men and horses. Stoney Castle Camp is admirably sited, a small island of two green fields set in the midst of pinewoods and gentle heathery slopes. Filled in with neat rows of tents and lines of tethered horses, it made a delightful picture.

The horses, adorned with white fly-fringes on their browbands, grew quite frisky under the kindly influence of sun and open air. What a wonderful treat for the poor brutes after their long twelve months in Barracks standing tied with their noses up against a whitewashed wall for twenty-two hours out of every twenty-four !

Men, lightly clad, basked in the sunshine. Life was, as far as possible, just go-as-you-please. The authorities showed sound common sense in permitting this.

Our evenings in the canteen were something to remember. Beer and good companionship were to be had there in plenty. The former, though costing only a modest three-halfpence a pint, was of marvellously good quality. Anyway, it seemed to produce no ill effects. A piano adorned a corner of the marquee, and smoking-concerts were often organized. An old soldier, very often Bob Roberts, would take the chair, announce all items, and keep order. He was assisted by a runner, whose duty it was to get around among the assembly and make a list of people able and willing to give a turn.

Suddenly the chairman would strike three blows on the table with a mallet, and roar : " Order please, gentlemen ! Trooper Adlam will oblige with the first song of the evening." A shout went up which nearly lifted the roof off the great tent : " Good old Jack ! " Jack Adlam mounted on the table, cleared his throat in the best professional manner, and proceeded to sing in a very pleasant baritone ' As we go down the vale.' The chorus was taken up by all and sundry. There was more vigour than harmony in the combined effort, but that did not matter, all was well with the world. Adlam earned and duly received a generous meed of applause, and invariably rendered as an encore ' The difference between East and West.'

Five minutes' interval followed, during which pots were drained and replenished. Then the chairman's mallet came again into action, and he could be heard summoning in stentorian voice one Trooper Wilkinson to give the next song. This announcement was greeted with enthusiasm in which there was much merriment. Wilky was a sturdy, dour Yorkshireman, with a round, red face, and huge black moustache. His whole repertoire consisted of one song. He sang it in all seriousness and with quavering voice. You could have heard a pin drop as he did so, though the audience all through held its sides which threatened to burst with suppressed mirth. No wonder. Wilkie's song was entitled 'Daddy's on the engine.' I sometimes wonder now whether he was really serious. I believe he was.

Victor Burton, the Sergeants' Mess cook, was a man whose leisure moments were few and far between. He was celebrated in the regiment for his geniality, for the amount of beer he could drink, for the amount of work he could do, for the amount of sleep he could do without, for his excellent cooking, and for his concert number, 'Martha.' Besides being a talented chef, he was a born Cockney comedian. If he happened to put in an appearance in the canteen during a smoker, he was given no peace till he mounted the stage. As the applause at the end of an item died away, a howl went up: " Come along, Victor! Martha! Martha!" In response to the chair Victor would take his stand on the table, holding a pint pot in his hand. Very deliberately he took a drink, put the pot down, wiped his mouth with the back of his hand, and, giving his slacks a hitch, broke into a spate of Cockney patter. He described, all in the first person, the adventures of an East End family on holiday at Southend. He looked the harassed Cockney father to the life, and gradually wound off his yarn to the point where they were enjoying their first bathe. The adventure ended in disaster. " There we was," he would say, " right in the middle of it, bobbin' abaht like a lot o' corks, when all of a sudden—(here he sang)

> Marfa swallered a jelly-fish ;
> Jinny she got the cramp ;
> Mar in lawr began to jawr
> Because the sea was damp.
> Uncle Bunkum stuck in the mud ;
> A crab caught 'old o' me,
> An' when we looked for the bathing-machine
> It was driftin' aht ter sea."

This refrain was bellowed by the assembled soldiers in chorus and then the patter went on : " Well, 'ere's a nice kettle o' fish," says Marfa (that's the wife). " Wot'll we do nah ? "—" Ne' mind, old gal," I says, " let's stop 'ere till

the seaweed grows all rahnd us."—" We won't do nothin'
o' the sort," she says. " Let's go acrost an' arsk the old
boatman for a bit of tarpaulin." And so he continued with
the family argument till finally a policeman strolls up.

" Allo ! " says the copper. " Wot's all this ? "

" Well, it's like this 'ere, guvnor," I says. " Me an'
Marfa (that's the wife) comes dahn 'ere with the family for
our annual wash. Everything was goin' lovely. We
wasn't arf enjoying ourselves. There we was, right in the
middle of it, all bobbin' abaht like a lot o' corks, when all
of a sudden—

> " Marfa swallered a jelly-fish ! " etc. etc.

Victor invariably brought down the house. Indeed he and
his turn would have been a success on any variety stage.

Our beer was supplied by Messrs. Flower. One of their
draymen, old Charlie, was another of our stars. He was
always about the canteen in the evenings, and it was only a
question of time before some wag raised the cry : " Wot
abaht the old dust-cart ? Come on, Charlie ! " Old
Charlie just revelled in the limelight. He was a living
advertisement for the Brewers who employed him, and the
very sight of him singing a serious song (he, at least, took
it all seriously, and seems to have been a pioneer of
the ' Buy British ' campaign) was painfully funny. His
principal item had for chorus :

> " Poor old England's fairly in the dustcart.
> Everything is foreign, you'll agree.
> The tables and the chairs, the carpet on the stairs,
> Were made in Germany.
> When I go out into the garden,
> There, growing in a tiny plot,
> Is a pretty little rose that in the summer blows,
> That's the only bit of English wot we've got."

Pretty awful stuff, perhaps, but the air has a fine swing and
Charlie was worth seeing.

Thus the evening wore on. There were many other
singers and performers, but those mentioned were, for all
sorts of reasons, the most popular. Military songs of the
death or glory type were completely absent from these

occasions. The audience wanted good singing and good fun. We wanted to sing together and laugh and be happy.

Outside the stars shone on the restive, neighing horses asking for their night-cap of hay, and giving the line-guards a busy time keeping them out of mischief. At ten o'clock the clear notes of the trumpet rang out summoning us to roll-call. All stood up when Bob Roberts shouted: "Gentlemen, the King!" In half an hour's time we were sleeping soundly in our tents, or, as many of us preferred, out in the open beneath the summer sky.

There was a serious side to this camp life. Every soldier had to reach a high standard in shooting if he was to qualify for the full rate of pay. Proficiency Pay, as it was termed, was a brilliant idea on the part of the authorities. Although the old soldiers, to whom the innovation seemed a dirty trick, groused loud and long about it, the younger men accepted it as a challenge and got down seriously to work. The most searching test in the course was rapid shooting, at which one was required to fire fifteen aimed shots in a minute at a range of three hundred yards. The whole course lasted three weeks. There were intervals of a day or two here and there. These non-shooting days were devoted to field days on the rolling downs about the camp.

A rifle has always had a peculiar fascination for me, so I enjoyed the shooting from beginning to end, and had no difficulty in holding my own with the older soldiers. I reached marksman's standard, the highest classification.

One morning, when there was no range work, the Squadron was ordered to parade mounted with rifle and sword on the saddle, for drill in the field. Although I had a horse of my own at the time, I was only a novice at riding, and as such not eligible to take part in field days. My pride was hurt at the idea of remaining behind in camp, so when the time came I saddled up and fell in on parade in the rear rank of the troop beside Will Franklin. My horse, D. 27, was a little short-backed, brown devil as quick as an eel. I was very fond of him, though he had more than once disgraced me in the riding-school by shedding me unexpectedly in a corner, and then trotting on without me, with an innocent look on his face, as though he didn't know what had happened. He had a tremendous reputation. As soon as I entered the school with him for the first time, Joe Ratcliffe, who had won the Empire Championship on him at Olympia, yelled: "Hallo! You ought to do all right now on 27. You've got the best horse in the regiment under you there." I paid dearly for that honour before I was dismissed rides.

When the Troop Sergeant, Snuffy Webb, approached and saw me sitting coolly amid the other members of the troop he nearly collapsed. To my surprise, and against his better discretion, he allowed me to remain. Of cavalry drill in the field I knew absolutely nothing, except to keep close to Will Franklin.

The troop moved off at a walk and joined the rest of the Squadron on the open downs to the west of the camp. I felt very pleased with myself at having at last a place among the trained soldiers. The Squadron Leader, complete with Trumpeter, set about putting us through the usual wheelings and turnings, first at a trot, then at a canter. Everything was going fine. I had kept my place with ease, both on 27's back and in the troop, and had not been cursed once for anything.

Along we went at a loping canter in column of troops. On our left was a gentle slope rising to a skyline a mile or so away. The Squadron Leader spoke to the Trumpeter, who then sounded: 'Left wheel into line.' We wheeled like a machine. Horses began tugging at their bits and plunging. They knew what was coming; I did not. Suddenly another call rang out. This time it was: 'Gallop!' It conveyed nothing to me. I was too busy, anyway. Amid a thunder of hoofs, the whole line bounded forward up the slope. My mount got off the mark like a crack sprinter, and the next thing I knew I was out of the saddle and perched somewhat precariously on his hind quarters. The little beggar, catching me unawares, had jumped clean from underneath me at the first bound. His back seemed to spring two feet into the air at each stride he took. I was in a blue funk. When all seemed lost I heard Will Franklin shout in my ear: "Get hold of the saddle, you ruddy fool, and pull yourself back into it!"

With a desperate effort I managed to do as he advised. My feet found the stirrups somehow; my body found the rhythm of the galloping horse, but not a moment too soon. The trumpet sounded: 'Draw Swords!' and the next second: 'Charge!' Hell for leather, and roaring like mad fiends, we raced up the remaining part of the slope. On the top we halted, dismounted, and looked round our horses. The worst was over now, but it had been a near thing for me. Fortunately nobody but Will had noticed my predicament, and he kept his mouth shut on the subject. I learned more about riding in two minutes that morning than in a whole month of riding-school work.

A few more concerts, a few more gallops in the field on 27, and then early one morning we struck camp and marched back to London. Here rides and drills started again from scratch. I continued to attend the Garrison School, as I wished to obtain the first-class educational certificate at the next examination.

I was dismissed rides in September, though we all knew in our hearts that none of us could ride with any confidence. Foot-drill on the square was a long-drawn-out process. Owing to the small number of recruits who were then joining the regiment, it was not possible to get together a squad sufficiently large to be dismissed before October. Think of that, some of you duration of war soldiers, nine months' recruits' drill on the barrack square!

Just before our dismissal I was examined and obtained the first-class educational certificate. A boy named Osborne and I, both recruits, got it together. The day the result was announced Tom Phillips shook hands with both of us at drill and said we had done him credit. We knew, of course, that he regarded us as his own. All the same, this was one of the great moments of my life.

From the beginning of November the furlough season was in full swing. I now fulfilled the conditions governing the granting of this important privilege. I was 'dismissed all drills and out of debt.' I applied and was granted a month, which I spent with my people in Ireland. Up to now I had no regrets. Every moment of my first year as a soldier had been worth living.

c

III

ON returning from Ireland after my furlough I took my place in the Squadron as a full-blown duty-man. I figured on the Squadron rosters for King's Guard, Barrack Guard, Night Guard, Stable Guard, spare horses, chaff-cutting, dunghill fatigues, and any other fatigues that might crop up or be invented by the more or less nimble wit of the Orderly Corporal for the week.

The furlough season went on into March. Many men were away. This meant that one was presented daily with a horse and kit, sometimes two, in addition to one's own. At times it was with the greatest difficulty that one could keep up with guard duties and at the same time have the stipulated break of two nights in bed between twenty-four-hour guards. I have actually known a man come off King's Guard at 12 noon and go on Barrack Guard the same evening at 6.30 p.m. No officers' servants, cooks, clerks, or tradesmen—in short, no staff-wallahs—ever went on guard or any other duty.

I now made the acquaintance of a typical London winter. There were days when a soupy, clammy mist hung in the air and penetrated every nook and cranny in the barracks. No alteration in routine was introduced to combat the effects of winter conditions. Kits in stables were cleaned and hung up daily with leather shining black or brown, and all steel burnished till it shone like glass. Next morning the leather oozed greasy moisture. Steel was as red as if it had lain for the night at the bottom of the canal. It needed a stout fellow to carry on from day to day under these conditions and at the same time preserve his sense of humour. Yet it was all accepted in a fatalistic sort of way ; the grousers groused a bit more, that is all. 'Mucking out' at reveille was a pretty repulsive business, but one can get used to anything, especially if there is no way out of it.

Exercise on slippery London streets in the early mornings was a nerve-racking job. We became experts in the art of side-stepping whenever a horse slipped up on the icy surface and hit the ground like a sack of potatoes.

It was not long before I was detailed for King's Guard. This adventure was enough to fill the heart of the novice with awe. On evening stable parade the Orderly Corporal read out the names of men and horses for the following morning. The actual parade took place about 9 a.m., and the guard mounted at Whitehall at 11 a.m. on weekdays and at 10 a.m. on Sundays.

A soldier warned for King's Guard washed his horse's mane and tail straight away. This done, he tackled the problem of the collar-chain. This contraption was about two yards of steel chain, worn round the horse's neck and attached to the head-collar. Its purpose was to replace the leather reins, which are easily cut in a rough and tumble with a riotous mob. It was scrubbed in wet silver sand, then placed in a clean cloth and shaken vigorously for upwards of an hour till every link sparkled. This gaudy article was then taken upstairs and kept overnight in a dry place. The horse was then groomed till the trumpet sounded ' Feed ' and ' Dismiss.'

Uniform and personal equipment were cleaned in the barrack-room the same evening. A smart soldier would have everything shipshape before 9 p.m.

At morning stables the horse's feet were carefully washed out and any white socks or stockings he may have possessed washed with soap and water and dried. Nose and eyes were sponged clean.

After breakfast the saddle and all its appendages were brown-polished ; head-kit blackened and polished ; brow-band and girth pipe-clayed ; bit and stirrup-irons burnished ; brass head-stall and breastplate polished, and all buckles polished inside and out. The horse was then saddled, and sheepskin and cloak placed in position. He was then tied short, and somebody asked to keep an eye on him lest he lie down.

There followed a dash upstairs to shave, wash, and dress. By that time the Trumpeter would be looking up

at the clock to see if it was time to sound 'Turn-out!'
It took a clever man to dress without soiling some of his
equipment. A comrade was always handy to give one a
final dust over with a cloth and alter a buckle here or there
before going downstairs. Another would lead out the
horse, rub away any spots of dust, and make any final
adjustments that were necessary.

For the King's Guard there were actually two parades.
The first was on foot. We were marched on to the parade-
ground by squadrons. The inspection which ensued was
something of an ordeal. The Adjutant, Quartermaster,
and R.S.M. turned everything inside out, and there was no
getting through with a half-hearted turn-out. At last we were
dismissed and hurried back to the stables for our horses.

On mounting we were marched on to the square, where
we formed up by squadrons, in open order. The Riding-
Master now added his presence to the inquisition, and the
mounted inspection was a thousand times worse than that
on foot. This was where the poor devils who had a bad
name came to grief. It is always possible to find *something*
not quite right about a Lifeguardsman in King's Guard
Order. It is only a question of looking long enough. Our
black horses were a special source of trouble. Even
though they shone like polished ebony in the morning sun,
a little patient scratching of their coats was bound to reveal
scurf in minute quantities. The experts knew that nothing
short of a bath will completely remove this deposit, and
even if the horse could have a bath, it would start forming
again immediately the animal was dry.

We sat there like so many graven images. When your
turn came one would examine your horse's mane ; another
would pick up a hoof to see if it had been washed out ; a
third would beat a tattoo with his whip on your sheepskin
in the hope of making the dust fly. Perched up in the air
as you now were, any of them could look at the insides of
your boots and spurs. Unless you had a kicking horse there
was not the flimsiest chance of getting away with anything.

Finally, the four who were considered the smartest on
parade were ordered to advance and form up facing the
others. The horses were paired to match as nearly as

possible, and these four performed the duties of mounted sentries or ' boxmen ' during the guard. They also formed an advance- and rear-guard to the main body during the march to Whitehall. The post of boxman was much coveted, partly because of the honour attached to it, but largely because the boxmen did one hour on and one off as mounted sentry between 10 a.m. and 4 p.m., and in addition had all night in bed. The dismounted sentries did two hours on and four off throughout the day and night.

At last the Guard formed up as a guard on the *manège*. The Captain took command, and the Drill Sergeant handed the Standard to the Sergeant-Major, who sat in the centre of the front rank. The Guard then moved off in half-sections, Trumpeter on his grey horse leading and sounding the ' Royal Salute.'

My own horse, D 27, was too brown to go on King's Guards, so I was ordered to take Joe Sykes' D. 15. This was a stroke of luck, as horse and kit were always in good condition. I was picked out for boxman. This was a feather in my cap, and Joe, my regimental father, was very pleased too. When we marched out I was one of the half-section forming the rear-guard. My companion was Gladman. We had to keep some fifty yards behind the main body, join up with it at all crossings and turnings, where we halted and faced about till the Guard had advanced another fifty yards. Then we turned round and continued.

Little Jimmy was as steady as a rock on parade. Once, in the street, however, he became a thoroughly bad lad. We turned down Albany Street, and into Regent's Park through Cumberland Gate. In the park he began to frisk and gambol like a very giddy little lamb. I could not persuade him to behave. As we passed the Reverend F. B. Meyer's chapel, the door suddenly opened, and a crowd of devout persons came pouring out. Their appearance was sober and correct in the extreme, but they affected Jimmy as if they were Red Indians in full war paint. His conduct was so very disgraceful that I actually lost a stirrup, and he raised such a clatter with his heels on the road that the Sergeant who rode between us and the main body came trotting back to glare at me and demand, none too amiably : " What the hell do you mean by this Buffalo Bill business ? "

My first King's Guard was a great success. During the remaining three months at Regent's Park I did fifteen altogether. I was boxman a few times, but not on Jimmy. Another horse was eventually given to me, D. 11, a bad character, who was a very treacherous brute, and had nearly kicked Hans Blitzer's head off before he was allotted to me. This scamp was well behaved in the streets, but sulked in the sentry's box, and wanted to lounge with his head down and feet splayed about any old how. He showed his resentment when I tried to pull him together by rearing up on his hind legs till he almost fell backwards. Every time the clock behind us struck a quarter he tried to rush out of the box. Taking him all in all, D. 11 was a thoroughly unpleasant customer, and an expert with heels and teeth. He was one of the very few horses for whom I never could feel any affection.

The Horse Guards, Whitehall, is a miniature barracks, complete with canteen. Here, when off sentry-go, it was possible to be very comfortable, and the men were left largely to themselves. There was seldom or never any trouble on King's Guard, but there have been some exceedingly narrow escapes. I can vouch for the truth of the following.

One Christmas morning there mounted a ' Short ' guard, that is, a N.C.O.s' guard, which goes on when the King is out of town. Two famous characters, George and Gus, were Sergeant and Corporal respectively. There was the usual supply of free Christmas beer. The Quartermaster lectured George, before going on, about the advisability of setting a reasonable limit to the amount allowed per man. The two N.C.O.s set out with the best of intentions. Four o'clock parade was successfully passed and evening set in. They remembered nothing more till, at dawn next morning, they were awakened by a tapping on the window of their little room. George scrambled up and saw a policeman looking rather anxious. " Oi ! " said the man in blue. " You'd better go and have a look at your sentry." Out went both George and Gus to the front yard, and there they found the sentry, Trooper Miner, lying peacefully asleep on his back midway between the two gates. His sword and helmet lay some distance away. He was dressed in jack-boots, underpants, and vest, with his red cloak on top. With feverish haste they collected Miner and carried him inside, then went in quest of someone to take his place. On entering the day-room they encountered a sight never to be forgotten. In the coal-box lay the tallest man in the regiment, Bill Dithers, sound asleep. His spurs hung over one end of the box, his plume over the other. He was fully dressed in King's Guard Order. What a night it must have been! Things were ultimately straightened out and the guard relieved without mishap. George and Gus determined to hold their peace. Not a word ever leaked out till one night in a billet in France George told us about it.

Barrack Guard was much more strenuous than King's. Here one was continually under the observation of the R.S.M. Anything was liable to happen on Barrack Guard. Some of the N.C.O.s, too, behaved rather childishly when in charge. I did my share of these interesting duties, and was always glad when relieved and away from the vicinity of the guard-room.

I was now getting to know my comrades better. There is nothing like community hard work for welding men together and bringing out their several qualities, good and bad. It gives me great pleasure to say that the great majority of my fellow-Troopers were excellent men, decent and straightforward, always ready to lend a hand to anybody who needed it, and with few exceptions always good-humoured and quick to see the funny side of our somewhat monotonous existence. The routine of our lives now appeared to consist almost entirely in soiling articles of equipment and arms in order to clean them again.

The men drifted into groups, according to common tastes. One party of half a dozen were inveterate music-hall goers. The chief attraction, however, was not to be found billed on the programmes of those places. It lay rather in the erratic bahaviour of George Levy, one of themselves. George's name was a byword in the regiment for all that was honest and decent, besides which he was a smart soldier. Red-haired, jovial, rather stoutly built, possessing an inexhaustible fund of good humour, he suffered from one awful disability; once he started to laugh heartily, he completely lost control, and could not stop. Every Friday evening he visited the old ' Britannia ' in Camden Town and took his seat among his pals. If anything really funny happened to be staged, George began to laugh, and soon the whole house was in an uproar. Nothing could arrest the flow of laughter, least of all George himself. He had simply to choose between walking out and being fired out. His chums left with him, and the laugh was kept up in fits and starts amongst them till the next Friday.

Most of us dutymen were stay-at-homes, who wandered round to the canteen when our evening's work was done. We sat there and talked about everything under the sun till closing time. We were not allowed to gamble, but there was practically no supervision. Men were left alone in their leisure hours. That was a blessing, and we appreciated it. Now and then, however, some adventurous fellow with a craze for getting rich quickly would start a ' Crown-and-Anchor ' school in a remote corner, and carry on quietly all evening without arousing suspicion.

Occasionally an attempt was made at a concert, but with the furlough season in full swing, the result was never up to standard.

There were certain old soldiers, just a select few, who seemed to spend much time simply engaged in drinking beer. One night two of these, Mack and Twanky, being exceedingly full of this beverage, resolved to try a small flutter. Twanky found the necessary apparatus and opened a bank. In a short space of time he had relieved Mack of the residue of his cash. All passed off quietly; the canteen turned out at ten, and we went off to bed. We had scarcely put out the lights when the peaceful atmosphere of the barracks was rent by a revolver-shot, soon followed by others. We jumped up and ran to the windows. Beneath us we saw a regular Wild West drama being enacted round the block. Mack, being very full of beer and brooding over his financial losses, had gone straight to the Squadron, where he procured a revolver and ammunition. Thus armed he set out to hunt up Twanky. Round and round the block they raced. When Mack turned a corner he sighted Twanky's heels disappearing round the next one. Each time he let drive with the revolver at the fleeting figure till his ammunition was exhausted. By then the guard had turned out. The two wild, woolly desperadoes were rounded up and locked away in the cells.

We were fortunate in having for our Commanding Officer Lieutenant-Colonel E. B. Cook. He was a thorough gentleman, sympathetic and approachable, though always a stickler for having everything done with absolute correctness. He had absolutely no use for what the army terms 'crime.' He detested inflicting punishment on his men, though he knew how to hit hard. He was one of those rare C.O.s who knew *when* to punish a man, and when the circumstances of any particular case called for leniency. A bachelor, he had one or two amusing eccentricities, and his favourite curse was 'blast.' He blasted all and sundry when the occasion demanded it. He was exceedingly popular. If he had a fault, it was that, in common with all the senior officers, he did not get about enough among the men. Hence much that he would never have tolerated went on in the regiment without his knowledge.

Next morning Messrs. Mack and Twanky were marched in under escort to the orderly room. A sorrier sight than they presented it would be hard to imagine. They both bore, hitherto, irreproachable characters. They were thoroughly ashamed of themselves, and looked it. They trembled in every limb as they stood together before the C.O. The latter let them stand for some time before looking up at them or speaking. This was a period of unspeakable agony for them. They were reduced to a state bordering on collapse, when at last the C.O. looked up sharply and addressed Twanky.

"Well, blast you, you've been playing 'Crown and Anchor,' eh?"

" Ye—Ye—Yessir."

" And you took all Trooper Mack's money, eh ? "

" Ye—Ye—Yessir."

" And you're a blasted fool, eh ? "

" Ye—Ye—Yessir."

" And you," addressing himself abruptly to Mack, who nearly fell down, " you were playing ' Crown and Anchor ' too, blast you, eh ? "

" Ye—Ye—Yessir."

The C.O. considered a moment, then turned to the R.S.M., and said : " What am I to do with these two old fools ? If I give them detention, or even C.B., their beer will be cut off and then they'll both die, blast them ! Take them away ! Allow them into the canteen only at certain times, and ration their beer."

As the culprits marched out he roared after them : " Don't let me ever find you up here again, blast you ! "

Mack and Twanky were free men, and considerably wiser. They never got into trouble again. Goodness knows what might have been their fate if they had staged such a show in any other regiment.

Lord John Cavendish, second in command, and a most popular officer, allowed his servants much rope in many directions. His groom purchased all materials necessary for cleaning his master's horses and saddlery, paid for them himself, and kept an account of the expenditure in a book which he presented monthly to the officer for payment. One day, about the first of the month, Lord John was making an inspection of the canteen. On the counter he noticed a lofty pile of yellow brickbats. These cost a halfpenny each, and were much in demand for scouring. Lord John, who had not come across such things before, asked the canteen manager what they were. The latter answered : " Brick, sir. A gritty substance used for cleaning steel." " Oh," said Lord John. " So that's brick, is it ? Damned expensive stuff ! My groom gave me his book this morning, and one entry in it was : ' Brick—Two pounds ten.' "

There was little time in our busy lives for sport. I never saw any sign of football at Regent's Park. Boxing was

taboo. The C.O. did not like it. Rifle shooting was to be
had in plenty as soon as the fine weather arrived.

Some cycling enthusiasts formed a cycling club. Jackie
Kitson was the moving spirit in this activity. I believe he
was in a position to obtain cycles cheap somewhere.

In April the regiment entered a rifle team for the *Daily
Telegraph* Cup Competition. This annual event was open
to all units, Regular and Territorial, in the London District.
It was keenly contested. We had won it two years previously. The team consisted of a platoon under an officer
and Platoon Sergeant. The competition involved marching
some twelve miles in full marching order and in a limited
time. Firing on the range followed. This was entirely of
the 'field-firing' variety. The platoon advanced from
about 700 yards and targets bobbed up anywhere in front at
unknown ranges. The range had to be judged and given
before these could be successfully fired on. When they
bobbed down, the advance continued till another set of
targets came into view. The whole provided a searching
test of marching, judging distance, fire-control, and
accurate shooting.

I was given a place in the team. Our Platoon Officer was
Lieutenant Smith, and the Platoon Sergeant Paul. Charlie
Wright, then a Corporal, was also included. True to the
traditions of the regiment, we carried out no practice
whatever in marching, so that when the day arrived I found
I did not possess a pair of boots sufficiently stout to stand up
to the march. Jock Donaldson kindly lent me a sturdy
pair. I take nines; Jock's boots were in the neighbourhood of twelves. Like the young fool I was, I set out in
them. Before we had covered two miles my feet felt red
hot. Mr. Smith set a scorching pace. We finished the
march with too much time to spare. It was evening, so we
had to sit down as we were in the comparative cold and
await our turn to shoot. Anyway, we were not in the first
half-dozen. I don't think we greatly cared, somehow. On
returning to Brookwood Station we found the winners,
whoever they were, had filled the cup with whiskey and
soda at the Station Hotel. They were kind enough to invite
us in and passed the cup round. It was a mighty vessel,

rivalling a village pond in capacity, but of beautiful work-manship. I shall always remember getting my nose over the edge, peering at the bottom through the sparkling amber liquid, and taking two deep draughts before passing it on. We were badly in need of something of the kind. I learned a lesson about boots that day.

Quarterly kit-inspections were occasions for much excitement and mirth. Every man on joining received a free issue of clothing and necessaries. No further free issues were made to him. He was credited quarterly with a generous allowance to replace unserviceable articles. The serviceability or otherwise of the soldier's property was determined once a quarter by the Squadron Leader, who held a solemn inspection to that end. It was well worth while practising economy, or even a little sleight of hand, in order to survive the ordeal. If no kit was seized as unfit for further wear, the soldier drew his allowance intact, and a nice little round sum of ready money always came in useful. Very wisely the Squadron Leader gave us as little notice as possible of the impending search. All our belongings had to be laid out on our beds in a certain way. An actual photograph of a perfectly laid out kit was available for guidance.

It was not enough to have a complete kit. Everything had to be in a state of best. One dodge was to borrow new things from another squadron and pray that the numbers would not be too closely scrutinized. At the very worst, one folded things with their best sides outwards, and hoped for the best. On one occasion, as soon as the Squadron Leader entered the room, we were called to attention, and were supposed to stand to our beds till the whole room was finished. Our room was in the shape of a right angle, so that it was impossible to see from the beds near the door what was taking place round the corner. Daddy Long's bed stood right round the corner, and when we were called up to attention Daddy was not there. He was actually away on an errand of supplication and was not missed. Before the first kit was inspected we heard a light tap on the veranda window, and on looking round we perceived Daddy standing outside, all on pins and needles, and carrying a tunic and a pair of overalls under his arm. The window was raised without noise; in crept Daddy; down went the borrowed clothing in its place, and he stood by waiting his turn with a look of sublime innocence on his face. He got clear all right, but he had one bad shock. A piece of yellow soap had an allotted place in the display. Daddy had no soap, but at the last moment found a piece of cheese that looked about the right size, so he put it down as a substitute. The Captain's little dog started sniffing about his bed, located the cheese, carried it off, and ate it. "Dear me!" said the Captain. "First time I've ever known a dog eat soap."

Regarding the remaining weeks at Albany Street, there is little of importance to record. On every dutyman's lips were the comforting words: ' Wait a bit. We'll soon be going down to Windsor. Things will be much better there.'

Joe Sykes was promoted to Corporal and posted to another Squadron. I was too young a soldier not to miss him. He now began to attend school to study for the first-class certificate. In the regiment these were few and far between. Joe was no dud. He passed comfortably at the next examination.

There was a change of Adjutants. The chief clerk in the orderly room, Sergeant-Major Peter Jackson, retired on pension. His place was taken by the clerk next in seniority, and a vacancy occurred for a junior. Osborne, who had got his first-class certificate with me, was appointed.

On the nearest Wednesday to the first of May we left Regent's Park Barracks early in the morning and marched down to Windsor. Staff-wallahs went by train or car. I was the last of the long column of horsemen, and rode one horse and led two. It had been raining. Albany Street was coated with a film of slippery grease. Fifty yards outside the barracks, as I turned in to the right at Cumberland Gate, my riding horse came a cropper under me and pulled down the other two. A lively scramble ensued. We sorted ourselves out, and after an otherwise uneventful ride, reached Windsor about noon.

IV

COMBERMERE BARRACKS, Windsor, lie on the edge of the Great Park, and alongside the 'Lord Raglan.' The Park is too well known to require description. I was destined before long to know every inch of it. Of the 'Lord Raglan' I can say no more than indicate its position ; I never crossed its threshold. Across the road from the barrack gate the King Edward VII Hospital was almost completed when we arrived.

Early summer in all its freshness and beauty lay everywhere about us. We experienced a welcome feeling of room in which to breathe ; our horizon was not, as in London, bounded by walls and housetops. The barracks itself, with its extensive grass lawn lying in front of the officers' house, and bounded at the sides by the men's quarters and stables, looked peaceful and spacious. All barrack rooms were lofty and airy ; verandas ran the whole length of both wings. As summer quarters they were ideal. In winter, owing to ill-fitting doors and windows and inadequate heating arrangements, they were cold and damp. The only warm place at that season of the year was in bed.

Field days began at once. For a short while these were Squadron affairs ; but soon the whole Regiment left barracks daily in the early morning and returned covered with dust and sweat about 1 p.m. I found these daily excursions thrilling. There was much galloping. To gallop in the ranks in various formations, but especially in line with the whole Regiment, was sheer joy. Horses soon became hard and fit. To see them at work and to work with them made life worth living.

Plenty of hard riding improved our horsemanship tremendously. The carrying out of mounted evolutions in Squadrons, and at a cracking pace, called for the exercise of intelligence and skill on the part of the individual Trooper.

This was particularly so when the ground was soft after rain. Then the flank men really had to ride. When wheeling, distance and interval had to be judged to a nicety.

The weather grew hotter as the summer advanced. Mounted drill gradually gave place to what were known as 'schemes.' The regiment went out after an imaginary enemy, sometimes represented by half-a-dozen mounted men carrying flags. In these games we were taught the duties of scouts, and advance-, flank-, and rear-guards. Dismounted action played a large part. Riflemen, panting and perspiring, doubled for miles over the countryside, while some distance behind the number-threes struggled with armfuls of contrary led horses, each one of which seemed to have its own ideas as to the best way of conducting the battle. It was all very strenuous, but excellent training. I believe everybody thoroughly enjoyed it.

When we turned out for the field, every fit horse had to be mounted. From remote nooks and corners of the barracks staff-wallahs would come along and take their mounts all ready saddled for them by the long-suffering dutymen. On returning in the early afternoon these gentry handed over their horses and then retired to carry on with their important duties elsewhere. Thus we dutymen had always two, and often three, horses and kits awaiting our attention after dinner. The kits presented no great difficulty. They had to be cleaned; but then Windsor is not London. As regards the horses, it was another matter. Some of these came back dirty but dry; others arrived dirty and sweating; the worst were those who reached stables dry, commenced to sweat as soon as they were off-saddled, and continued to sweat for hours. All had to be thoroughly dry and spotlessly clean before we could leave them.

Ted Castle and I hit on a plan to simplify this long-winded process of grooming and drying. On sunny days we were allowed to tie up our horses and feed them outside in the open air. The trumpet sounded 'Dinner up,' but we just hid round a corner till the big noises had disappeared. We then emerged armed with buckets, drew water from the trough, and one swilled the horses down, while the other went over them from ears to heels with a button-stick and pressed the water out of their coats. In a few minutes they dried in the sun and were as clean as new pins. The whole operation took just a few minutes. Then we dashed away and secured something to eat.

Cleaning horses by the pail and button-stick method was against orders. We were never caught, but one afternoon we had a close call. On returning to stables after dinner we found the Riding-Master scrutinizing our little bunch of horses. He felt their coats and examined the ground about them for traces of water. The sun had done its work well, so he drew a complete blank. But his suspicions were aroused. Doubtless the old boy had seen the same dodge long ago in the Royals. The operation called for great caution after that.

Guard duties at Windsor were simple, though the Barrack Guard was still a source of entertainment for the R.S.M. When he had nothing important to do, which was frequently the case, he would stand and glare at the sentry, and threaten him with extra guards and pack-drill if he did not move up and down more smartly. One day he happened to drop on me standing at ease and gave me a bad quarter of an hour.

Our existence was divided between field, stables, and bed. There was little time to go out into the town. Although I was stationed at Windsor for a year, I know nothing of the place, beyond the way to the river and the two railway stations. The more energetic ones spent their leisure on the river. A boat club was formed, and we wore ourselves out pulling oars in all types of craft.

In another part of the town was a barracks which held a battalion of Footguards. Individually we got on rather well with them. Their outlook as a unit was in many respects the reverse of ours. We believed in giving our men as many and as generous privileges as possible, and then leaving them to themselves. Woe betided any man who made a fool of himself and abused this freedom; he was severely punished. Besides any C.B. he might collect, the C.O. could deprive him of all privileges for a year, and the Squadron Leader for six months.

The Footguards, on the other hand, seemed to have little in the way of liberty. They had to walk out in uniform. Every evening they put a picket of twelve men under the Provost Sergeant on the streets, whose business it was to look out for buttons undone, gloves off, caps not straight, civilian boots, and a thousand other things. We considered this as manufacturing ' crime.'

And so the weeks passed. We worked like mules all the time. There was a pleasant break of a month at Pirbright. That season again I qualified as a marksman. I was second shot in the Squadron and third in the Regiment. The Squadron Leader in an unguarded moment offered a pound for the Squadron shot and ten shillings for second. Gus Russell and I drew our prize-money exactly a year after we had won it.

After Pirbright the same old routine went on again through the autumn. It began to grow monotonous. Ted Castle had been made a Corporal, and taken his departure to ' C ' Squadron. For some time now I had no particular chum. I grew restless and disgruntled, and longed for a change of any kind.

It must not be imagined there was no laughter in our lives. There were plenty of comical characters about, and now and then something would happen to set us laughing for days on end.

Some minor official, I think the Barrack Warden, possessed a parrot. He occupied a small house beside the guard-room just inside the main gate. In fine weather Polly was perched in a massive cage on the edge of the square. One day on coming in from the field, the Squadron orderly corporal, Jimmy Gotheridge, got permission to fall out at the guard-room to get the troops' letters. He dismounted, looked round for something to tie his horse to, and noticing the parrot's cage, made the head-rope fast to a large ring in the top. Jimmy entered the guard-room, and Horace, his little grey horse, attempted to scrape acquaintance with the parrot by sniffing at the bars of the cage. Polly resented this forward behaviour and straightway bit him severely in the nose. This was too much for Horace. Without a moment's hesitation he galloped out

D

through the gate, jumped the railings round the hospital, and started careering madly round the hospital lawn with the cage swinging wildly on the end of his head-rope. The parrot screamed for all he was worth. This made Horace go all the faster. At length a party of us ran across and caught him. Neither of them was any the worse for the escapade.

A crowd, hearing the screams and commotion, collected around the gate, and Bill Whitehorn, who was having a wash in a lavatory which overlooked the scene, could not resist having a peep at the fun. Now Bill possessed the largest cranium in the regiment, and he did not like being reminded of it. In the little circular washhouse were loopholes in place of windows. In his curiosity Bill poked his head through a loophole, and then found he could not get it back.

The parrot having been rescued, and Horace pacified and fed, the attention of the crowd was now directed to Bill's sad predicament. There was, alas, nothing for it but to fetch hammers and cold chisels and chip away the bricks around his ears. The laugh raised that afternoon will re-echo down the years.

A regatta was arranged on the river. No end of trouble was taken to ensure its success. Every soul in the regiment flocked to the scene. Coloured tents were pitched on the river bank. There were swimming and boat races of every kind. Funny men in fancy dress, especially some dressed as ladies, vied with one another in choosing the right moment for falling into the water and screaming. The chief attraction of the whole gala lay in the married pairs' race. But the greatest joke of the day came from a totally unexpected source. Half-way down the course a boat containing a famous N.C.O. and his wife came into violent collision with another craft. Both were capsized and the two pairs flung into the water. The wife took the water with a head of wavy auburn hair, but on emerging from the flood she was seen to be almost completely bald. Everybody stood still and gaped. The husband, instead of going to the rescue of his spouse, absolutely disowned her, refused to recognize the lady, and struck out all hot and bothered for the bank. Some brave man in the audience went to her assistance and brought her ashore. The subsequent meeting of the pair in their quarters must have been interesting, but fortunately no record of it exists.

The London District Rifle Association held its annual Individual Competitions on the Pirbright ranges during the Summer. There were events open to all ' other ranks ' on payment of a small fee. A reduction was made for a general entry. The fees were pooled, and as the entries were always very numerous, they provided quite substantial money prizes. Woodward and I both made a general entry.

We had to be on the ranges early. Competitors were swarming there before nine o'clock. The first event was grouping at 100 yards. Conditions were ideal. There was not a breath of wind. We took plenty of time. I managed a four-inch group ; but so did a good many more. Woodward scored a two-inch. That was good shooting, and meant a prize of over three pounds. At this meeting the standard was exceedingly high. There followed some slow events, in which neither of us earned distinction, and about eleven o'clock we found ourselves mighty hungry and thirsty, and faced with a break of about half an hour before the ' rapid ' event.

There was a canteen just off the ranges. We strolled across and sat down. Woodward was elated at his success, so he treated me to rolls, sausages, cheese, and a pint of brown ale on the strength of it. When we had demolished this it was time to get back and report at the firing-point.

The range was 300 yards. The targets were khaki head and shoulder silhouettes, which bobbed up behind the butts and remained visible for thirty seconds. Each competitor received ten rounds in two clips of five. These had to be placed on the ground and the rifle-breach kept closed. As soon as the targets appeared one could load and carry on. I remember on my left lay a hefty Sergeant of the Scots Guards.

Up came the targets and away we blazed. One was so frantically busy as to be deaf to the din of the hundred or so rifles round about. I was still struggling with my last two or three when I noticed through the corner of my eye

the Scottie on my left quietly picking up his empty cases.
With a tremendous effort I got my tenth round off just
before the silhouettes vanished. The marker signalled me
nine bulls and one inner. That was a certainty for a prize.
Woodward and I spent a very pleasant and profitable day.

A new officer joined us about this time. He was a
large, good-natured man, but so frightfully jumpy and
erratic in his ways that he, with the best intentions in the
world, led his Squadron, and especially his Sergeant-Major,
a pretty dance till they got accustomed to him. His original
methods and ideas caused much merriment amongst those
of us who were fortunate enough not to be in his Squadron.

Little Nobby Clarke, the Trumpeter, returned to Barracks
one day some minutes late. He was marched up before the
new officer, and his offence stated by the Sergeant-Major.

" Stop his leave for ever ! " hissed the officer.

" Can't do that, sir," cooed the Sergeant-Major.

" Well, stop his leave for six months."

" Can't do that neither, sir."

" What can I do, then ? "

" You can stop his leave for a week, sir."

" Very well, then. Stop his leave for a week."

Here Nobby, who so far had held his peace, butted in
politely : " Beg pardon, sir, but I very particularly want to
go out this week."

The officer considered a moment. Then he had a
brain-wave. " All right then, Sergeant-Major. Stop his
leave when he doesn't want to go out."

He became such a famous character that before long
legend got busy, and the canteen rang with tale after tale
of his exploits. There were the stories of how he attempted
to put Stribling in the clink on Salisbury Plain ; and the
even better one concerning how Alan Lovell eventually
disposed of his sandwiches. Many of these are excellent,
though of doubtful veracity, and for various reasons they
had best be left unrecorded. The case of Nobby Clarke,
which is authentic, will throw sufficient light on this
strange personality.

A humble Sergeant, one Freddy Andrews, was also
responsible for much amusement. He was married on the

strength, and had quarters outside in the town. In the precincts of the Barracks was a large strip of land divided into gardens and allotted to the married men. Freddy was an enthusiastic gardener, even if somewhat one-sided in his ideas. He developed a mania for cabbages. But he aimed specially at producing tall cabbages. It didn't matter a straw to Freddy what breed of cabbages they were, so long as they were lofty. His absorbing ambition was to grow cabbages that would be the tallest in Barracks, if not in the world. One morning Gus Horsman actually saw him at daybreak, complete with tape-measure and stick, wading laboriously through the dewy allotments and recording the heights of all cabbage plants which threatened to rival his own in stature.

Freddy had a sort of *pied-à-terre* in a room in Barracks, which was the regular habitation of another Sergeant, George Hindy. He had to be in every morning before reveille and change into uniform before going to stables. One morning George was awakened well before reveille by a noise in his room. He peeped over his blankets and perceived Freddy, with a look of hopeless dejection all over his countenance, pacing to and fro on the floor and mumbling something to himself. He looked as if he had been up all night and was obviously worried. George made no movement, but straining his ears to their utmost, he caught the words : " I shan't purchase him. I'll see him damned first ! Let the beggar stick it, like I've had to."

" What are you jabbering about now ? " inquired George.

" I shan't purchase him. I tell you I shan't," replied the other.

" Purchase what ? " asked George.

" My youngster. He was born at one o'clock this morning. If he goes and joins the Army, I tell you he'll have to stick it, like I've had to."

In August one fine evening a cricket match was being played on the lawn. Young Osborne, the orderly-room clerk, who was playing, was taken suddenly ill. He was carried to the Hospital and discharged from the army a few days later on medical grounds. His place in the orderly-room was given to me.

V

IF there was one saving grace in the life of the pre-war soldier it was the remarkable suddenness with which anything was liable to happen to him. Just when existence had touched the lowest pitch of boredom, he might be hurled at any moment, and without the slightest warning, into a completely new and unknown sphere. On the other hand, just when he was enjoying every moment of his days, the bottom might suddenly drop right out of everything and leave him in a hopeless mess.

Not only was it possible for a thoroughly conscientious, smart, hard-working soldier to go whistling or singing to his work at reveille, and find himself that same evening an inmate of the local clink, and the next day safely lodged in the 'Glass House' in Aldershot. It was also a commonplace occurrence for a poor bored soldier, actually contemplating suicide or desertion, to be violently uprooted from the dreary daily round and transplanted with stunning suddenness elsewhere as a clerk, a cook, a cobbler, a clipper of horses, a casualty, or a corporal. Anybody was liable to be thrust into any kind of job without the smallest consideration for his fitness or his choice. The motto of all soldiers was: 'If anyone asks you whether you can do this, that, or the other, always say you can.' The amazing thing about it all is that the uprooted ones carried on in their new roles in most instances with a fair amount of success, and in some with distinction. Kitchen employees formed the one outstanding exception. Hence the saying: 'The Lord sends grub, but the devil sends cooks.'

In filling vacancies which occurred for specialists no notice was taken of a man's pre-army trade or calling. Thus a regiment was largely a collection of make-shifts. For example, it was quite in the natural order of things that the Rough-rider may have been a sailor before enlistment, the Farrier a baker's apprentice, the Cook-Sergeant a bookmaker's clerk, or the Sergeant in charge of the young horses a ladies' tailor. This is not exaggerating. The whole point is that they were nearly all jolly good make-shifts. Almost every specialist ultimately became a first-class man at his job.

This haphazard method of producing specialists was not without its advantages to the individual and to the army as a whole. It fostered adaptability, and encouraged men not to be afraid of trying their hands at something new and strange. It bred and developed self-confidence, and above all, initiative. On paper we compared badly with the French and German armies in respect of the classification of personnel. In both these nations a conscript was posted to that branch of the service in which he would be able to turn to account his civilian calling. Farmers' lads found their way into horse units; mechanics entered the A.S.C. and Artillery; skilled tradesmen went to the Engineers, while the unskilled masses found a niche in the Infantry. Yet, when the test came, our men stood head and shoulders above the continental troops in resource and initiative.

The great majority of our officers were fine fellows, gentlemen, and good leaders; but, unlike foreign officers, they were not dependent on the service for their livelihood; they were not obliged to regard the Army as a serious profession, wherein efficiency was of vital importance. They simply did what was absolutely necessary and were promoted, as time went on, by seniority. Few of them were students. The ideal officer is, of course, a blend of the two types. He was always to be found in small quantities in every unit of our army. There were, perhaps, some half-dozen specimens of him in our own regiment.

When I enlisted, and in so doing shook the dust of the schoolroom off my feet, nothing could be more remote from my ambition than the idea of developing into an Army clerk. I wanted to ride in the ranks, to march and shoot and sing with the crowd. In my heart I despised pen-pushers and ink-slingers, as we called them. It is true I had found soldiering in a Troop dull work after the first novelty wore off. It was also, at Windsor, gruelling hard work; and it could not, with any degree of truth, be called clean work. But I had earned a good name. I was a marksman. I held the highest educational qualifications then obtainable. I was as good a horseman as anybody else in the Troop, and I had always managed to avoid trouble with the N.C.O.s. As a matter of fact I was beginning to see myself as a favourite of our Troop Sergeant. On field days he would have nobody but me ride next to him on his left. This was flattering till I found out the real reason. It was quite simple. It would appear that the old lad had a colossal corn on a toe of his left foot. My horse was the tallest in the troop, so when riding in close formation my right foot was always well up in the air above his tender spot. I always rode in the same position by special request.

I was still very young. Promotion seemed a very long way off when I had a mere eighteen months' service, and I was more than tired of the pointless drudgery in stables. So when the vacancy came in the orderly room I was carried away by the prospect of a change, especially a change to something cleaner and more comfortable, and I accepted the appointment when it was offered.

Many times afterwards I wished I had declined and remained where I was. If only one could have foreseen the nearness of the war! Like a fool I became a clerk in July, 1912. I spent two years of unspeakable misery in the orderly room until the outbreak of war. When war was declared I tried everything I knew to get out of the orderly room and back to the Squadron. In the end I only succeeded in getting clear with loss of rank, and for months afterwards I bore upon me the stigma of a miserable clerk wherever I went.

Anyway, the morning after Osborne became ill, I was taken in by the R.S.M. before Colonel Cook. Like the great gentleman he was, he explained the situation to me and pointed out all the pros and cons connected with it. If I had been his own son he could not have treated me with greater consideration or shown more interest. When I accepted he said: " Very well, then. Do your best to learn the routine, and make yourself as useful as you can to the Orderly Room Sergeant. I shall promote you and look after your interests." I thanked him and was marched out. I was set to work without delay, and in a few days' time promoted to Corporal.

The orderly room contained two offices, an inner sanctum where the C.O. and Adjutant carried out their office routine, and an outer office for the R.S.M. and clerks. The clerks' room was furnished with a broad, three-sided, stand-up desk, which jutted out from a wall, and was constructed so that three people could perform on it at once, one on each side. There were high stools, officially known as ' Stools, wooden-headed, Sergeants ',' two or three tables, a couple of typewriters, piles of army forms and books, and pens, ink, and paper.

On the side of the broad desk farthest from the door the R.S.M. had staked out his claim. This corner was his holy of holies. In it he stored his complete stock-in-trade —a biggish book, containing the Sergeants' and Corporals' duty rosters, his whip, and his gloves. He was the same merry old soul who had watched over my training as a recruit and my efforts as a sentry. All day long he haunted the place. He saw and heard everything that went on and missed nothing. He seldom spoke. Now and again he would laugh at one of the Orderly Room Sergeant's witticisms, and the resultant sound was like the lowing of a distressed calf down in the depths of a well.

The Orderly Room Sergeant was an excellent clerk, in fact a super clerk. He possessed other accomplishments. As a shop-walker he would have been worth his weight in gold to the proprietor of a departmental store. He was endowed with powers of persuasion which would have made his fortune in the Caledonian Market or Petticoat Lane. His talents as a diplomat were of a high order. The ease with which he handled refractory officers of all ranks was an absolute eye-opener. I have seen an irate Major dash into the office with murder in his eye, and after five minutes' conversation with the O.R. Sergeant melt into the very personification of gentleness and affability, and depart beaming on all and sundry. It would not have surprised me in the slightest had the O.R. Sergeant attempted to sell him a typewriter before he left, and I believe he could have done it too. In the first weeks of my noviciate he was tremendously fond of me. Then he gradually changed, till at last he detested the very sight of me. Naturally, the R.S.M.

and the Adjutant followed his lead in this respect. I had jumped from the frying-pan into the fire with a vengeance.

I was now expected to cut all my old pals and assume a haughty, condescending superiority to them, as befitted my lofty destiny. The O.R. Sergeant would one day have to retire. Then the mantle of Elijah would fall upon Elisha. I must prepare myself if I was to wield with due dignity the great power which would then be thrust into my hands. I am afraid I was not impressed. I soon saw through a good many little pettifogging things which to the R.S.M. and O.R. Sergeant were matters of the highest importance. I was amused. But unfortunately I was too young to have sense enough to conceal my amusement, which in their eyes amounted to blasphemy and treason.

After a time, therefore, the atmosphere in the office could not by any stretch of imagination be termed friendly from my point of view. I might speedily have been sacked had I not soon shown signs of becoming a useful clerk, and there was at the time a dearth of suitable youngsters in the regiment to replace me. For my own part, I was determined not to give up the post and clear out of my own accord. The job carried many valuable privileges with it, and I made up my mind that they were worth all the discomfort and humiliation of the actual work in the office. So I just held on and said nothing. I believe now it would have been considerably wiser and more to my advantage to have pocketed my pride and cleared off back to the Squadron.

A short time after making my debut as a clerk, the regiment left Windsor for manoeuvres. For this purpose a Composite Regiment of Household Cavalry was formed, consisting of one service squadron from each of the three Regiments. In addition, we furnished the Regimental Headquarters. This necessitated the departure of the R.S.M. and O.R. Sergeant. When I saw my old Troop ride away I felt completely out in the cold. I had to remain behind and look after the office. "If anything out of the way should turn up," said the O.R.S. as he took his departure, "just ring up old Sam Keyworth of the Blues. He'll tell you what to do about it." Nothing of importance cropped up.

Manœuvres finished, I got on with my clerical duties, typing, rejoicing, sorrowing. Out of office hours the N.C.O.s' Mess offered a comfortable retreat. Unlike regiments of the line, the Household Cavalry do not run a mess exclusively for Sergeants and upwards. They have a N.C.O.s' mess, of which everybody, from the most junior Corporal to the R.S.M., is a member. This system yields many important advantages. It is good for the youngster to move freely among his seniors; and it does the older N.C.O.s no great harm to be reminded by the presence of juniors in their midst that they themselves were once young and green.

The food in the N.C.O.s' Mess was excellent. Victor Burton saw to that. Instead of having one's midday meal served up all complete on a plate, the joint, or whatever we had, was carved on the spot by a Sergeant at the head of the table. A corporal in attendance shared it out on to the plates, and they were then passed along the table in a civilized way. Vegetables and gravy were housed in appropriate dishes from which people helped themselves. There was always plenty of everything. This was not obtained at the expense of the troops. We had to pay for it, and by the time all subscriptions were deducted from my meagre pay (I was not yet on Troopers' full rate) I was left with the princely sum of nine shillings a week in cash.

There were two bars in the mess, or perhaps it would be more accurate to say the bar had two sides, namely, 'the glory-hole' and 'the half-crown side.' In the former assembled junior members, all those betting men who were invariably hard up, and thirsty seniors who took their libations in pints. The half-crown side was the rendezvous of the 'upper ten,' seniors who consumed 'short' drinks, and affected superior manners and expensive cigarettes. There, too, were entertained as guests many notables and influential friends from the civilian community outside, and known among the humbler fry as 'fitters.'

Among the senior N.C.O.s with whom I scraped acquaintance in the Mess were some fine men. Peter Bruce, Harry Tapsell, Frank Oram, Charlie and 'Fender' Wright, and the brothers McFeeley were some of the best.

It was impossible to be dull anywhere in their neighbourhood. In addition to being a blessing from a social point of view, they were the most efficient N.C.O.s in the regiment.

In my new vocation I missed the company of the horses. I often took a stroll round the stables to see my old long-faced friends and have a word with them. They may have remembered me. I hope they did; but I have no great opinion of horses' intelligence. One reads and hears much on the subject. I never came across any outstanding examples of it among army horses. Lovable creatures they certainly are. But their fascination lies, to my mind, in their beauty of form, great strength, willingness to exert themselves at our slightest bidding, helplessness, absolute dependence on us for their every need. A good horse always gives of his best without stint. He will suffer hunger, thirst, pain, and still work on till he drops. All these are virtues, but they are no indication of intelligence. Other animals, the mule and the dog, for instance, are different in make-up. They will jib at a hard task, and absolutely refuse to attempt a job beyond their powers; they will squeal and wince under pain. These are not attractive qualities, but they indicate intelligence.

Horses are exactly like very young children in their nature. They are foolhardy, mischievous, prone to injure themselves if not constantly under supervision and control, and quick to give an empty-handed old friend the cold shoulder for a new one with a lump of sugar.

Anyway, I went when I could and had a word with old Freddy (D. 48), little Jimmy (D. 15), and was greeted with open jaws by old Jock (D. 13). Whatever they may have felt, they always looked pleased, and it cheered me up to feel them nosing about me again.

Many changes in personnel took place before we left Windsor. Old Tam Wilson and Q.M.S. Jones, both of my old Squadron, left on pension. Their places were taken by Barney Rudd and Bob Harrison. Nobody could wish for two better men at the head of the Squadron. I felt more grieved than ever at being a castaway when they were appointed.

In May 1913 we returned to London, this time to Knightsbridge Barracks.

VI

IT is strange how London gets a grip on those who
have dwelt there. Even though many aspects of a
soldier's life in the metropolis were hateful to me, yet
after a year at Windsor I, in common with all my comrades,
felt the pull of ' town.' We were glad to get back to it.
In any case, it meant a change. Knightsbridge Barracks
was a fresh field to all in the regiment with less than three
years' service.

This time in London there was, for me, no incessant
going on and coming off guards. I was, in fact, to all
intents and purposes, a civilian. My work in the orderly
room began at 8 a.m., and very often finished at 1 p.m.
Only on very rare occasions was anybody to be found in
the office after 3 p.m. The rest of the day was absolutely
my own. With a weekly wage of nine shillings, I had
perforce to restrict my pleasures and pastimes. I was not
at all likely to paint the town red. Still, it is surprising how
far a few shillings went in 1913.

I was well fed and clad. My quarters were comfortable,
and there was no dearth of good fellows who were finan-
cially in a plight similar to mine. I lived in a small barrack-
room with some other staff N.C.O.s. All my room-mates
were men with ability in one direction or another. There
was no lack of intelligent conversation and discussion, any
more than there was lack of fun.

Harry Tapsell was an authority on political matters. He
was a well-informed and quick-witted opponent in an
argument, and an admirer of Horatio Bottomley. Often he
reminded me strongly of Goldsmith's schoolmaster, ' for
e'en though vanquished, he could argue still.' ' Fender '
Wright was in those days a most versatile individual. He
owed his nickname to his novel methods of physical culture.
On getting out of bed in the morning he would perform a

series of exercises with the barrack-room fender, a piece of furniture made of solid iron in three sides of a rectangle, and weighing about a hundred pounds. He was a brilliant signaller. In the London District Tournament he won the bayonet-fighting championship, beating the Footguards at their own game. As a musician he was talented, and possessed a somewhat weird-looking instrument called a cithera, with which we whiled away many a wet evening. Chock Hodgson, who lived in a room opposite and played the guitar, used to bandy serenades with him on summer evenings across the intervening space. Their duets were worth listening to. Frank Oram was a gymnast, signaller, and rifle-shot of the first rank. He possessed intellect, humour, and was well educated. Jimmy Stoole, the school corporal; Howard of the Blues, orderly at Buckingham Palace; Joe Ratcliffe, the Rough-rider; and Jerry Sheppard, another young Rough-rider, who was seriously contemplating matrimony, completed the little company.

We did not go out a great deal, for the simple reason that we could not afford the expense. Outside, the Music Halls provided our chief source of entertainment. Acquaintance was renewed with the 'Britannia,' Camden Town; with the old 'Met.' in Edgware Road, and occasionally we patronised the Palladium or the Coliseum. At the latter place I remember having a good laugh at Charlie Chaplin in a very minor part, long before he was known to the community at large. We were familiar with Albert Chevalier, Harry Tate, Marie Lloyd, Little Tich, George Formby. Not a very intellectual or cultured form of entertainment perhaps, but nevertheless very brilliant in its own way. It was the hey-day of the great comedians, and we were in search of laughter, even though our quest entailed the assimilation of large doses of what George Robey so aptly calls 'honest vulgarity.' People had still the stomach for robust fun. There were no milksop crooners about the Halls yet; nor were there milksop audiences.

On fine Sundays we strolled or sat in Hyde Park and listened to the band or studied the crowds. On such occasions we always made a point of being smartly dressed.

On arrival from Windsor in the Summer of 1913 'Fender' and I had each a fairly extensive and serviceable wardrobe. The rigours of winter reduced this considerably, so that the early summer of 1914 saw us pooling our resources and purchasing a smart grey suit between us. This we called our 'Band-stand suit.' We were identical in height and build, and by mutual arrangement the suit did valiant service with each of us in turn. Of course we still retained our 'ratting suits,' which owing to long service had lost their original spick-and-spanness, but were good enough for evening excursions to nowhere in particular. In many cases a 'ratting suit' was all a poor devil possessed. Thus it was fairly common as one dashed out of barracks about dusk, looking none too well tailored, to be hailed from the windows with shouts of: "Oi! You've forgotten the ferrets!"

Meanwhile my relations with the great powers in the office grew neither better nor worse. I had my own special share of the routine work. I did that and no more.

When autumn came all staff N.C.O.s and men were sent on 'Staff Rides.' This amounted to nothing more nor less than an hour's riding drill in the school once a week. Many rare and wonderful sights were to be seen on those occasions. Portly officers' servants with paunches worthy of aldermen, and stiff old tradesmen and clerks from workshops and offices, combined to make an impressive pageant. These dignitaries had to be handled with care. The staff ride was no slap-dash affair; it bore no sort of resemblance to a rodeo. The fastest thing in the way of pace was a comfortable jog-trot.

That was all the exercise provided for the staff-wallah by the regimental authorities. One or two of us, however, were still young enough to find pleasure in riding, so we set about finding ways and means to augment this feeble effort. Bertie Channon and I hit upon the plan of carefully watching the officers' stables. When an officer departed on long leave, a modest spell of from three to six months, he sometimes left his horses behind in charge of a groom. Many grooms were very paragons in attending to the interests of their master and the welfare of his cattle. Some few here and there were the reverse, and celebrated his absence by a bout of drinking which lasted till the day before his return.

We soon discovered a very fuddled groom. He had two fine chargers in loose boxes, but he had already reached that stage when he no longer had the nerve to go in to them. All he did was to give them water and forage across the half-door and then leave them to themselves. Every morning at 5.30 or 6 a.m. we took those horses out into the Park and put them through an hour's hard work. The poor brutes were mad with delight at being able to stretch their legs again. After a while Channon went to the Cavalry School and our early morning scampers in the Row ceased.

I now hunted up another early bird in the shape of 'Cabby' Dawes, the N.C.O.s' Mess Sergeant. Cabby was a good soul. He had little opportunity for taking exercise, so I arranged to come and dig him out of bed every morning at 6 a.m. and take him out riding. None of your chargers for Cabby, though! He was more staid than Channon and I, so he stipulated that we should obtain a couple of quiet old stagers from the Squadron. This presented no difficulty, as the Troop Sergeants were always glad to get their spare horses exercised. The first few mornings saw us cantering sedately round Hyde Park, keeping well within a modest speed limit. Then one morning Cabby had an idea. What about quitting the park and having a little promenade round the houses? Seeing London in the early morning sort of thing? Out we went.

This was no haphazard sortie on Cabby's part. He made as straight and as sure as a bloodhound for a little public house in the backblocks of Kensington, knocked up the landlord who happened to be a friend of his, and ordered some rum and milk. Very good it tasted too in the early morning, but it was the beginning of the end of our outings, for very soon they showed signs of developing into a common pub-crawl. I decided Cabby would be better off in bed, so in bed I left him. He was a charming fellow. I do not believe he ever had an enemy except himself. For years he had been engaged to be married, and spent his time trying to get together enough money for the venture. He never led the lady to the altar. He was still saving when the war broke out, and then, one morning shortly afterwards, he was lost with many another good fellow on Zandvoorde Ridge.

Andy Kealey, the Sergeant-Cook, was a man of a different mould. He weighed somewhere round about twenty stone, but he carried out an elaborate slimming process with a determination which was the admiration of the whole regiment. Dawn every morning found him, in all weathers, far out in the waters of the Serpentine. Here he swam hard for an hour, scaring the lives out of the water-fowl, and leaving a wake behind him like that of an ocean liner, while the level of the water rose appreciably all round the edges of the lake. One morning in late autumn a fog descended suddenly and thick upon him. He completely lost his sense of direction and it was only with the utmost difficulty that he ultimately reached land. But that sort of thing would not deter Andy. The slim lines of his youth must be retrieved at all costs, so he persevered with his exacting regime in spite of everything.

If the troops could be believed, this morning swim was followed by a breakfast of gigantic proportions, consisting of mountains of liver, sides of bacon, several loaves, and tea by the pailful. After breakfast he rode in the Park for a couple of hours. Poor horse! However, there was nothing wild or dashing about Andy's riding. It was a gentle exercise designed to aid digestion and to land him back just in time for another small snack about half-past ten. This sufficed to keep his body and soul together till dinner-time. His dinners, eaten in the seclusion of his 'office' adjoining the kitchen, were gargantuan in variety and extent. (Here again I am relying solely upon the word of the troops.) Then followed three hours' siesta till tea-time, a drink or two till supper-time, then a quiet game of cards, and so to bed. In spite of his strenuous attempts at reducing, old Andy never lost an ounce. Evidently something was not quite right in his self-imposed regime, but be that as it may, he stuck to it like a hero.

Only very rarely did anything out of the ordinary crop up in the orderly room. Its sober dignity was seldom

E

disturbed by anything in the nature of a joke. I can recall
only one noteworthy happening during the whole time at
Knightsbridge.

A Corporal named Bella Bently was promoted to
Sergeant. Quite naturally he was pleased with himself, but
when week followed week and he was never warned for
guard, he began to grow uneasy within himself. His
fellow-sergeants were perplexed, and to some extent angry,
for Bella was not pulling his weight as a sergeant. They
even chipped him about the matter, and being a sensitive
soul, he was grieved. At length Bella plucked up courage
and approached the R.S.M. about it. The interview took
place on the veranda outside the orderly room door. The
old man was in a corner. A case of this sort had never
happened before. Anyway : ' The King can do no wrong,'
so he was not going to admit he had made a mistake and
passed Bella over or anything like that. No ! He would fall
back on the good old heavy father touch, so he glared at
Bently and barked : " Have you been warned for guard,
young fellow, or have you not ? " " No, sir," replied Bella.
" Then you don't go on guard." A feeble protest was
struggling on Bella's face, but the old man got in first with
a still fiercer bark : " If you haven't been warned, you don't
go on. That's all." There was no more to be said. Bella
walked away more perplexed than ever.

For some moments after returning to the office, the
R.S.M. was in a brown study. He took his sergeants' duty
roster and pored over it. Apparently this threw no light on
the matter, for he soon closed it with a bang and put it back.
Presently when all was clear, my curiosity got the better of
me, so I looked in his book, and there at the end of the list
of sergeants' names was a name which no living man could
read. I had no doubt the old man had written it in for
Bently, but could make nothing of it himself, so he simply
passed it by and started at the top of the list again. Not long
afterwards he was engaged in earnest conversation with the
Orderly Room Sergeant. The latter wrote something in
the R.S.M.'s book ; Bently was soon warned for guard,
and went on.

Attempts at social functions in the N.C.O.s' Mess were

not looked upon with favour by the R.S.M. But there was a young Corporal in the regiment against whose powers of persuasion even the old man was not always proof. This was none other than Charlie Wright. Two or three times he performed the miracle of obtaining permission to hold a supper and sing-song. These were more lofty and dignified than the canteen affairs, but they could be very pleasant evenings for all that. Victor Burton could be relied upon to furnish a good supper, and Charlie would always have him in to give us his celebrated 'Martha.' That was, of course, well on in the evening when the rough edge had worn off things.

The sing-song was, as befitted a gathering of N.C.O.s, very superior to a Troopers' concert in material, if not in mirth. Tom Phillips really could sing 'The Bandolero' and 'Tommy Lad.' A very superior young Sergeant-Major Roughrider always treated us to 'Glorious Devon.' A pawky individual from Manchester, lately become a Drill Sergeant, sang a Lancashire dialect song, 'Tha's welcum lad.' This was considered clever work by the Cockneys present, as it amounted, in so far as they were concerned, to singing in a foreign tongue. Last of all came something really funny—old George Beasneys recited 'Kissing Cup's Race.' That was the one thing in the whole world old George could do without making a mess of it. He put his whole heart and soul into the effort, and the effect more than compensated for any flatness there may have been in the early part of the concert.

Very soon, although we had not the remotest suspicion of anything brewing till the very end of July, the war was destined to break in upon us and sweep us away from the old familiar surroundings.

VII

AS July 1914 drew to a close, echoes of vague rumblings on the Continent reached us, but did not, so far as I can remember, cause any uneasiness or excitement. In the last week of July Hans Blitzer went out one evening and did not return. Nobody attached any significance to his disappearance. He was duly posted as a deserter, just as anybody else would have been. To-day it seems fairly obvious that he had inside information concerning the storm which was brewing. We were still in a state of peace, and desertion in peace-time is not quite the same as desertion in time of war. He realized it would never do for a British soldier bearing the name Hans Blitzer, and hailing from Königsberg, to fall into German hands, so he made a wise move.

The actual declaration of war caused a tremendous stir among the civilian population of London. It was difficult to recognize the reserved, highly respectable, live-and-let-live Londoner of 3 August in the wildly excited, cheering, bloodthirsty patriot of 4 August. A wave of enthusiasm swept over the metropolis. A mysterious something had touched a chord which had lain dormant since the days of Napoleon. The ranting, roaring mob who cheered and sang 'Rule Britannia' in the streets little realized the extent to which the conflagration would spread. They were under the time-honoured delusion that a little British Regular Army would once more go a long way, while they remained comfortably at home, read of its valour in the newspapers, joined in the singing of jingo songs in the music-halls, and then welcomed home the victors with pride and rejoicing. Could they but foresee that this time the little British Army was destined to go but a short way, and that thousands of themselves were to follow on the same road, they would not, in all probability, have been so very enthusiastic.

In the regiment we received the news calmly. War was our business, our calling; and the latest move simply meant business. We saw no glamour or romance in warfare; neither were we stirred to the depths of our souls by the thought of upholding the great traditions of our Corps. At the Battle of Waterloo, as the Life Guards returned after routing the French cavalry, Wellington raised his hat and said to them: " Life Guards, I thank you." But we were not aware of this. To ninety per cent of us the mention of the name Waterloo conjured up nothing more in our minds than a railway station where one took train for Pirbright. No. The things that mattered now were a stout horse, a serviceable rifle and ammunition, and a leader who was not a born fool. Plenty of hustle there certainly was; but it was devoid of noise and excitement.

Outside in the streets we were acclaimed by civilians who wanted to treat us to everything. Most of us were repelled by this sudden gush of favour. Our memories were not so short as to have forgotten in a couple of days that the great bulk of those who now hailed us publicly as heroes looked upon us forty-eight hours previously as outcasts, and would have been ashamed to be seen in our company. I myself have actually seen posted in places of public entertainment before the war the words : ' Soldiers and dogs not admitted.' The good old, self-satisfied, highly respectable British citizen was about due for a rude awakening.

The privilege of plain clothes was withdrawn, so ' Fender ' and I folded up our ' band-stand suit,' bade it farewell, and put it away in my box. The King's Guard continued to mount in full dress, but for ordinary wear our blue jackets and slacks gave place to khaki.

A Composite Regiment of Household Cavalry was formed at once, each regiment contributing one service squadron of four sixteen-file troops. In addition, our regiment provided the Headquarters of the Composite Regiment. This effort pretty well cleared out the whole of the old regiment. The Composite Regiment immediately began fitting out in order to proceed overseas with the first expeditionary force. Those who were left behind would be made up to strength with reservists and retain the title of 1st Life Guards. Colonel Cook took command of the Composite Regiment, and my old colleagues, the R.S.M. and O.R. Sergeant, were to fill parallel roles in that unit. This meant that I should be left at home, for the time being at any rate.

The formation of the new unit necessitated a split in the orderly room staff, so a day or two after war was declared the R.S.M. and the O.R. Sergeant collected their various odds and ends and dissolved partnership with me. The young Sergeant-Major Roughrider who sang ' Glorious Devon' was appointed R.S.M., 1st Life Guards. The evening he left our office, the O.R. Sergeant said to me as he passed out : " If you had played the game, you'd now be Orderly Room Sergeant, 1st Life Guards." This parting remark set me thinking, but I could make nothing of it, and in my extreme childishness I could see nobody except myself to take his place.

Next morning, when I arrived in the office from which my old friends had now gone, whom should I find sitting in state on the O.R. Sergeant's stool but George Beasneys of ' Kissing Cup ' fame.

" Hallo, George ! " I greeted him. " What can I do for you ? "

" My dear old chap," he replied. " I'm damned if I can see any sense in it, but they've appointed me Orderly Room Sergeant of the 1st Life Guards."

To say that I felt mad would be expressing things too mildly. My mind worked rapidly. I must get out of this hole at once. There was still time. The position was quite impossible. Old George had fifteen years' service. He had spent all his life in the stables, the last five years as a Troop Sergeant. What did he know of office work ? What could he learn ? The most he could do was fill the vacant post while I did all the work. That was exactly what he was meant to do.

I went at once to the old R.S.M. and asked to see the Colonel with a view to getting sent back to the squadron. But the old boy had been expecting some move of this sort. He was much too fly to let me see Colonel Cook. The R.S.M. met my request with : " You have nothing more to do with me now, young fellow. You don't belong to my regiment." That was solid fact ; there was no getting past it, so I jogged along and asked the new R.S.M. if I could see my new Commanding Officer, who happened to be the Duke of Teck. He could not very well refuse, but he first consulted my old friends and between them they prepared the Duke for my reception. When all other business was finished I was marched in at one door. Immediately the Duke saw me, he lifted his silk hat from the table and made for the other door. As he went he turned round and addressed me over his shoulder : " You want to go back to the Squadron, do you ? Well, you won't. You'll stop here and work like hell." With that he disappeared through the door, and I was left standing. The R.S.M. said nothing.

Back in the office old George was in a frightful mess. He could not even answer the telephone. As I entered he pushed the receiver into my hand. " Ah, here you are, old boy," he said. " I'm damned if I can make out what they want." I put things straight, and when a lull occurred in operations George proceeded to make friendly overtures. " Come along, old chap," he said. " Let's go and have a drink. We're getting on famously now. You and I have some busy times ahead of us."

I was in need of a drink. But carry on under such conditions ? Not if I knew it ! The more I studied the situation, the less I liked it. I did not stand an earthly chance of getting away from the office now. The only alternative was to get rid of George. I deliberately hardened my heart and staged a one-man strike. The telephone was ringing day and night about all sorts of things. As soon as a voice at the other end demanded : " Is that the orderly room sergeant ? " I handed George the receiver and left him to it. He stuck it valiantly for two whole days. By that time he had a nasty glint in his eye ; but he was beaten. He went and asked to be sent back to his old haunts. His request was granted. The same day he was given a troop of Dragoon Reservists in ' C '

Squadron. Next day the troop refused to soldier under him, and sent a deputation to the Squadron Leader, Lord Hugh Grosvenor, asking to be rid of him. George was moved on again, but his guardian angel did not fail him. He dropped into the not too strenuous position of Musketry Instructor. Nobody else came to the office in place of George. I was not promoted, but I was left in peace.

On the morning of 15 August the service squadron marched out from Knightsbridge Barracks *en route* for Mons. There was no crowd to see them off. That was just as well. The men and horses looked fit. Joe Ratcliffe and I stood together just outside the gate as they passed, exchanging a word here and there, and now and then a handshake, with one or another of our special chums. The Band turned out to play them off. It struck up the most inappropriate tune that could be found, ' Where are the boys of the old brigade ? ' I felt like going across and throttling the Bandmaster.

When at length the Squadron had moved well up the road towards Hyde Park Corner, Joe and I turned quietly round and came back into Barracks. Without feeling distressed or in any way inclined to weep, both our eyes filled with tears. All of us who remained behind felt bereaved. We had, however, a brand-new regiment to create and shape, and that process provided us with occupation sufficient to divert our thoughts from the handful who had just gone on.

A few days later a draft of some twenty men was formed to proceed overseas to the base as a first reinforcement. It was composed of hard cases, mostly reservists of our own unit. They were due to march out dismounted at 10 a.m. The King, who was riding in the Row with Princess Mary, got wind of this somehow, and said he would come in to see the boys off. At ten minutes to ten the party formed up on the square. One man was missing. Apparently none of the others had seen him. It came to light that the delinquent was a famous character nicknamed ' Squeaker.' Suddenly the canteen door opened and the absentee appeared looking not exactly intoxicated, but just about three sheets in the wind. At the top of the landing stairs he let his rifle fall down ; then he followed it himself with a rush, collected his gun, and fell in on the left of the others. A second afterwards the King rode in. He sat on his horse beneath the clock as the draft marched out, and ' Squeaker,' keenly alive to the humour of the situation, and pulling himself together with a desperate effort, faded away into the distance with the others. Goodness only knows what would have been the end of him if the King had not come in just at the critical moment. The presence of His Majesty seemed to paralyse the new R.S.M. and render him incapable of dealing with ' Squeaker ' as the situation normally demanded.

VIII

MEANWHILE the formation of the new regiment of 1st Life Guards had been proceeding steadily from the day after war was declared. Terms of service in the Household Cavalry had only recently been altered from twelve years with the colours and no reserve service to eight years' colour service followed by a period of four years on the reserve. Our reservists therefore, when mobilized, were a mere drop in the sea. So far as I can recollect, they amounted in all to some sixty men. The King's pardon brought deserters to the number of about a dozen, but few of these were still fit for service. One was a wild man from Scotland, with flowing red whiskers. He was well over fifty and had deserted some thirty years before. His record was unearthed from among the regimental archives, and he was sent back to the ' land o' cakes ' with a free pardon in his pocket. Many men whose time had expired presented themselves at once for re-enlistment.

Officers came from many sources, and were, like the men, good, bad, and indifferent. In the very first days of mobilization we were startled by the appearance of an officer who had come back from retirement dressed in a rig-out which was a sight for the gods. His khaki jacket fitted him where it touched him ; his riding-pants were of coarse material, baggy, and reminiscent of knickerbockers at the knees. He wore in addition a pair of thick greased, hob-nailed ankle-boots, rough puttees, and a cap from which the wire had been removed and which looked as if it had been slept on. On his Sam Browne belt was a stout iron hook from which dangled a pair of hedging-and-ditching gloves. Before he had advanced ten paces inside the barrack gate he was unanimously christened ' Sinbad the Sailor.' The nickname seemed to jump to the minds of all those who saw him, and Sinbad he remained. In spite of his wierd uniform, Sinbad was a fine soldier and a fine gentleman. When somebody chipped him about his turn-out, I heard him reply in the deep, deliberate voice with which we were soon to be familiar : " My dear sir, you'll all be dressed like this, or worse, before Christmas." He was right.

A Veterinary Officer, Captain Tagg, the smallest man on earth, came and took over his duties, and for Quarter-master we were sent Captain ' Billy ' Garton of the Grenadier Guards. The latter appointment seemed a mistake, and there was no excuse for it. Captain Garton was a splendid old soldier whom everybody liked, but as a Footguardsman of some thirty years' service, he could know little concerning the equipment of a cavalry regiment. We had more than one man among our senior N.C.O.s who could have filled the post with efficiency and confidence, but no attempt was made to give any of them preference. The same policy of ignoring the advancement of our own men persisted throughout the whole campaign. In fact no regular soldier of the 1st Life Guards ever got a commission during the war, except one, a clerk somewhere at the base.

Owing to our scanty reserves, the authorities decided to build the three Household Cavalry regiments to war establishment with line-cavalry reservists. Accordingly we filled up with Dragoons and Dragoon Guards, the 2nd Life Guards with Lancers, and the Blues with Hussars. Our Dragoons began to arrive almost immediately in batches of from twenty to a hundred, and within a week or so we had reached the full complement of six hundred men. About 70 per cent of the whole number were Inniskillens (for some reason or other, which I could never ascertain, spelt ' Inniskillings '). The next largest faction came from the 1st King's. Office work in connection with the documents and posting of our guests provided me with some hectic days.

A merry dance they led us for a time. The ' Skins,' being the most numerous section, regarded mobilisation as a reunion and an occasion for great and prolonged jollifica-tion. Their high spirits were understandable to me at least. Most of them were Irishmen, but of the Liverpool, Glasgow, and Tyneside varieties. Only comparatively few came from ' the old country,' and there was the never-failing sprinkling of Cockneys. All of them had served together for seven years in India, except for a short spell in Egypt on the way out. For about a year on an average they had been home on the reserve, and had not quite settled down to the comparatively drab existence of civilians. Now here they were, quite unexpectedly collected together again in one place, as if by magic. No wonder they felt inclined to make merry. Their N.C.O.s were few and feeble. Naturally the ' Skins ' were not going to send us their very best N.C.O.s.

As a whole they rather resented being attached to us at first. They accused their own regiment of breach of faith in casting them out. They had a high opinion of their own value as soldiers, and their main grievance was that they had been drafted to a miserable regiment of tin soldiers in order to prevent us by their gallantry and soldierly qualities from disgracing ourselves when we came into action. Anyway, their behaviour was, to put it very mildly, somewhat wild.

Horses for the new regiment could not begin arriving till room was made for them by the departure of the original ones. Thus for the first fortnight the Dragoon reservists had no occupation and not much room to enable us to get to grips with them. They lounged about in groups and were always obsessed with a burning desire to get drunk and sing. In this respect they seemed to be remarkably successful. Most of the day and half the night the barracks rang with the song of the ' Skins,' a somewhat melancholy lay, especially when keened in the small hours by a couple of dozen more or less tipsy Irishmen, in a medley of brogues from the four corners of the Kingdom. The chorus of their regimental song was familiar to me since my boyhood days, when I had heard it sung during the Boer War. It ran as follows :

> " Fare thee well, Inniskillen,
>   Fare thee well for a while,
>   And all the fair borders of Erin's green isle.
>   When the war is over
>   We'll return very soon,
>   And they'll all welcome home the Inniskillen Dragoon."

By way of a change they sometimes fell back on an Indian ditty, partly in Hindustani, or at least what the British soldier took for that venerable language. The song seems to have had an only verse, and a refrain which appears to have made a tremendous appeal to them. To the best of my recollection the whole ditty went like this :

> " Seven long years you've drunk my waters ;
> Now you're off to Blighty O.
> May the boat that takes you over
> Go to the bottom of the pawnee O !
> Hoolam da-a-a.
> Hoolam da-a-a.
> Cha rann archig archig
> Doh pye spukkaree."

We Lifeguardsmen were scandalised at the continuous carousals of the Dragoons and their complete lack of interest in all our attempts to make them comfortable and promote their welfare. The greatest shock to our innate respectability came one day when the ' Skins ' were visited by their old Riding Master, Bill Judd. They seized him and bore him to the canteen, and when that place of entertainment closed, they carried him shoulder high, all in their shirt-sleeves, across Knightsbridge to the ' Trevor,' while the sedate thoroughfare echoed with the strains of ' Fare thee well, Inniskillen.'

The rest of the Dragoons were quiet and orderly, not being sufficiently strong in numbers to compete with the redoubtable ' Skins.' The whole contingent and its ways puzzled us a great deal to begin with. They all looked very much alike, and we found it difficult to pick out and remember individuals. Many of them did not give us much opportunity to cultivate their acquaintance, because they soon developed the habit of being in full strength on pay-day, and then vanishing in gangs for the rest of the week. The Londoners had their friends at hand, and the others soon made friends. However, with the departure of the service squadron on 15 August, we were able to enjoy more of their society, and got to know them gradually. For all their wild and woolly ways, they were fine soldiers and good fellows, apart from a very small gang of toughs. These were separated in the various squadrons, and eventually we came to live, and later to die, with them in perfect harmony, and to regard one another as part and parcel of the same unit.

A few of the Dragoons had run to fat since leaving the colours, and were now stout, portly gentlemen. Harry Pudney, later a very great friend of mine, was one of these. When at last he was fitted out with uniform and given a pair of horses in the transport lines, he discovered to his profound disgust that he could not mount. The dimensions of his waistline prevented him from putting his foot in the stirrup. That was serious. It might even mean being left behind, if the war lasted long enough for our new regiment to be sent out. A stout heart beat behind Harry's distended waistcoat, and staying at home was for him a dreadful prospect. After serious contemplation of the situation, he lowered the stirrup down to the full extent of the leather. He could now get his foot in all right, but was too low down to throw his right leg over his steed. It was hopeless. He begged and prayed to be kept where he was, and Tom Phillips, now acting as Transport Sergeant, who had an eye for a good soldier, and was not himself quite so slim as he used to be, gave Harry the post of wheel-driver on the box of a wagon. In course of time, the rigours of the campaign reduced his waist to such an extent that he was able to mount with the best of us.

Another interesting case was Norman Scott, one of our own reservists. He, too, found his way to the transport. His difficulty was worse even than Harry's. Norman could mount quite easily, but the reverse operation greatly perplexed him, for so large were his feet that he could not withdraw them from the stirrups when ordered to dismount. This was also solved. Jock Faid of the 'Skins,' Norman's fellow-driver on the same wagon, provided himself with a mallet which he always carried on his saddle. When the time to dismount arrived, Jock sprang to earth like a squirrel and knocked the irons off Norman's boots.

Horses were supplied almost entirely from private sources. They came from stables all up and down the country, and were of all sorts, sizes, and colours. Some were sober-minded old stagers, who took to soldiering as a duck takes to water; but not a few were violently opposed to conscription, and many a rider came a cropper in Rotten Row as a result.

Our efforts to weld the reservists and ourselves into something resembling a regiment met with little success. Tattersall's and Ward's Yard were acquired for additional stabling and men's quarters. The whole of the transport camped in Hyde Park. This distribution of groups here and there, with strings of public houses as connecting links, did not tend to improve our prospects. The utter futility of the whole business was soon realised, and at the end of August we were moved away down to Salisbury Plain. Here, on the slopes of Windmill Hill, above Ludgershall, the three regiments pitched camp; 'K' Battery, Royal Horse Artillery, Signal Troop, and Field Ambulance soon joined us, and one fine morning, early in September, we were in a position to behold ourselves in a compact mass as the 7th Cavalry Brigade.

Field training was begun in real earnest; all were under constant supervision and in continuous employment during the daytime, and far removed from the many pitfalls of London. In an incredibly short time men and horses were all in good condition.

During the first week or so a healthy hustle pervaded the whole vast camp. Then some rumour-merchants started broadcasting the interesting information that we were to be retained in England for home defence. No steps were taken by the authorities to enlighten anybody. The troops were satisfied that the rumour was true. Where in the whole British Army, they argued, was a better regiment to be found? Almost every man was an experienced soldier of eight years' service; the war had already been started over a month; if the authorities had any intention of using us in the field they would have sent us out long ago. What were we hanging about for on Salisbury Plain?

It would have been so simple to tell the men we were waiting for certain units to arrive from abroad, in order to make up a complete cavalry division. We were to proceed to the front as a division, not as a brigade. But nothing was said. Even I, who was in the orderly room, knew nothing of the reason at the time.

Once the day's training and duties were finished, the men had the evening and night to themselves. All were convinced that the war would be over before Christmas, and therefore we were wasting time. In another couple of months they would be back again in civilian life without having struck a blow. A jolly fine way to treat old soldiers ! So away they went as soon as 'Dismiss' was sounded, into the neighbouring villages, where they played merry hell.

There were, of course, camp bounds, roll-call, police, a guard-room ; in fact, all the approved means of preserving good order and military discipline ; but they were all rendered quite impotent, simply because the reservists did not care a hang for any or all of them. Possessing nothing in the nature of conduct sheets whereon entries might be collected to the prejudice of their future careers, they scorned the whole machinery.

The canteen which served our regiment was housed in a huge marquee at the bottom of the hill, and run by a civilian firm. The manager went in constant fear of his life. Night after night, when the camp was abed, a gang of toughs raided him, and rolled barrels of beer out under the tent walls and down into the ditch beside the railway line. Here they held all-night carousals. The echoes of the Plain rang with 'Fare thee well, Inniskillen' ; and Kitchener's Army, away over on Perim Down, attracted by the sounds of revelry, came across and joined in.

Then, especially at week-ends, many men left camp and stayed away for two or three days without leave. On Mondays and Tuesdays the muster of prisoners outside the C.O's. office was like a squadron parade. The offenders were marched in one by one, made no excuse for their absence, and received their punishment with complete indifference. They believed it was going to be a short war, so they determined to make it a gay one.

All those punishments, together with promotions, allotments of pay, and a thousand and one other things, made the proper carrying out of the work in the orderly room impossible. The business of preparing a regiment for war has its paper side as well as its practical side. Many matters of vital interest to the men and their dependants have to be dealt with in a regimental orderly room. However, training seemed to be the only thing that mattered. Sometimes of an evening Jim Fleming came and gave me a hand. I just did my best under the circumstances and let the rest go, hoping daily to be ordered abroad.

It must not be thought, from what I have said of the men's attitude to life in general and soldiering in particular at this period, that we were a disorderly rabble. Nothing could be farther from the truth. The disorder set in at the end of the day, after work was finished. During the day's work everything went as smoothly and efficiently as could be desired. But the preservation of discipline called for strong N.C.O.s, especially Sergeant-Majors. Some dear old dodderers, who had been the bane o many a poor young devil's existence in the old regiment, had to be removed.

Tom Phillips became one of the new Sergeant-Majors, and he at once set about restoring and maintaining order by getting in among the toughs in person and throwing his jacket off when he considered it necessary. He gave one or two stiffs a sound hiding. The result was a complete success, and the men soon held him in profound admiration and respect. Bob Harrison and Barney Rudd had used the same line of treatment from the very start, with equally good results. In fact, their Squadron soon became rather like a large, happy family, with the Sergeant-Major and Quarterbloke as father and mother. They treated every man as a man, without fear or favour, and insisted on receiving similar treatment themselves in return. I know from my own mixing amongst them that every man in the Squadron, whether Lifeguardsman or Dragoon, regarded these two N.C.O.s as his own personal friends. The Squadron was also fortunate in its Captain, the Hon. A. F. Stanley, whom the boys called ' Old Digger.'

The formation of Troops necessitated the promotion to Sergeant of some Corporals who were junior to me. Being in the orderly room I was not in the running, and I had to put the matter very plainly to the Adjutant. After a while I was made Acting Sergeant, like many others,

F

including Fleming and Channon. I was now an Acting Corporal just changed into an Acting Sergeant, all of which meant actually that I was a Trooper wearing three chevrons. I had no substantive rank, and could be summarily ' broken ' by the C.O. There was, however, one great advantage, namely, all acting ranks were paid at the rate for the substantive rank.

It suddenly occurred to somebody that, as a member of a cavalry regiment, I ought to be provided with a horse. Barney Rudd made a survey of those in his squadron and selected one sufficiently useless to bestow upon me. With it he sent me a batman, a very young Grey, named Macfadyen. Both could easily be spared. The horse was old and over at the knees; Mac spoke the broadest Scots I have ever heard, so they could make nothing of him. He was, however, a good youngster. I was glad to meet him afterwards on the Somme as a corporal in his own regiment.

Towards the end of September, although I had been given no information, I could see that the authorities were daily expecting orders for the front. There were signs, too, that they feared, when the orders came, that half the troops would be on French leave. It would have been so much wiser not to have kept us all in the dark.

At last, on Sunday morning, 5 October, we were ordered to entrain at Ludgershall at 6 p.m. Hundreds of men were on leave, French and otherwise; and hundreds of telegrams were sent by me to the addresses left by the permissionaires. As in most cases the said addresses were fictitious, the results of my effort to rally the clans may be imagined. However, some of the telegrams must have got home; cars were sent out on all the neighbouring roads; officers and other ranks on leave in London collected anybody they came across. Incredible as it may seem, when the moment came to march out, not a man was missing. As a matter of fact, we had one extra, though nobody noticed him at the time. He was a civilian friend of one of the reservists, who, determined to go to the front with his chum, secured a suit of khaki somewhere, and passed unnoticed in the crowd.

While saddles were being packed and put on, including mine by the faithful Macfadyen, I laid everything in the shape of papers and documents out on a table in the orderly room, so that they might easily be taken over by an officer who had come down from London to take over the camp. But he, like everybody else, seemed to forget that the orderly room existed. When he arrived he refreshed himself at the mess, inspected cook-houses and latrines, but kept well away from my department. The troops began to file towards the station, and, not wishing to be left all alone on Windmill Hill, I dumped all papers into a large box and banged down the lid. I then called Mac, mounted my poor old nag, and proceeded cautiously towards the train. I was never again to function within an orderly room, and I thanked heaven for my release.

Darkness had begun to set in while the horses were being run into the trucks. This proved to be an exciting job. Our regiment alone had six hundred to entrain, and they stood on a narrow platform waiting their turn. There was a line running behind them, on which trains kept continually passing, and it was a miracle nobody got dragged on to the rails and run over.

It was here I first made the acquaintance of Herbert. He belonged to a young Corporal named Lister. He was the tallest horse in the unit, and he had a dislike amounting to violent hatred for trains, buses, steam-engines, and all huge things which moved mechanically and made strange noises in their insides. He absolutely refused to enter his truck, but there was no time for ceremony, so half a dozen hefty soldiers slipped a surcingle round his hind quarters and gave him a lift. This decided him to make a plunge through the door of the truck, but being so tall his saddle caught in the roof, and he bounced back amongst us, more obstinate than ever. We then turned him round, removed his saddle, and backed him in without more ado.

My steed made no objection to travelling by rail. It was quite dark by the time all horses were aboard. Then I found myself seated in a third-class carriage among my fellow-warriors, puffing away from the Plain, and wondering in what direction we were going.

IX

A SHORT journey of a couple of hours brought us to
Southampton. To the accompaniment of much
lurid language, horses were detrained and we
mounted and formed up. Then began what threatened to
become an endless promenade of the outskirts of the town.

At long last we turned up on the Common. Horses were
pegged down on ground-lines, after which we bivouacked
beside them. I rolled myself up in my blanket, stuck my
head in the saddle, and slept through the remainder of the
night in fits and starts. There was a heavy ground frost,
and when day dawned I was glad to get up and stretch my
legs. The bivouac and horse-lines presented a comical
sight. In the darkness lines had been badly put down. The
curled-up forms of the men making the most of the last few
moments before reveille, lay about like shapeless, floating
logs. The funniest was old Jack Harrison of the 1st
King's, ' the Sad old Saddler,' as Charlie Wright christened
him on account of his venerable age and hairless pate. As
he poked his bald head from beneath the blanket he rubbed
his eyes, and with the air of a half-frozen chimpanzee,
mumbled : " Heck ! I wur as cowld as hell, I wur ! "

After breakfast the Adjutant sent me to Headquarters for
secret orders. The receiving of these from the hands of a
venerable brass-hat was an awe-inspiring and ceremonial
occasion which caused me much amusement. They
resulted in the regiment embarking that afternoon.

Soon after midday we rode through the town towards
the docks. Nobody in the streets took the slightest notice
of us. We might have been a troop of boy scouts going to
week-end camp for all the citizens of Southampton cared.
No time was wasted at the docks. Our transports stood
ready, and the task of putting horses on board began
at once. One vessel was allotted to Regimental Head-

quarters and 'D' Squadron. It contained three decks.
The horses were not slung on board, but rushed one by one
up a gangway on to the ship, and then down two or three
more into its depths. The lower deck was filled first, then
the middle and upper ones. The gangways were steep, and
the man-handling of the horses a tricky business. I brought
several on, including Herbert.

During the embarkation of the horses, some of our
officers, who believed their presence vital to its success,
gave up their chargers to little Johnny Hume, the Colonel's
Trumpeter, and hurried to the front to get in the way.
Johnny, a very tiny man, soon had eight horses making
rings round him, and was right at the end of the column.
Nobody gave him a thought. As the head of the column
became swallowed up in the boat, an ever-widening space
separated him from the rest of us. As the last few horses
were being rushed up the gangway, Johnny's eight decided
it was time for them to get aboard. Simultaneously they
raised their heads, neighed loudly in unison, lifted the wee
man off the earth and made a dash for the gangway. They
bore him along like a fly, gradually increasing their pace,
till luckily some of us saw his perilous predicament and
went to his rescue.

Our transport bore the name *Huanchaco*, but I failed to
discover her port of registration. Part of her history,
however, was written on the walls of her latrines in the
shape of nursery rhymes in Spanish and Portuguese. From
these I concluded her peace-time calling was the trans-
portation of emigrants from the Peninsula to South
America. Whatever her nationality or line of business, she
was a perfect sea-boat. That was a blessing, not only for
us, but also for the horses. They were rather crowded
down below and thoroughly disgusted with their surroundings and with the water supplied them for drinking.

As darkness fell on the evening of 6 October, we
crawled slowly down into the English Channel and turned
eastwards. All of us sought out a suitable place on deck to
sleep. Lister and I, like two good land-lubbers, arranged a
fine double bed on top of a hatchway. We thought our
position excellently situated up in the open air and out of

danger of being trodden upon. Everything went well till we got out into the open Channel and the breeze freshened up. It nearly blew us out of our blankets, so there was nothing for it but to scrap our beautiful bed, and as all other space on deck was crowded, find a sheltered corner where we kept falling off to sleep as we stood up, and spent our waking moments cursing the cold, the ship, and everything we could think of.

Daybreak on the 7th October saw us out in the Channel and steaming eastwards at a snail's pace within view of the South Coast. Our skipper paced his bridge as though looking for something to turn up. Very soon it did. A patrol boat raced alongside, and the naval officer in command bellowed at him through a megaphone. Our skipper seemed somewhat hard of hearing, so we heard him being roundly cursed and ordered with great picturesqueness to proceed to the Downs.

During the whole of that day we continued our crawl along the coasts of Hampshire, Sussex, and Kent. In the evening, just as darkness was gathering, we joined a huge convoy in the Downs containing the 7th Division and 3rd Cavalry Division. That same night we set out in inky darkness. All sorts of destinations were predicted, including Davy Jones' locker. We had no idea what route was being followed, so we just gave it up and tried to get some sleep.

At dawn next morning, 8 October, our vessel lay a short distance from a long concrete arm sticking out into the sea about half a mile. Still the curious ones were baffled. Our line of vision shorewards was blocked by the concrete wall. From time to time a head with a fantastically-shaped head-dress peered over it in our direction. Orders were at length received for us to get alongside the mole. Here we ascertained the place was Zeebrugge, and the gentry with the pantomime hats Belgian gendarmes.

So far as we could see, there was nowhere in the neighbourhood any sign of war. Indeed the only warlike folk anywhere about were ourselves. Several civilians came alongside as we were awaiting orders to disembark, and tried to converse with us in broken English. They got little information, as the troops refused to discuss anything beyond the prospects of getting something to drink. It struck me at this moment that my French, however rusty it may have been just then, would prove very useful to me in the days ahead.

Almost as soon as we got alongside, the Colonel sent for me, ordered me to get my horse, and go at once with an officer and an interpreter to find billets for the Regiment in the neighbourhood of Blankenberghe. I had my poor old steed off the boat in quick time. He looked about as sorry and hopeless a mount as one could well wish for on the first day of a campaign such as we had before us. It was not his fault, and I was deeply sorry for him. The poor old fellow was not fit, and had no business to be there at all. When I mounted him he nearly collapsed under me. Still, he stuck it bravely, and I now found myself one of a group comprising the two officers, with their servants, and a stout signaller named Sammy Hughes.

It was a glorious autumn morning. A clear sky, bright sunshine, and a bracing breeze combined to put us in excellent spirits. We also felt elated at being ashore again, and making our way into the unknown in advance of the remainder of the regiment. The road was paved, so we took to the left side in Indian file, where the going was soft on the turf. We had yet to learn, by dint of being cursed, that on the Continent the rule of the road is ' Keep to the right.' The flat, clean landscape, dotted here and there with windmills, seemed somehow quite familiar to me, and I felt thoroughly at home, in spite of the fact that I had seen no country of a similar nature before.

Half an hour or so brought us to Blankenberghe. We dismounted on a triangular patch of green turf at a fork road on the edge of the town. Here the two officers and one servant left us to go in search of the Burgomaster. They gave us no instructions as to how long they would be away; so when they had been gone some time, we off-saddled, and allowed the horses to graze.

We lay down on the grass, stretched our legs, and basked in the warm sunshine. A crowd, composed for the most part of flappers, surrounded us. We failed at first to grasp what they were after, but they soon enlightened us by making a combined assault on our badges and buttons. This forward behaviour on the part of strange maidens who appeared to be of the better class, astonished, not to say shocked us. Finally someone gave a lass a button. She vanished with it, and then the affair looked like developing into a free fight. One hefty damsel, who discovered I spoke French, pestered the life out of me for my cap-badge. She was so persistent that I'm afraid I was rude to her. She kept on rolling her eyes and repeating : " Je le garderai toujours, toujours, toujours ! " It struck me that she may have wanted it for purposes of identification.

In order to escape, Sammy Hughes and I beat a retreat to an *estaminet* close by. Here we were able to procure bacon, eggs, and beer. The food tasted good, but the beer, though a good dark colour, tasted like vinegar. We tried some light-coloured beer later, but it was almost tasteless. This discovery was the cause of intense forebodings on the part of Sammy. His optimistic outlook on the campaign received a severe shock. He could not see how we could possibly win a war on beer like that. I gave the waitress half a crown. She seemed to know its value and actually gave me some change.

The day wore on without a sign of our two officers. Late in the afternoon the head of the regiment made its appearance in the direction from which we had come in the morning. 'A' and 'C' Squadrons had disembarked at Ostend, joined the others at Zeebrugge, and waited there all day for orders. They came along on foot, leading their horses in half-sections. The two officers appeared as if by magic. We saddled up and fell in in our places in the moving column.

Here one of the strangest happenings in my life took place. As I was moving along in my place, there occurred a block in the traffic ahead which caused us to halt. We drew up in front of a large private house with a tier of steps going up to the door. On the steps stood a group of girls, all dressed and wearing hats as if about to set off on a journey. One tall girl about eighteen years of age and dressed all in black came down the steps and made straight

for me. To my amazement she addressed me with:
" You're Irish, aren't you ? " I owned up, and we shook
hands. She told me she came from Tramore and was at
school there in Blankenberghe. The school had broken up,
and they had orders to get away home as best they could.
She asked my advice, and I told her to make straight for
Ostend. Just then the column began to move, so we shook
hands again and I got along. I never found out who she
was or what became of her.

As we passed through the town, the civilians turned out
to give us a reception. They swarmed round us offering us
cigars and beer. A certain senior officer was furious when
he saw a man accept a glass of beer. He shouted to him:
" They'll poison you, you damn fool ! " I happened to
ride alongside that thirsty soul, Farrier Ted McKlosky.
Once as we halted, a fat lady ran across from her doorway
and handed him a pot of foaming light-coloured beer. With
one mighty swipe Ted drained it, then handed back the pot
with a perplexed look on his face. When the good lady had
disappeared from view he spat viciously on the ground, and
with a look of despair in his eye exclaimed : " Crikey !
Kids' beer ! "

We duly passed through Blankenberghe, and we of the
billeting party began to wonder what had become of the
billets, as we bivouacked beside a railway line, with a ridge
of sand-dunes between us and the sea. Everything soon
became smothered in damp sand. I think it was here I first
experienced a feeling of loneliness, and realised the grim
business ahead. This was especially so when in the middle
of the night I heard the boom of guns in the direction of
Antwerp. That was the first firing I heard in the war.

X

I BELIEVE the immediate objective of our little force,
consisting of the 7th Infantry Division and the 3rd
Cavalry Division, was the relief of Antwerp. The
Belgians, however, had already begun their retirement from
that city on the day we landed, and it actually fell into
German hands on the following day, 9 October. We
tried to cover the Belgian retreat, and at the same time to
find touch with General Allenby's Corps, so as to establish
a line of sorts between the Germans and the Channel ports.

On 20 October the stage was set for the first battle of
Ypres. The allies were placed as follows :

The 3rd British Corps across the Lys.

1st and 2nd Cavalry Divisions from Messines to
Zandvoorde.

7th Division from Gheluvelt to Zonnebeke.

3rd Cavalry Division from Zonnebeke to Poelcapelle.

Haig's 1st Corps from Zonnebeke to Bixschoote.

French Cavalry Corps between Haig and Dixmude.

Belgians reinforced by French Marines, Infantry and
Territorials, from Dixmude to the sea.

The part played by an individual soldier in a big operation like the retreat from Antwerp is necessarily insignificant. His chief interest and responsibility throughout the
whole scheme is to keep himself, his horse, and his weapons
in the best possible condition ; to endeavour always to have
a bite in his haversack, corn in his horse's nosebag, and a
full complement of ammunition in his pouches. Owing to
his very limited knowledge of whys and wherefores, and
the rapidity with which places and incidents follow one
upon another, he is apt to retain but a hazy impression of
the whole period when he tries to look back upon it.

The actual retreat covered the days between 8 October
and 20th. For me they were chock-full of interest, and
often excitement. The role allotted to us as cavalry,

namely, the protection of the left flank of the 7th Division and the finding of touch with Allenby's Corps about Kemmel, kept us continually on the move. We lived a 'here to-day and gone to-morrow' life. Billets were unthought of; indeed, till the end of November, we never slept under a roof. We simply got out of the saddle and slept, when we had the chance, on the ground beside our horses. The regiment was seldom collected in one body, but split up into patrols of varying size, from a section to a Squadron, and these were scattered in all directions. The distribution of rations was, therefore, largely a matter of luck. If we happened to run across the supply column we got some rations; if we did not we got none.

On 9 October we marched via Bruges to Lophem. We halted for an hour in Bruges. Here I was struck with the serene and ancient beauty of the old town. Its cobbled streets, canals, gateways, and belfry seemed to have gone to sleep centuries ago and to be still slumbering. At Lophem we remained till midday on the 10th. We bivouacked in the grounds of a large château whose inhabitants were most hospitable. I felt thankful I was still master of sufficient French to be able to talk to them.

When we reached the château grounds Lister tied Herbert to the wall of an outhouse while we went to fetch water. On the way to the well we were startled by a tremendous crash and hurried back. There stood Herbert with the wall lying in a heap at his feet. His hair stood on end with fright; his eyes stuck out, and he was snorting like a grampus. He wanted to go exploring on his own account, so he just pulled the wall down as if it had been a piece of stage property. He did not injure himself; but it was a lesson to us, and in future he was made fast to a decent-sized tree.

Here we received the first news of the enemy. Patrols were out all the time towards the south and east. One of these under Sinbad the Sailor reported running across him in the vicinity of Ypres and Dickebusch. I took out a patrol of four men myself that afternoon, but we saw nothing, as our scope was limited, and we were responsible only for the district within about a mile of Regimental Headquarters.

October 10 saw us on our way to Ruddervoorde. We

reached this place next day after a tedious march, due to the cobbled roads and the masses of retreating Belgians who hampered our movements. We met no Belgian infantry, only small bodies of cavalry and a considerable amount of artillery. The latter were a picture of desolation. The guns were covered with mud and dirt, limbers piled up mountain high with miscellaneous baggage thrown on any old how, harness cracking for want of attention, and horses exhausted.

We went and had a look round a battery which halted near us. The horses were a pitiful sight. They were quite worn out with rapid and continuous marching, and everywhere the harness touched them was a raw sore. The gunners and drivers were men of a big stamp. These never dreamed of dismounting to ease the wretched animals, but sat perched in the saddle calmly smoking and waiting for the word to march on. This was an eye-opener to us, who, however much we may have grumbled at them, thought more of our horses than we did of ourselves. We found in the end that this is the great failing of the continental cavalryman and artilleryman. French, Belgians, and Germans were all alike in this respect.

The following day found us at Rumbeke, a small town rejoicing in the possession of a race-course, on which we spent the night. On marching out next morning a German Taube monoplane hovered above us at a great height. It looked a sinister object, rather like a gigantic black hawk.

At midnight on the 13th we reached Iseghem. So far as I could make out, in the rain and darkness, it was a large, prosperous town. I have a vivid recollection of that place. The rate of marching during the day had been very rapid. On reaching the town many of us were dead-beat for want of sleep. The night was pitch black, and it rained cats and dogs. The Germans were not far away, but I had reached that pitch when nothing else but sleep matters, and, anyway, the Germans were the business of the outposts.

We were too weary even to go in search of something to eat and drink. So I just sat down on the edge of the pavement with my horse's reins over my arm, and was soon fast asleep. I knew nothing more till about 5 a.m., while

it was still dark, when I was awakened by shouts of
" Mount ! " When I awoke I discovered I had been sleeping soundly in the gutter, where the stream of muddy
water from the street had converted me into a waterlogged
island in the middle of a small lake. My poor old horse
stood there like a wet rag, waiting for me. I mounted,
and we hurried out of the town.

We were now on the way to Ypres. The morning broke
fine and clear ; but neither the sunshine nor the water in
my clothes could keep me awake. I kept falling asleep in
the saddle, and Freddy Cotton of the 'Skins' kept waking
me up. German patrols had been all over this part of the
country in the last day or two, and traces of them were to
be found here and there as we went along.

Ten a.m. on 14 October saw us make the acquaintance of
Ypres. We were fated to see much of it in the future.
Many of those who entered the smiling little town that
morning were destined to leave their bones somewhere in
its neighbourhood, and to those of us who survived, it was
our pet nightmare for years to come. Ypres was carrying
on with its normal peace-time activities. The town had
the day before received a visit from a body of German
cavalry, and a few shrapnel shells had been burst over the
outskirts. The inhabitants received us with open arms and
made a tremendous fuss of us.

Not one of us who admired the ancient town then, with
its imposing buildings, tree-bordered streets, rows of
handsome shops, and spick-and-span townsfolk, could
foresee the ghastly dust-heap to which it was doomed to be
reduced within the next few months.

I happened to halt just outside a convent. The nuns
got busy at once and sent us out basins of delicious soup
and bread. They pressed us to have as much as we could
eat. Needless to say, this taste of ' Christian diet ' was a
godsend. Many of them were Irish, and they preserved
within the convent since the days of Marlborough a standard
of the old Irish Brigade which formed part of the French
army long ago. When the battle began the nuns converted
their place into a dressing station. They stuck to their post
till the building full of wounded crumbled in on top of them,

During our halt of about two hours in Ypres there was a short period of breathless excitement. A German Taube flew over the town at a fair height. He was greeted by a burst of fire from a machine-gun which perceptibly staggered him. He did not crash, but lost height slowly and started coming down directly over the square. Civilians came rushing out of their houses with shot-guns and revolvers, and finally, when he was low enough, they actually bombarded him with bricks. He was brought down in the square, so we did not see what eventually became of him, though it was not difficult to guess.

At noon on 14 October we moved off towards Wytschaete. Guns were roaring just in front of us. This was Allenby rushing his left wing over the Mont des Cats in order to join up with us. The junction was successfully affected without drawing our Brigade into the main operation. That same evening Regimental Headquarters bivouacked about a sugar factory at Groote Vierstraat.

We were now definitely at grips with the outer fringe of the enemy. As we ourselves corresponded to this fringe, inasmuch as we were the feelers, eyes, and ears of the British force in this locality, brisk skirmishes with bodies of Uhlans were of frequent occurrence. The latter were shy of coming to close quarters, and, taking them all in all, not very likeable customers. In their methods they resembled prowling packs of wolves rather than soldiers. Hereabouts the country was a patchwork of villages, all connected up by light railways which ran along the roadsides. The trains were still running, and a favourite trick of the Uhlans was to leave their horses somewhere handy just outside, then board the next train and enter the village, where they terrorized the inhabitants, cut telegraph and telephone wires, looted the shops, and played up general old merry hell.

A patrol of ours, consisting of 'C' Squadron, had several small engagements on the 14th. They discovered the village of Gheluwe occupied by German cavalry, and promptly rushed it with two troops dismounted. A lively five minutes followed. This form of village fighting was particularly nasty, as the bullets ricochetted off the cobblestones and performed ugly tricks. Soon the party of

Uhlans was wiped out, all except two. One of these managed to reach his horse, sprang into the saddle, and galloped away. He went tearing along a straight road at full speed, and was gradually becoming a mere speck in the distance, when Sergeant Johnny Arthurs of the Skins took his rifle, sighted it at twelve hundred yards, and shot the Uhlan dead.

The second one took to running across country and was pursued by the Hon. Gerald Ward and a couple of mounted men. Soon he stopped, raised his carbine, and aimed straight at the officer. As the latter rode direct at him, he changed his mind, threw the gun down, and put up his hands. A wild fellow, named Bellingham, of the 'Skins,' galloped at him and ran him through the body with his sword. He then calmly wiped his sword on his horse's mane and remarked: "That's the way to serve them bastards." Those present were shocked at the cold-bloodedness of the deed, but there was some weight in the remark which followed it. At any rate, what might have been a nasty business for Master Bellingham was suffered to pass unheeded.

Casualties now began to be frequent, and no day passed without one or another of my old friends being killed. Bill Leggett was the first to go.

We remained about Groote Vierstraat till the morning of 16 October. I have no recollection of a village there, but I remember distinctly an inn, or *bierhuis*, opposite a large sugar factory. At the inn the Uhlans had behaved like wild beasts the day before we arrived there. Here we happened to be quite close to the Composite Regiment of Household Cavalry containing our Squadron which had left Knightsbridge on 15 August. Our officers motored over to see them, but they were still too far away to permit of an exchange of visits between the other ranks.

On the morning of the 16th we marched via Ypres to Poelcappelle. On the way one Squadron had news that a strong party of German cyclists was moving towards them. The Squadron dismounted and lined a hedge alongside the road in order to trap them. Suddenly a solitary Belgian soldier on a bicycle came up from the opposite direction and ran slap into the Germans round the corner. He sprang from his bike, fired into their teeth, then mounted and scooted back like the wind. The Germans, to our great disgust, turned tail and must have tried another route.

Once or twice during a halt outside a small village between Poelcappelle and Passchendaele we heard the report of a rifle close at hand. Thinking it was some idiot who had fired his rifle accidentally, we took no notice of the first report. But as the firing was repeated, and in the end somebody was hit, we could only come to the conclusion that we were being sniped. A search of the surrounding gardens was made, and two young men, apparently Belgian civilians, were caught red-handed. They had been keeping up the appearance of working in a garden a short distance from the road, and they were varying the monotony of gardening by taking pot-shots at us with a mauser rifle when an opportunity offered. I saw them marched away under escort, and a surly, square-headed pair they looked.

In the same village I could scarcely believe my own eyes when I saw a bent old man, about eighty years of age, hobble out from his house and cut our telephone wires which were laid past his door. We hustled him back into his cottage, closed the door, and the wires were repaired. Out he came to cut them again; so he, too, was arrested and marched away towards Ypres after the other two.

Just in the neighbourhood of Ypres were some weird specimens of civilians. Many were openly hostile to us. They may have been planted Germans, but I had an idea they were Boers, who, dissatisfied with British rule in South Africa, had emigrated to Belgium. Whatever they were, they hated us like poison, and we continued to suffer at their hands. Others, on the contrary, were clearly glad to help us in any way possible. I shall always remember the burly farmer who came along and attached himself to the 2nd Life Guards. He brought with him two magnificent Percheron horses which he insisted should be employed on the transport. Whatever might happen to the other wagons, our Belgian driver, with his laughing round face and battered slouch hat, and old Biffer Birch sitting beside him on the box, was always in the right place at the right time.

XI

ON the evening of 16 October our little game of hide-and-seek with the enemy came to an end. We were relieved by French troops and dropped back into Passchendaele. It was, in those days, a clean little country town, with rows of whitewashed houses, cobbled streets, and a large market square, on one side of which stood a church which seemed much too big for the size of the little community. When we marched in, about 9.30 p.m., the place was full of troops actually sleeping on the pavements and even in the middle of the streets. It was all we could do to avoid trampling on them.

My little party went right through and pulled up outside a large *estaminet* on the far side. Having seen to our horses, we trooped in, and found that the landlady, a buxom woman of some fifty summers, had already prepared a big dining-room for our reception. She had made an inexhaustible supply of excellent coffee, which she distributed to all of us, and refused to take payment. While we drank this she collected our ' Maconochies,' and we had them piping hot from her oven in less than no time. This was about the first issue of Maconochie we had received. It was tinned cooked meat with vegetables and gravy. If you had a fire and a little patience you made a hole in the tin and warmed it up; if not, as was generally the case, you simply ate it cold.

Having finished the first square meal we had eaten for some time, we drew up round a big fire, and while smoking and basking in the heat, fought our battles over again. Madame produced a bottle of rum, gave us a nightcap all round, and we cleared out about midnight to sleep beside our horses. Ducky Tennison and I collected some hay, which we spread in the shelter of a wall, stretched our weary bones upon it, and, covering ourselves with another layer of hay, slept peacefully till daybreak on the 17th.

I can remember the morning of 17 October quite clearly. It broke more like an August morning than an October one. We were soon astir, but Madame was before us, and coffee was ready for everybody. We numbered about twenty all told, and between mud and whiskers, we must have terrified any ordinary woman. Madame, however, was not an ordinary woman. She took us under her wing and mothered us like a hen with a brood of chickens during the time we were there. This treatment made a deep impression on all of us, and it began to dawn upon us what we were fighting for.

We had breakfast under civilized conditions. Before that it was rumoured that Madame had some daughters. That piece of news startled us so much that some of us had a shave and general brush up before breakfast. I am glad we did. The daughters were three in number, comely, cultured girls of eighteen, sixteen, and fourteen respectively. They were typically Flemish, with blonde hair, fresh complexion, and of sturdy build. The youngest became very friendly with me, and we managed to converse freely in French. The family appeared comfortable and well-to-do. The little girl was very nicely brought up. Her French was the product of a boarding-school, but her sisters would not speak anything but Flemish. Poor child, I'm afraid she had a thin time later on when the village fell into German hands. I know she got away, because one day, some weeks later, as the regiment rushed through Ypres at a trot, I saw her standing at the door of a tumble-down house. She recognised me and waved her hand, but I had to keep moving. She looked pale and haggard. I could not help wondering what had become of her mother and sisters, and I wished her well out of Ypres. It was a death-trap just then.

During the day outposts were placed to the east of the town, and protective patrols went out. No fighting took place, but a patrol reported late that evening that a château a mile to the east was occupied by the enemy. At midnight an officer and two men (Lord Somers, Hayden, and Hibberd) went out to verify this report. They approached the château and found it surrounded by sentries. The first sentry they met was killed silently, and they went on farther to see what they could find out. On their return they reported the château full of Germans. At daybreak ' A ' Squadron rushed the place, but the enemy had found their dead sentry and were clearing out when our people arrived. They managed to shoot a few Uhlans and capture half a dozen horses.

The captured horses were reduced to skin, bone, and sores. The saddlery was superior to that of our officers. The wallets were huge, and contained more odds and ends than a whole troop of ours. The horses' nose-bags were either deficient or empty. No wonder the much-boosted Uhlan is a poor cavalryman. Each of them ought to have had a lorry instead of an unfortunate horse. The ideal cavalry soldier travels as light as possible and is always nursing his horse. The continental horse-soldier, on the other hand, treats his horse like a bicycle, pushes it along all day, and expects it to keep going on air.

Each Uhlan was armed to the teeth. He carried a long straight sword, which was an extremely useful weapon, and could be used for cut as well as thrust. In addition, he carried an iron lance as long as a telegraph pole, and known to our troops as a ' gas-pipe.' For firearms he had an automatic pistol, and a short carbine sighted to six hundred metres.

As soon as ' A ' Squadron returned, the regiment moved out to Staden, where, in conjunction with the French cavalry, they became slightly engaged. Still, there was practically no fighting that day. I had orders to remain behind in Passchendaele to deal with a large mail which had arrived, so I spent the day in peace and quietness. Ducky Tennison stayed with me, and that night we slept again in our hay bed. As the regiment did not come in, there was some anxiety on the part of our sentries lest we should have a visit from the Germans while we were short-handed.

Next morning there was heavy artillery-fire to the northeast. It was rumoured the Germans were up in strength and making an attack on Roulers. The regiment accordingly took up a position on the Roulers–Menin road, where it was attacked by infantry and artillery in superior force. It held on for three hours, and then retired in conformation with the general retirement to Moorslede. We had several casualties, but our rifle-fire gave the enemy a bad time.

Not being with the main body of the Regiment in that action, I had a chance of seeing things from a spectator's point of view. In order to keep in touch with the movements of the troops in action, and to ensure the safety of the body of odds and ends in Passchendaele, I was placed with a few men on a windmill to act as an observation post. The mill stood on the edge of the town just where the main road from Roulers entered it. Being fairly lofty I was able to see Roulers and two or three villages in a semicircle to the north-east.

We took our stand there about 9 a.m., and one could see by the dense columns of black smoke and red brick-dust which were going up into the air like so many waterspouts from Roulers that the Germans were violently shelling that town. Suddenly a mob of French Territorials with red trousers, and packs as big as wardrobes on their backs, came running for all they were worth down the road towards us. They seemed to have a violent dislike for shells, so they ran till they fell down for want of breath, then gasped on their tummies till they got their second wind, jumped up again and continued on the shortest route for France.

It was bad policy on the part of the French authorities to send those poor old men to fight alongside us. They were long past standing up to an attack and quite incapable of delivering one. We held them in absolute contempt. They got us into all sorts of tight corners all the time they were mixed up with us. One thing they could beat us at was retiring. They marched back at a cracking pace, and often when we reached our billeting area we found every house in the place full of the little black-moustached imps, lying up to their necks in clean straw and smoking and gossiping as if the war was a thousand leagues away.

After the French came the villagers, a long procession of whom soon filled the road and came streaming past us into

Passchendaele. Such scenes are described in numerous war books, so there is no need for me to repeat the description. Anyhow, the poor people would have stood a slender chance of escaping if the British Tommy had been so careful of his skin as the French.

Before noon we were recalled from the mill and proceeded to join the main body of the regiment, which remained at Moorslede till the evening. We then retired behind the French to Zonnebeke.

While at Moorslede we had a chance to compare notes with our opposite numbers in the French army, the Cuirassiers of the Guard. They would not believe we were British Lifeguardsmen on account of our appearance in mud-stained khaki and rusty steel equipment. They were dressed in the glad rags of their review order. Many of them lay on their backs in all their glory asleep in a turnip field. They were fine men, not so tall as ourselves, but of a more sturdy build. They would have made magnificent infantry ; but for all the use they were then, they might just as well have been in Madame Tussaud's. Later in the day I saw one of them shot through the head by an infantry outpost of ours, who took them for Germans.

On the way to Zonnebeke, as darkness set in, the flames of four or five burning villages lit up the sky on our left and made the country-side as clear as day. Here the Colonel was taken ill and returned to England. All that night I was worried by the thought that the miller at Passchendaele was a spy. He had kept working his mill until right after we had left the place, when everybody else was collecting a few belongings preparatory to clearing out. It certainly looked fishy, but it was too late now to worry about him.

On 19 October 1914 the war of movement in open country lapsed into a state of trench warfare. The British dug a line beyond which the Germans, in spite of repeated attempts right up to Christmas, were unable to advance. The portion of this line which was most bitterly contested, and in which our lot happened to be cast during the whole operation, was the salient which bulged out to the north and east round Ypres.

During the eleven days which had elapsed since landing we had been continually marching and fighting. The German front had now stiffened everywhere between Lille and the sea. They were massing with the object of rolling up the allied line before them in an impetuous rush towards the Channel Ports. They did not keep us long in suspense as to their hopes and intentions. The ensuing battle, ' first Ypres,' was a grim business, a soldiers' battle. There was neither time, room, nor sufficient troops on our side for brilliant tactics. The actual battle lasted for three weeks.

During this time my regiment, with the 2nd Life Guards and the Blues, formed the 7th Cavalry Brigade under General Kavanagh, and with the 6th Brigade made up the 3rd Cavalry Division under Byng. We had all been issued with bayonets, and the part played by us was mounted infantry work. A portion of the line was allotted to the Division, and, when possible, the two Brigades relieved each other every forty-eight hours.

The brigade not in the line stood saddled up a short distance behind in reserve. Whenever any part of the line within a few miles was hard pressed or in danger of being broken, or whenever the French ran away and left a gap, the reserve brigade was called upon. It straightway galloped to the danger point, dismounted, and going in with the bayonet, put things again in order. It then held the line till relieved, after which it got back to its position in reserve.

Our Brigade seemed to get a call almost every time we were out, so we became known to the troops in the salient as ' Kavanagh's Fire Brigade.' We did this sort of job at least half a dozen times during the battle, and considering the desperate nature of the work, casualties on those occasions were comparatively small, but as luck would have it, they always seemed to claim our very best men. The shortage of casualties was largely due to the masterly way in which we were handled by our Brigadier. He never spared us, but wherever the Brigade went he took the lead, and there was no braver man in it than himself.

We now passed through a month, which, when looked back upon to-day, has the appearance of an ugly dream.

Several features stand out vividly, but the whole is so blurred as to defy any attempt at grasping it and presenting it as a correct and ordered sequence of events.

All idea of time was soon lost. Nobody could have named the date or the day of the week, and nobody cared. The only factors which reminded us of the passing of time were daylight and darkness. Our horses ceased to be employed as cavalry horses. Their role was similar to that played later by the omnibus, the rapid conveyance of rifle-and-bayonet soldiers to the line. The exciting scampering along country roads and through neat villages gave place to an existence comparable only to that of a water-rat in a swamp.

The autumn vanished suddenly and along came the winter with rain and sleet, which quickly changed the low-lying country into a quagmire. We became almost amphibious animals, wallowing in a sea of mud which normally reached our knees, and in shell-holes and trenches which threatened to swallow us up. Roads developed into paved causeways, ten feet wide, with a river of mud on each side of the *pavé*. Two vehicles were unable to pass on the solid surface, and to leave it meant disaster. The state of the roads presented a serious problem to those concerned with the transport of wounded, rations, guns, and ammunition. Soon we ceased to worry about roads, and always travelled across country, wading to our destination on a bee-line through the mud.

All through the battle there was no shelter either in or out of the line. When out, horses and men occupied a field, wherein every man and his chum tied their ground-sheets together and made a bivouac. These bivvies, especially towards the end of the battle, when we lay round about 'Mud Farm' at Verlorenhoeck, looked like pre-historic lake-dwellings, or roofed islands of sodden straw. Communication between them was rather like getting about in Venice, except that there were no gondolas available.

Being cavalry, we had no travelling kitchens like those of the infantry, so we seldom had a hot meal. The best one could do was to attempt to make some tea in a mess-tin, at the risk of being shot for making a pillar of smoke by day or a pillar of fire by night. All those little amenities were extra to the shelling, counter-attacks, and beating off of attacks which made up the ordinary day's work. During the whole time there was a steady drain of casualties, until a regiment was lucky if it could still furnish a hundred rifles for the line.

In these days of peace it is impossible to believe that one could carry on under such conditions. Yet our losses through illness were almost negligible.

XII

WE entered upon the first battle of Ypres under a new Commanding Officer. We still had two Wyndhams, a Grosvenor, and a Stanley left with us, so we were not exactly lost sheep.

On 20 October a defensive position was selected, and we marched to our allotted sector at 6 a.m. The Germans had not yet advanced to within rifle range, so we dug a line of trenches in broad daylight. We were on the left of the 7th Division at Zonnebeke. Slight rifle-fire broke out about 8.30 a.m., and soon afterwards the German artillery livened things up somewhat. It was recognised that a heavy push was threatened, and later in the morning orders were received to hold on to our position at all costs till the arrival of Haig's Corps. He did not, however, reach our front till next day. About noon the French on the left of the line were pushed back, so we were obliged to retire in order to preserve an unbroken line. The Germans made no advance towards us, but sprinkled us with shrapnel as we left the trenches. We retired on St. Julien.

The 7th Division remained about Zonnebeke, and during the night of the 20th the village was heavily attacked. The 22nd Infantry Brigade found itself hard pressed as there was a gap on its left flank. They called on the ' Fire Brigade '; we assisted in beating off the attack, whilst ' A ' Squadron filled the gap and remained in it for twenty-four hours.

Next morning we formed a flank guard to Haig's Army and conducted it without incident to Staden. No sooner was this job done than our old clients of the 22nd Brigade gave us another call. They were again having a thin time. We advanced and helped them on the west of Zonnebeke, held on till about 4 p.m., when the attack died down and we were relieved. We moved into reserve at St. Eloi.

I spent the night in an orchard behind a farm with old

Bill Whitehorn. It was bright and frosty. There was a lull in the firing and the night was the sort that keeps one awake and inclined to talk. Bill had had a busy day. As Doctor's right-hand man he dealt with the wounded, and a fine fellow he was at his job. If he had one fault it was his irrepressible urge to talk about it afterwards. This was due to no strain of boastfulness in his nature. A more modest man never lived. But with him talk was a safety-valve. If Bill could not talk he would just burst.

Well, it was a perfect night and we had settled down for a nap together on a tobacco-screen. Bill had some rum, which we shared. This lubricated his talking-machine, and I lay there in the calm moonlight listening, at first, with interest, to what sort of wounds Snuffy Webb, Joe Ratcliffe, and Harry Tapsell had received, and how he had treated them, and what he said to them and they to him.

Bill was one of those decent, sensitive souls who are all too scarce in this life. I would not have told him to shut up for the world. So at long last I snored loudly. He concluded I had fallen asleep and proceeded to follow my example. We could not have been asleep many minutes when we woke up with a start. The Germans, probably acting on information from spies, had started to drop shells into our orchard, nineteen to the dozen. We woke up in the midst of a generous display of fireworks and made to untie our horses and get into the open. Bill and I managed this without any trouble, but Jim Pearson, whose horse was tied with ours, was in the act of lifting the saddle on to its back when it dropped at his feet in a heap and left him standing holding the saddle in the air. The shelling went on for some time, the farm-house suffering badly, but nobody was hit. I'm afraid I said nasty things to myself concerning old Bill for keeping me awake so long. Sleep was valuable just then.

At dawn (22 October) we moved up to Hooge, where we remained in reserve all day. At 6 p.m. we retired to Klein Zillebeke for the night. I had made up my mind to have some sleep that night, come what might, but I was doomed to disappointment. I lay down with some others beneath a hedge within a short distance of the line. Rifle and machine-gun fire was pretty lively and loud all the time just in front. That, however, would not have kept us awake. To our unutterable disgust and surprise, we were awakened at least half a dozen times during the night by cheering and the sounding of trumpets. We could make nothing of it all.

Next morning we found the explanation in an adjacent farm, where we witnessed a parade of a French infantry battalion. We held our breath when we saw them. Here was something new. Finer infantry I have never seen. They called themselves 'the Ironsides,' and apparently lived up to their name, for they had attacked the enemy several times during the night and inflicted severe loss on him. We could have worked with fellows like those. If only the French had sent us a division or two of them instead of the little old men, then I believe the story of the October fighting in West Flanders would certainly have been different.

At 8.30 a.m. we moved up to Zandvoorde to relieve the 6th Cavalry Brigade in the trenches. Every man paraded except the very smallest number necessary to look after the horses. On reaching the ridge we received a snappy greeting with shrapnel. Some of the officers, including the C.O., were hit. It was then decided to postpone the relief till the evening, as it was evident that the Germans were now in a position to make daylight reliefs costly, if not impossible. We moved back again to Klein Zillebeke, where we spent a peaceful day. When darkness came in the evening we advanced and took over the line. Our position was on the left of the Brigade, next to the 2nd Gordon Highlanders, who were on the right of the 7th Division.

The ensuing forty-eight hours in the line were my first spell of actual trench work. It proved so interesting that every detail connected with it is still fresh in my mind and never likely to be forgotten.

When the regiment paraded to move off, it was found that thirty men of 'D' Squadron were engaged on some job which prevented them from mustering with the rest. I was ordered to wait behind and collect them. Having done this I was to proceed about half a mile along a road to the bottom of Zandvoorde Ridge, where a guide would meet us and conduct us to our position.

There was a moon somewhere hidden behind the clouds, but when my little bunch assembled it was quite dark. We had no difficulty in getting to the spot where the guide (Clements) met us. He did not give a very inviting description of things in the line. However, this was neither the time nor the place to hold a meeting, so we took in across country, Clements leading, the men following in single file, and I last of all. Soon we were climbing up the back of the low, broad ridge, on the forward slope of which were our trenches. The men immediately in front of me were John Lawrence, a Belfast Orangeman; Tom Birch, a Wexfordman; and Harry Pudney of Tooting. They were a fair sample of the whole thirty, and about as bright a trio as anybody could wish for.

We got along famously till we gained the top of the ridge and entered a garden beside a small farm-house. As the moon just at that moment peeped through a crack in the clouds, I expect we became visible to the enemy on the skyline. He immediately let fly at us with machine-gun and rifle fire. We straightway fell flat among the vegetables and listened to the bullets clipping the turnip-tops and zipping into the ground in our immediate neighbourhood. It was pretty accurate shooting, too. Although none of us was hit, Will Franklin discovered later that a machine-gun had fired a spurt right underneath him, between his stomach and the ground. His cloak was torn in shreds just as if it had been slashed across with a very sharp knife.

After a few minutes the firing died down, so we made for the wall of the farm-house, going all out on hands and knees. When all were up I passed the word to move on, when Lawrence abruptly announced that he very desperately needed to fall out. I could not refuse his request, and being responsible for seeing them all into the trenches, Birch, Pudney, and I stayed with him.

As soon as John was ready to proceed, we found to our dismay that the guide and the remainder of the party had vanished. Of course they had made a dash forward when given the word to move on, and had disappeared in the trenches farther down the gentle slope. The night was now as black as the pit. Here then were we four beauties— three Irishmen and a simple Cockney—behind the wall of a burnt farm, without the haziest idea of where our trenches were, and nothing to guide us to them except the none too attractive flashes of rifles below us. However, none of us wished to let the others see he was in a blue funk, so we made a rush down the slope only to flop and flounder once more when Fritz hailed us with another sprinkle of bullets.

Then we set off crawling, and Lawrence's language became lurid when we found ourselves crawling up into the necks of our long cavalry cloaks which got under our knees. As luck would have it, we actually crawled in the darkness right between two of our own trenches, thus getting in front of a portion held by Sergeant Dapper Smith and a few men. Dapper was a bloodthirsty fellow, so he turned the fire of his section on us at point-blank range. By a miracle none of us was hit, and when the language issuing from the trench caused the true state of affairs to dawn upon us, Tom Birch called them a few complimentary names and requested them, none too politely, to turn it off. They ceased fire and we set about distributing ourselves in the line.

This process of distribution of ourselves was an almost hopeless task. There was no continuous line. The trenches were a series of holes, for all the world like large graves, not connected, and running zigzag across the hillside. At the point where we struck them each trench was chock-full of men who absolutely refused to admit us into their already cramped space. Our best course, we concluded, was to separate and seek admission where there was less crowding. I soon dropped into a hole manned by a corporal and three men (Davy Deas, Gillman, Keefe, Lebentz). My gate-crashing gave them cause to grouse, and grouse they did, but I found favour in their sight when I let it be known I had a cargo of Woodbines on my person.

Birch and Lawrence kept together, and after crawling round for some time at the risk of their lives, and getting roundly cursed everywhere they went, eventually came across an empty trench, which they speedily occupied. This was almost too good to be true. They began to put their house in order, when suddenly their hair stood on end at the sight of a crouching figure approaching them from the front. Birch was all for shooting at once, but Lawrence challenged the visitor. A faltering voice replied something which sounded like "Pardon!" Birch raised his rifle, exclaiming: "Pardon be damned! Shoot the bastard!" Lawrence, however, suddenly realized who the stranger was, and knocking Birch's rifle aside, he shouted: "Holy Jasus, don't fire! It's poor ould Harry Pudney."

They gave Harry a hearty welcome. The poor devil was about done up and bubbling over with indignation. For half an hour he had been crawling about in a spray of bullets, seeking an opportunity to hold a portion of the line for his King and country and being grossly insulted everywhere he showed his nose.

We were now all safely in the line, so I passed word to that effect along to Captain Stanley. I then set about finding my bearings by questioning the original occupants. It appeared that the Germans, like ourselves, had no permanent line, but occupied a series of similar holes from a hundred to two hundred yards from ours. They had the range of our position to an inch, and kept sending over bursts of machine-gun and rifle fire which whistled along our parapet. We were within a hundred yards of the edge of Zandvoorde village, and Jim Fleming's Troop occupied the holes between us and the Gordons.

The farm through which we had passed on our way up was still smouldering. I inquired how they were off for rations and found they had a seven-pound tin of bully beef, no biscuits, and no water. Rather a pleasing prospect for five men for forty-eight hours. I had a pocket-full of small biscuits, but so long as I had plenty of Woodbines the thought of hunger did not worry the others.

The trench was about ten feet long, two feet wide, and five feet deep. I set about enlarging the left end with my bayonet, we had no entrenching-tools, till I had made a small cave in which I could sit without cramping the other four. I then fixed my bayonet and laid my rifle on the parapet. Just as I was doing so the machine-gun on our right opened fire and a bullet went through the fore hand-guard, knocking the rifle out of my hand. This was a warning I did not neglect. I kept well under cover and so did my trench-mates.

For about an hour things were fairly calm. Then a terrific fusilade began. The air was thick with bullets. Everybody seemed to be firing on both sides, though for our part there was nothing to aim at except the flashes of the German rifles. We expected an attack, and Captain Stanley passed word along to the Gordons in order to find out what their plans were in case it developed. The reply came back, shouted from trench to trench: "The Gordons will hold on to the last man." The Gordons' answer was received with a cheer, and needless to say we were determined that the Jocks should not stick it alone.

The bout of mad firing gradually died down, and save for an occasional burst of machine-gun fire along our parapets, and a single shot now and then, the situation was comparatively quiet. There were no Very lights in those days, but the Germans had a searchlight, apparently mounted on a lorry, which they shone across towards us for a few minutes at a time, and then moved quickly to a new position in order to dodge our artillery. They had small need for caution on that score. I cannot recall hearing a British gun fired at any time during the night.

During the remainder of the night one man at a time stood up and kept a look out. The others squatted huddled up in the bottom of the trench and slept with one eye open. When the night was well advanced, the senior sergeant, Snuffy Webb, crawled along the back of the holes and gave each of us a tot of rum. It went down to our very toes and made us as warm as toast, but without food and drink as we were, it created an intense thirst afterwards.

Later on I exchanged compliments with Jim Fleming in the trench on our left. He was highly delighted, as he had just run across his brother, who was R.S.M. of the Gordons, and actually in the next trench to him, though the Gordons seemed to see nothing extraordinary in that. They had not previously met for years, the R.S.M. having been stationed in India up to 1914.

While all was still quiet, a Major of the Gordons came along behind the line and spoke with a man here and there. After he had been gone some time word was passed along that he was a spy, and we had orders to collar and examine any person not actually known to us, whatever his rank or uniform.

A small kitten, probably from the farm-house behind, kept wandering about on the parados just out of our reach. Its piteous mewing began to get on our nerves, so we attempted to coax it into the trench with a morsel of bully beef, but it refused to approach closer. When morning came it was still roaming around, and a sorry sight it looked, with singed whiskers and its fur burnt in patches. Presumably it had had a job to escape from the burning building.

When it was still pitch dark, but getting on towards morning, suddenly, away among the Gordons, a bout of wild firing broke loose. It spread rapidly to us. Everybody was up at once and standing to his rifle. For nearly an hour it was like hell let loose. The whine of bullets passing across our trench was like the singing of telegraph wires in the wind. Though we expected an attack at any moment, nothing happened, and no target beyond rifle-flashes was visible. It seemed as if all at once everybody had become bored to the limit with cold and waiting, and was resolved to smarten things up somehow or other. In the trench on our right a man was killed by a bullet through his head, and his companions, instead of growing more cautious, kept on firing at nothing, exposing themselves, and wasting ammunition. They paid dearly for their rashness, for before morning broke they had Sir Richard Levigne and three others killed in the same way. The occupants of my trench were more level-headed, and all five of us saw daylight without a scratch.

Dawn broke amid comparative peace, and my feelings on seeing the sun rise again were rather mixed. We tried to swallow some bully beef, and a Wild Woodbine completed breakfast. The ensuing day was as monotonous as a day could be. It was impossible to stretch oneself either standing up or lying down, and there was nothing for it but to keep down and, at the same time, alert. We all knew there was nothing behind us, and when the attack came, if we did not stop it nothing could.

During the forenoon Lebentz, a lively soul and an exceedingly comical fellow, provided a little entertainment by engaging in a shooting duel with a German in a trench opposite ours. For a long time they kept up a game of fire-and-duck. The German wore no cap and was bald, so his pate, shining in the morning sunshine, provided a fairish aiming mark. Lebentz, though keen to register a hit, and funny beyond description in his antics and accompanying remarks, was not an extraordinarily good shot. The German missed him once or twice by an inch. In the end, like a sensible fellow, and in response to our advice, he gave up the contest, and in consequence he is walking about London till this day.

A few times that day we sat down tight in the bottom of the trench and waited with bated breath while the enemy sent salvoes of shells into the farm-house. It was about thirty yards behind us, and when a shell dropped half-way between us and the building showers of earth, mud, and splinters came hurtling in on top of us. Every minute we fully expected to receive a whole one all to ourselves. There was a feeling of relief each time the spasm finished, and we plucked up enough courage to joke about it. It was fortunate for us he did not try a sprinkling of shrapnel, as we had no head-cover of any sort.

At long last the sun showed signs of settling down into the west; shadows began to lengthen, and finally disappeared. We set about bracing up our spirits to face another night and all it might have in store for us. Immediately after sunset rain started. It poured as it can only pour in Flanders, and the darkness was like ink. The rain served to make us liverish, and a brisk fusillade began on both sides. This was kept up for about half an hour, till, I suppose, the Germans, as well as ourselves, were too soaked to continue. By 6 p.m. we were all wet to the bones and the trench had become a mud-bath.

To our intense surprise, word was now passed along that we were to be relieved almost at once. Every man was to collect his odds and ends and stand-to, in readiness for the word 'File out' as soon as the 10th Hussars came on the scene to replace us. Filing out was going to be no simple matter. The business of getting out of a hole six feet deep, with its sides covered with a foot of sticky mud, while the rain still fell in sheets, would have presented a sea-lion with serious difficulties.

It was not long before the 'Shiny Tenth' made an appearance, and we set about the feat of handing over our places to them. Fortunately, the terrific rain had stopped all firing. We threw all caution to the winds, and men struggled and splashed and swore to their hearts' content. In my long experience I have never heard such expert swearing. The task was accomplished at last, and we stood behind our line with the rain running through us, waiting for the word to file on.

Then out of the darkness the voice of Captain Stanley could be heard calling for volunteers to carry the dead men back. There were four in our section, but everybody was so fed up that his call went absolutely unheeded. Then I heard him shout : " For Christ's sake, will somebody come and carry these unfortunate fellows back." This appeal had effect, and the dead were straight away lifted on anything available. All this took place in a few seconds. It was bad policy to remain where we were. Now we moved quickly a hundred yards along behind the Gordons till we struck the road running from Zandvoorde down through the two positions. Here we turned left, passed through the village, and over the crest of the hill.

In the village churchyard the dead were hurriedly interred. It was still raining in torrents, and spent bullets flopped about here and there. It was discovered later that Sir Richard Levigne had been buried with the squadron's pay in an inside pocket of his jacket. Next night a party went up and recovered it.

While the burial was in progress, I dropped across Tom Birch. As he was the Doctor's groom, and I by way of being the Orderly Room Sergeant, we were to some extent independent of the common herd, so we set off together before the others to our bivouac at Klein Zillebeke. We had about two miles to walk, and though the rain was still running through us, we were both parched with thirst, and had no chance of getting a drink. Birch had lost his cap in the scramble and was bare-headed. He was bald, and being somewhat touchy on that point, in the old barrack-room days nobody had ever seen him without a head-dress of some sort. Invariably his cap was the first article of clothing he put on at reveille, and he always waited till after ' Lights out ' before removing it at night. I therefore had the honour of being the first person for years who had seen Birch uncovered. In spite of the wretched all-round state of things I had to smile to myself.

Half-way to our destination there stood a solitary house on the right-hand side of the road. We approached it and entered in quest of water. We found Bill Whitehorn up to his eyes in work attending to some wounded who had just arrived. On being asked for a drink of water, he abruptly told us to go to hell ; so out we went again and continued our walk.

While in the house I had noticed that Birch had slipped on a stocking cap. It was soaked through, and the water from it was trickling down his face and neck. I saw at once that our thirst was as good as quenched. I requested Birch to remove the cap carefully and squeeze it into his mouth. The result was a complete success. In a few minutes both of us had swallowed enough water, such as it was, to keep us going.

We had a bad scare shortly after coming out on to the road. Our ears caught the sound of the hoof-beats of galloping horses. They were coming from Zandvoorde in our direction. We wondered if it could possibly be Uhlans who had slipped through in the darkness. With hair standing on end and rifles ready we drew in to the side of the road and waited. The horses passed us like the wind. They were saddled, but had no riders. Being, both of us, superstitious Irishmen, the occurrence gave us quite a creepy turn.

Our bivouac was reached a good quarter of an hour

before the remainder of the squadron got in. Old Tom and I sat by a large fire in the open and had a drink of tea. The fire was a glorious and comforting sight as it blazed and hissed in the rain, while the tea warmed us up inside.

No sooner had the squadron arrived than a motor-cyclist bobbed up out of the depths of the foul night and asked for the C.O. He delivered a verbal message to the effect that the 6th Brigade were being attacked and required immediate support. Up to now only our squadron ('D') had come back. 'A' soon followed, and told us the sad news that, in the confusion caused by the rain and darkness, the relief had missed 'C' squadron, who would therefore have to remain in the line for another twenty-four hours. Just as we were, we turned out at once in response to the summons, but another order came almost at once to say the cyclist had misinterpreted his message, and should have asked us merely to stand-to.

Tempers were pretty threadbare by this time. Birch and I decided the night was not fit for a frog to be out in, so we had a scout round the farm in which the officers were billeted and found a pigsty, which we shared with its rightful occupants. We could make no attempt at drying ourselves, nor could we remove any of our saturated clothing. We just lay down on some straw and were soon asleep in an atmosphere that would have asphyxiated a polecat.

It seemed as if we were to have no peace that night, for just as we were dozing off, the door of our sty opened and a torch was flashed in. The R.S.M. stood outside and called, in his best Rolls-Royce accent: " Anyone theah ? " Luckily, a partition hid us from view, so we lay still till he had cleared off. He was looking for a party to draw rations. We consigned him and the rations to the devil and slept till morning.

XIII

THE following day, 26 October, was fine and sunny. Daybreak found us astir and prowling around like hungry wolves in search of food. Nothing exciting happened till the afternoon. In the meantime rations had been dumped at the corner of a small wood close at hand, so we managed a good meal. Rifles were then cleaned, pouches refilled, and we visited our horses. I discovered that my poor old charger had been sent away to the Veterinary Section, absolutely done up from exposure to the weather. Horses seemed to stand up to the foul weather conditions much worse than the men. This was in large measure due to lack of opportunity for sufficient exercise rather than to lack of shelter. I never saw the old fellow again. Lord Newry gave me another at once. My new mount was a hunter named Traveller. He was slightly run down from hardship and exposure, but was a fine horse.

About 2 p.m. the Fire Brigade had orders to go to the rescue of the 20th Infantry Brigade, who had been heavily attacked and forced to withdraw in the neighbourhood of Kruseik. The Brigade rode at once to the danger zone and dismounted for action. The Blues were detailed to lead the attack ; we went over as second wave, and the 2nd Life Guards were in reserve. The Blues went through the Germans with a rush, and advanced over half a mile to the original German line, which they occupied. We followed some two hundred yards behind, and when the Blues had cleared the old enemy line we dug in where we stood. The Blues then withdrew through us, and we handed over our hastily-dug line to the Infantry two hours later. We then returned to our horses and got back to Klein Zillebeke.

That evening, after dark, ' C ' Squadron returned, after having been relieved in the line. They had been through a rough spell. Their chief troubles had been cold, wet clothes, and hunger. The night passed without incident, except that as I was sleeping on a tobacco-screen beside Alf Rose I woke up to find a large rat calmly sitting on my stocking cap with his cold paws on my forehead. I think he had a much greater shock than I.

At 6 a.m. we were ordered to saddle up preparatory to changing our position. At 10 a.m. the order was cancelled. While standing to, a German plane was brought down by our artillery. This was the first time we saw that sort of thing happen.

About 5 p.m. we paraded on foot to relieve the 6th Brigade in the line. The night was fine but pitch dark. On reaching the summit of the ridge we again became the centre of attraction for enemy machine-gunners and riflemen. There was the usual swearing and floundering among the turnips. My squadron was the last up, and it transpired that no room in the trenches could be found for two Troops. Lord Newry sent me back to inform the Adjutant and to ask for orders.

I turned and went with my hair on end. It is one thing to be under fire among comrades, but quite a different matter to wade alone through the bullets in the inky darkness. It is also remarkable how easily one can lose one's bearings. After a creepy journey I located the Adjutant. He came back with me to see the situation for himself, and in the end it was decided to bring back the two Troops and let them remain in reserve about Regimental Headquarters. I remember I lost my cap. They were the stiff, peace-time issue, and did not take kindly to the shape of one's head. They were lost in large numbers during those days. I forget where I spent the night, but I congratulated myself on spending it at all after crossing the ridge four times.

The Adjutant sent for me next morning, 28 October, and made me a kind of flying secretary between our Headquarters and the Brigade Headquarters. First of all, though, he despatched me to the wagon lines to bring up the Veterinary Officer. This proved to be a longer job than I had imagined it would be. After a three-mile tramp on a fine clear morning, I arrived at the field in which the transport lay, only to find it deserted and in a state of chaos. The surface of the field was honeycombed with monster shell-holes, and scattered about among these were the carcasses of some twenty horses. It looked as if the transport had received marked attention from the enemy during the night.

I went out again into the road and continued walking away from the line. Soon I met an Irish Guardsman who informed me in a brogue you could cut with a knife that our people had moved back that morning to Verbranden Molen. I trudged along another mile, passed through a one-street village, and found the transport in a field on the left of the main road.

Everybody and everything showed signs of having moved in here somewhat hurriedly. Groups of excited drivers and pot-bellied quarterblokes looking rather pink about the gills were engaged in animated conversation round steaming dixies of tea. Jingo Brown stuck his eyes out and glared at me as he would at a stray dog attempting to come in at his garden gate. As soon as old Bob Harrison saw me he placed in my hand a pint mug containing tea with milk, sugar, and rum in it. He then proceeded to cut me with his jack-knife a doorstep from a slab of cold, boiled bacon, and this he handed me on a chunk of good white bread. While I was polishing off this princely breakfast with the appetite of a growing lad who has existed for some days on pieces of broken biscuit and Wild Woodbines, I managed to get hold of the cause of all the excitement.

It appears that during the previous night, while all and sundry were snugly asleep beneath the wagons, the Germans began trying to fill their field with 'Jack Johnsons.' The field was some two hundred yards square, yet from a distance of at least ten miles the enemy landed a large howitzer shell right in the middle of it every two minutes. Some twenty 'Coal-boxes' arrived in all. The men lay flat on the ground and nobody was hit; but the unfortunate horses, standing up and tied to lines, got the full benefit of it.

This accurate shooting at long range could not have been mere guess-work on the part of the Germans. When the shelling was over, some drivers raided a lonely cottage standing some little way from the field. They had remarked that the sole occupant of this house was a particularly ill-favoured, ill-tempered woman, who was openly hostile, and refused to allow them into the yard to fill their dixies at the pump. They now forced the door and seized the lady, who as expected, proved to be a man. He was handed over to the military police.

I routed out the Veterinary Officer when I had finished eating and drinking, and he promised to report to Regimental Headquarters at once.

The morning was now getting on, and as I had other work to do, I set about clearing off back. Just as I was leaving the field I noticed Howard of the Blues, who shared my room at Knightsbridge when he was King's orderly, riding out on a horse that seemed to bear a striking resemblance to Traveller. I ran after him and caught him up, but he swore the horse was his own. I was none too certain, as I had only spent about five minutes in his company when I first took him over, but luckily I remembered the number on his hoof, so I challenged Howard to dismount and have a look. I scraped off the mud, and sure enough there was the number. I asked Bob Harrison to keep an eye on Traveller for me till I came down again.

Captain Molyneux, a merry fellow, who performed miracles with rations, forage, and was actually the Brigade Supply Officer, overtook me in his old tin-pot car and offered me a lift. He perceived I had lost my cap, so he fished out a salvaged one from the depths of his car and handed it to me. In size it was something like a baby's cap. The man it had previously belonged to must have had a head like a gooseberry. However, we had a good laugh at my comical appearance with the ridiculous cap perched on the top of my, what Wally Webber had termed, 'ruddy great 'ead.'

The Adjutant sent me straight off to Brigade Headquarters with a bundle of papers in order to compare notes with the Brigadier's clerk, and to more or less put the paper side of the business ship-shape. Brigade Headquarters were located in a lone house about a mile away from our place, and at the foot of the Zandvoorde Ridge. On entering, as I was passing through the door, I heard the double crack of a German rifle away on the ridge behind me, and a bullet rattled among the tiles on the roof. I thought this a lively place for the headquarters of a general, but I was not there to criticise what he was pleased to make his temporary abode, so I went in and got to business.

The interior was bare and cold. The ventilation, through shell-holes in walls and roof, was somewhat over-done. The general was actually shaving. He was in his shirt-sleeves, and performed before a small hand-mirror stuck on the wall. The only other occupants of the billet were the Brigade Major (Captain Kearsey), and Private Titchener, A.S.C., who just then appeared to fill the several roles of general's clerk, cook, and bodyguard all in one. I had several things to check with both the latter, and found them most businesslike and devoid of all fuss. They were the kind of people one would be glad to meet in a regimental orderly room.

I was struck by the absence of all the pomp and eyewash one is apt to associate with a general and his suite. Here was one of the finest generals the army had produced up to now, actually sharing quarters, rations, and shaving-water with a private. What a contrast to many of our junior officers, who kept two men eternally running after them with hot water and other luxuries morning and night.

Having completed my business to my great satisfaction, I went out again through the door. Again the sniper fired and again his bullet hit the roof. The occupants of the billet could never account for his bad shooting, any more than they could locate his position. Though most persistent day after day, he never managed to cause a casualty. The poor chap probably had his rifle-barrel bent upwards.

That night the following message was received: 'Reliable information has again been received that the 27th German Corps will attack the Zandvoorde position at 5 a.m.' The attack developed, but did not reach the portion of the line held by our Brigade.

I spent the night of the 28th in peace and quietness at Regimental Headquarters. The day of the 29th passed off uneventfully. I occupied my time in getting rid of the outgoing mail, and then prowling round the immediate countryside. Everywhere were plenty of interesting things to which the enlightened Cockneys, of which the two Troops out of the line and the odds and ends on Regimental Headquarters largely consisted, were quite blind.

It became known about three o'clock that afternoon that the regiment could not be relieved that night, as the 6th Cavalry Brigade, which should have furnished the relief, was away supporting the infantry. This gave birth to a fresh adventure in the shape of a ration party to the line after dark.

During the whole campaign it was my fate to have much to do with the distribution of rations to troops in the line, but never have I seen such a hopeless mix-up as was made of the attempt to get rations into the line on Zandvoorde Ridge on the night of 29 October. The quarterblokes brought up the rations for their squadrons in wagons to Regimental Headquarters and dumped them down there. They then cleared off back to the wagon-lines.

Soon after dark we set out. In addition to a box of biscuits, bully beef, or tinned milk, weighing half a hundred-weight, each man carried his arms and ammunition. None of us minded sweating up to the line with rations for our comrades, but we all realized what it meant to divide a box of bully or biscuits among parties of five or six men distributed in holes on a front a quarter of a mile long. It was quite on the cards that when the rations reached them in bulk they would throw them on one side in utter disgust.

Progress up the side of the hill was slow and language flowed hot and strong. I collected four or five rifles from the most heavily laden and carried them myself. On reaching the village we came under fire, but all were too fed up to care, so without halting we pushed on over the brow of the hill and kept to the road. A few yards down the road a nasty spurt from a machine-gun caused us to make a dive for the ditch by the roadside, where we sprawled among the boxes and sacks till the firing stopped. If the rations had been properly divided up we could have run along the back of the trenches and handed them over ourselves in no time. The R.S.M., however, despatched somebody to inform the troops that rations had arrived on the road. After a wait of about an hour some poor devils came along and trundled the great boxes away towards the line. Heaven knows how they got on with them afterwards.

As we waited in the ditch reliefs were taking place here and there round about us. Bullets were being liberally sprinkled, and an occasional shell fell in the village. On our way back, the Gordons, who had just been relieved, were lying as thick as sardines on straw spread on the pavements. They dared not go back far. The situation was recognised to be critical. At dawn next morning, 30 October, the storm broke, but we had no inkling of this as we trudged wearily back to Regimental Headquarters that night.

Almost at the end of the village we heard weird moans coming from a house on our right. On going over to investigate we saw that a shell had just recently dropped on the house, blown it down, and trapped a cow beneath a fallen wall. The wretched animal was pinned down and burning to death.

XIV

AFTER delivering the rations in the line on the night of 29 October, I trudged back with the two Troops of 'D' Squadron to the horse-lines. The latter were located on the edge of a small wood near Verbranden Molen. The Transport of the 2nd South Staffords lay alongside us, and with it was Major White, its Quartermaster. I had met this fine old soldier long before in Ireland, and was actually at school with his son George, who in those days was destined for the church. To the great disgust of his father, George had enlisted in the 9th Lancers as soon as he was old enough, and he had already been killed at the Battle of the Aisne. I only found out about George's death a month later, when I ran across the 9th Lancers at Ypres. I was thankful then that I had not gone over to speak to Major White in Verbranden Molen Wood. My visit could only have reminded him of things better left undisturbed.

There was no tendency on our part to oversleep on the morning of 30 October. Round about our ears six hundred cold, hungry horses were splashing in the mud, and the morning was frosty and raw. We were up and about with the first streak of dawn, and spent a hectic half-hour trying to water and feed the poor brutes. Before we had quite got through this operation a hellish bombardment broke out upon Zandvoorde Ridge. It was the hottest we had heard up to then. Its suddenness and intensity caused us to stand still for a moment or two and gape. One idea formed itself immediately in all our minds—this was the expected big German attack. We felt, too, it was right on the little patch of front held by our own people. For upwards of an hour the ground trembled and the air was full of din. Then gradually the shelling subsided and machine-gun and rifle-fire swelled up into a roar. We finished feeding the horses, then rallied round the cooks' fires and snatched whatever there was going for breakfast. We had no orders, but had the need arisen we would have had our work cut out to get the horses away.

Gradually, about 8.30 or 9 a.m., the rifle-fire grew less lively. It is amazing how rumour travels at such moments of crisis. It was soon being whispered in detached groups round the various fires that the line had been broken and that the regiment had suffered heavily.

Presently, when I saw a chance, I took Andy Kealey's big white horse from the wagon-lines, mounted him, and rode out in the direction of the Ridge. Half a mile along the road I met Hubert Bussey with his forehead cut open and bleeding. He was walking calmly back, smoking a cigarette, and looking for the dressing-station. Obviously he was badly shaken. I could get no information from him. As he appeared to be in no immediate need of assistance I left him and rode on.

Round the next bend I met Gus Russell of my old Troop. He was limping along carrying a machine-gun tripod. He was glad to see me, and told me the shelling had been fierce and had played havoc with the trenches. His machine-gun had been hit and put out of action. Old Doctor Holmes, the Machine-gun Sergeant-Major, a fine fellow, had been killed when the gun was hit. In the midst of this havoc the Germans came over in masses, and by sheer weight of numbers had gained a footing in our trenches, which had been almost obliterated by the shelling.

I took the tripod from Gus and we went back together, I riding and he hanging on to my stirrup-leather. I felt a fool at being out in the horse-lines while my comrades were in the thick of it, but it was not my fault. I should have been there right enough if there had been room for us when the relief took place. I realize now it was just my luck.

As the day wore on, we outsiders were not called upon. There were a mere sixty of us, so I suppose we were forgotten. Bit by bit the details of the battle leaked down to us with the wounded men. We could scarcely credit these reports till, at dusk, the survivors hobbled back to the horse-lines on being relieved by the Foot Guards.

They looked bedraggled and weary to death as they marched in. Sinbad the Sailor, covered in mud, and with a rifle slung over his shoulder like a Tommy, walked alone at the head of what remained of his Troop. His Troop Sergeant, Cabby Dawes, had been wounded in the first bombardment, and as somebody tried to carry him back he had been hit again and killed. Sinbad and Cabby were kindred spirits and inseparable at all times. Neither had any thought for himself. Their horses were never short of forage, nor their men of rations. Better soldiers than those two and their Troop of scallywags and hard cases did not exist.

Both 'A' and 'D' Squadrons had sustained losses, but 'C' Squadron had, with the exception of Charlie Wright and six or seven men, been absolutely wiped out. Charlie and his little bunch were not in the same section of line with their Squadron, but in close touch with 'D' Squadron. When the order to retire was given it did not reach the main body of 'C' Squadron owing to its position being slightly detached from, and in front on the left of, the rest of the Regiment. Lord Hugh Grosvenor, 'C' Squadron Leader, was not the man who would retire without orders, so they just fought it out and died where they stood. No trace of Lord Hugh and his hundred-odd men was ever found.

An attempt was actually made, when the situation was realized and when, incidentally, it was too late, to get the order through from a trench on the left of 'D' Squadron. Here a handful of transport drivers were holding out under the command of a venerable officer called 'Santa Claus.' A man volunteered to go across to 'C' Squadron, but was killed before he got half-way. Another who went immediately after him met with the same fate. A cat could not have crossed that piece of ground with a whole skin just then. Bogey Giles, who was in this trench, relates an interesting argument between Santa and Driver Tapper. Santa, feeling the weight of his responsibility, decided to send a third runner and approached Tapper.

It was now too late, and Tapper knew it. "Look here, Tapper," said Santa. "I wonder if you would try to get through with a message to 'C' Squadron?"

"Wot, me!" says Tapper. "Look at them two poor blighters out there! No fear! It's too bloomin' late nah, anyway."

"I say, Tapper. Your nerves are all in pieces. Have a morphine tablet."

"'Ave a wot? Garn! My nerves is all right. 'Ave a bloomin' jujube yerself. I may be a bloody fool, but I ain't as big a bloody fool as you think."

Just at that point the argument was terminated by the appearance of a wave of the enemy, and the ensuing ten minutes were hot enough to try the nerves of both Santa and Tapper, who happily survived and seem to have forgotten the affair of the morphine tablets.

Far from sitting down to moan over its disasters, the Regiment was on Fire Brigade work next day (31st) and actually had two calls, neither of which led to action. That evening it relieved two squadrons of the 4th Hussars in the line. The trenches were shelled next morning by heavy howitzers, and a few casualties occurred, including the Commanding Officer wounded. The command of the Regiment now devolved upon Captain Hon. A. F. Stanley. He had a considerable reputation as a soldier, and he fully deserved it.

The French relieved us on 1 November, and we rejoined the Brigade at Hooge, again on Fire Brigade duty. That afternoon a call for help came from the 4th Guards Brigade at Klein Zillebeke. The Regiment moved up and remained in reserve till 7 p.m., returning then to its rendezvous at Hooge.

On the afternoon of 2 November the Brigade moved up to support the infantry before Gheluvelt. The Blues came into action, and our regiment was caught by heavy shell-fire while waiting mounted on a road. A German six-gun field battery got them almost over open sights, and there was some confusion among fallen horses as the Regiment galloped in half-sections to a flank out of range. Ted Pettit and his mount turned a somersault over somebody who had come down in front. Neither was hurt, but they parted company, and the horse galloped off with its tail in the air in the direction of the Germans. Ted started in pursuit, swearing violently and calling his horse loudly by name. Finally he rounded the brute up, mounted, and joined the main body.

The most weird experience in this 'joy-ride' befell Brum Morris senior. He was hit in the leg right at the beginning of the shelling. He dismounted, and, taking his horse's reins over his arm, started limping along with the animal following. Suddenly he felt his horse weighing heavily on the reins. On looking round he saw, to his horror, that he was now dragging its head along the ground. A shell had completely severed it.

November 3rd, 4th, and 5th found the Brigade called out again every day, but it was not involved in any actual fighting. On 6 November, however, it did the best Fire Brigade stunt of the whole battle. While waiting in reserve near Hooge a call came from the 4th Guards Brigade at Zwartelen. For some strange reason a Battalion of French Infantry was in the line between two of our Guards Battalions. At 3.15 p.m. the Germans put over a sustained attack. The French turned and ran. As they did so some of the Irish Guards turned round and fired after them. The Germans started passing through the gap on the Guards' front. Our Brigade galloped to within a short distance of Zwartelen, dismounted, fixed bayonets, and advanced up a road through the village. The 1st and 2nd Life Guards deployed into line and advanced towards the gap with the Blues in support. The counter-attack was completely successful, and the deserted trenches cleared and held. That night our Brigade was relieved. It will give some idea of the severity of the fighting in the salient when one recalls that at 2 a.m. the 1st Life Guards were relieved by a mixed force consisting of two companies of the Royal Sussex, two companies of the Munsters, and a few Irish Guards.

Back at Verbranden Molen were more spare horses than ever. Though the affair at Zwartelen had not cost us very heavily in casualties, we had only about thirty in all in this action; there were a few vacancies in 'D' Squadron which would be hard to fill. Joe Ratcliffe, Charlie Wright, and Jim Fleming had all been wounded and were on the road to England. Charlie and Jim were both shot clean through the left lung. Joe was hit in the arm. I saw them all depart for Blighty in an old horse-ambulance.

But the saddest loss was caused by the death of Sinbad the Sailor. He was killed in the advance. His Troop Sergeant, now Jim Fleming, led the Troop so successfully that he was later decorated for his gallantry and received the D.C.M.

So well liked was Sinbad among the troops that when darkness fell the same night two drivers from the machine-gun section, Rubber Reeves and Tinker Underwood, got two horses and a half-limber, galloped up to the scene of the counter-attack, and brought back his body for burial in the near-by churchyard. They received no official recognition for this action, but Sinbad's brother, Lord Leconfield, sent them both a token of his gratitude and a letter of thanks.

I mentioned that when we left Ludgershall for Belgium we took with us, all unknowingly, a gate-crashing ex-cavalryman, one Private Tingley. In our extreme innocence, and in the excitement of going on active service, we took no notice of him whatever. His name appeared on no squadron roll, so he had some bother in negotiating rations and that sort of thing. Bob Harrison, like the good Samaritan he was, took pity on him and gave him a job on a wagon in return for food and shelter. For a time Tingley was contented, but soon he wanted to go up into the line with his chums and see the fun. On 6 November he cut loose, got a rifle and a spare horse, and went along to join in the counter-attack. He was killed. His death was duly reported and the authorities at home raised Cain. It was apparently a serious matter to take a civilian out to the front and get him polished off.

Regimental war diaries are not as a rule given to the exercise of humour. On referring to the *1st Life Guards' War Diary*, which I helped to complete during first Ypres, I find this entry: 'Nov. 7th. 2 p.m. Regiment moved to

I

BILLETS round Verloren Hoek.' Some billets! I remember there was a farm which housed the officers and their servants, but the other ranks took up their abode in surrounding fields in the open. This particular 'billet' was christened 'Mud Farm,' and a soldier does not bestow a title like that for nothing. Here we spent ten days. Mud, cold, deep, and sticky, was over everything and in everything. It took half an hour to walk two hundred yards in any direction. There was, however, one compensation. Not a single shell dropped in or near the wretched place during our sojourn there, although other farms round about had plenty of attention.

Fire Brigade work now almost ceased. Horses were left tied to anything and stood up to their bellies in slush. Attempts at exercise were painful and futile. Water there was in plenty, but it was thick and foul. Nose-bags were horrible, mud-soaked, stinking rags, and hay was speedily walked into the slime. The Regiment now did regular spells of trench-work and only twice was it called upon for counter-attacks. For the first few days its strength was 150 rifles.

On 11 November the Composite Regiment of Household Cavalry, which had left Knightsbridge for Mons on 15 August, was broken up, and the three Squadrons sent to join their respective regiments. Our Squadron joined us at Mud Farm late that afternoon. I shall always remember the sad look on Jersey Randall's face as he dismounted, took stock of his new surroundings, and asked in his high-pitched voice: " Where's the billets?" Major Cowie mentions this return of the Squadron to the fold in his private diary. He writes:

'Regiment marched to Ypres under command of Captain Bowlby, Royal Horse Guards, and joined the Headquarters, Cavalry Brigade, at dusk near Verloren Hoek—the "muddy farm." The Cavalry Brigade were then doing "Fire Brigade." No sooner had we reached the muddy farm and night fallen than a sudden order came for the Brigade to turn out: " Composite Regiment—every man to his own Regiment." And struggling over the broken country in pitchy darkness, a cataract of rain, heavy squalls of wind, and oceans of mud, the Composite Regiment disappeared and was absorbed into the 7th Cavalry Brigade.'

The Squadron had suffered pretty severely. Frank Rogers, Steady Ford, George Levy, and others of my old peace-time friends had been killed. Saddest of all, Colonel Cook had died of wounds. We knew we should not see his like again. Lord John Cavendish, too, had been killed. The best always went first. Still, war is war, and two hours after their arrival in our midst the new 'B' Squadron turned out with the rest of us and moved up to support a counter-attack at Zonnebeke. All returned at 10 p.m. At 1 a.m. we turned out again and slogged up to Hooge Château to help the infantry. At noon next day, 12 November, we were relieved and returned to 'billets.' Of the ensuing five days three were spent in the line about Zwartelen and two at Mud Farm.

Our peace-time Veterinary Officer, Captain Rees-Mogg, now returned to us with the Composite Squadron. He was not very popular. A fortnight after joining the Regiment at Windsor in 1912 he had dared to interfere with some moth-eaten traditions in the forge. Farrier McKlosky was court-martialled and broke for rasping down the walls of horses' hoofs. Rees-Mogg believed in making the shoe fit the hoof, not the reverse process. I doubt if he ever lived this down. I had found him a most reasonable and business-like officer, and my dealings with him were always most friendly.

The V.O. was shocked at the state of our horses, particularly those which had been slightly wounded and whose wounds were now ugly running sores owing to lack of proper protection from the poisonous mud. He discovered there was a British Veterinary Hospital somewhere in the neighbourhood of Dunkirk, so he collected some forty sick and wounded horses, put them on a train at Ypres, and sent them to the hospital. Among the convoy was my horse, Traveller. He was so far gone that he could scarcely eat or drink. The V.O. begged or borrowed three men and put them in charge of the horses. Off they started. A week or ten days passed, and nothing was seen or heard of the three beauties. About a month later they rejoined and spun the yarn that as rail communication between Ypres and Dunkirk had been severed soon after they arrived, they had had to work their way back on foot. In doing so they had to pass from unit to unit and take part in any actions that were going on. This sounded quite feasible, so no more was said.

Months and years passed and no more was seen of our sick horses, which in the natural order of things ought to have returned to us as soon as they were fit. One day in the summer of 1917, while the Regiment was in billets at Camblain Chatelain, an old horse passed down through our lines, had a drink in the stream at the bottom of the slope, and jogged back again all by himself. He was a light chestnut, over 16 hands. His mane was scraggy as if it had been eaten by rats, he wore about two and a half shoes, and his poor old ribs were visible beneath his skin. But, on his near hind quarter was branded a large I.L.G., exactly as Farrier-Major Mackenzie had done it at Ludgershall in September 1914.

This set me thinking hard, but I could not get to the bottom of the mystery. At last, one evening at the beginning of 1918, as I was issuing the Troop's rum-ration I came across the sole survivor of the precious trio who had escorted the sick horses to Dunkirk in 1914. I sat down beside him and we drank our rum together. As we did so we talked about old times and famous characters who were no more. Under the mellowing influence of the rum he opened his heart to me and told me that he and his two pals did not hand over the horses to the Veterinary Hospital, but had sold them to Belgian dealers and had a month's holiday at Dunkirk on the proceeds. The worst cases among the unfortunate animals were slaughtered for food, and the remainder sold to farmers. That would account for the old horse at Camblain Chatelain.

I kept his secret from all except Jim Fleming. He and I had had our suspicions of the three rascals, but we hardly gave them credit for an exploit such as this.

My old horse now having departed, I asked Captain Rees-Mogg if he would use his influence to get me Herbert. I had had my eye on him since he joined at Ludgershall, and he was still as fit as a fiddle in spite of all the hardships he had been through. Herbert became mine the same day, and for the next three years I had a horse that was never sick or lame, in fact a horse and a half.

One night at Mud Farm it rained so hard that Tinker Bell and I were completely washed out of our bivvy. We gave it up and splashed our way to the wagon-park. Here we undid the canvas wagon-cover on one side of a G.S. wagon, and stood beneath it with chattering teeth, prepared for a three or four hour wait till dawn. The rain drove along in sheets parallel to the ground, and gusts of wind shook the wagon. Once or twice, however, we could have sworn it shook and trembled when there was no wind blowing. It was a terribly uncanny business, but there was no doubt about it, the great wagon was trembling from stem to stern. We were feeling like running away, till suddenly a series of violent coughs and smothered oaths came down to us from beneath the cover. We shouted up a few words of encouragement to the inmate, and found it was none other than Andy Kealy. The sly old dog had burrowed himself a cosy nest on top of the load, and with the cover drawn down all round was safe from the rain. This night, however, the cold was too much for him. He woke up shivering, and when Andy's twenty stone of all too solid flesh started to shiver, the G.S. wagon and load had no choice but to join in.

The Regiment went into the line for the last time from Mud Farm on 14 November. There was severe shelling, and about 3 p.m. 2nd Lieutenant St. George went back to headquarters to report. On his return he was shot dead by a sniper from a house on the Zillebeke road. I was interested in Mr. St. George because I had an idea he came from a West of Ireland family. The vicar of my native parish was a Mr. St. George, but I never found out whether there was any connection. The strange thing about this young officer's death was that it left his groom, Freddy Whittle, in a queer predicament. Freddy had been bustled into khaki at the outbreak of war, duly enlisted, and without doing any drill or training of any kind had accompanied his master on active service. He would have been completely at sea in the ranks, but, being a popular fellow, a post was found for him as groom and servant to a pot-bellied French interpreter who went by the name of Bon Sonty.

The same sniper wounded George Haywood that same afternoon. I mention this because George was to prove a good comrade to me later on in the war, when he returned after the battle of the Somme.

We vacated Mud Farm on 17 November, and moved to Begersburg, which is, I believe, a sort of suburb of Ypres. It was a decided improvement on Verloren Hoek. There were plenty of buildings about wherein one could take shelter and endeavour to keep dry when out of the line. Here we remained to 21 November. Three of the four intervening days were spent in the trenches, the worst being the 20th, when we had about forty casualties at Zillebeke. Here a dear old friend of mine, Peter Bruce, was killed, as well as Joe Rose, who was Corporal of the Guard the day I joined at Regent's Park, and Lizzie Helliwell, who weighed 9 stone and was 6 feet 3 inches in height when he joined at Knightsbridge.

An amusing rencontre took place between Captain Stubber and Trooper Dalton of my squadron during the intense bombardment of the trenches on 20 November. These two could not possibly have been in close proximity for very long without setting each other alight. Captain Stubber ordered the men to move along to the left out of the shelled sector. As they moved a terrific strafe opened right on the portion of trench where they happened to be passing. Some dug-outs had been constructed in the side of the trench, and the Captain ordered the men into these. There were four or five steps at the narrow entrance. Captain Stubber was in a hurry, and the last man in. Dalton was immediately in front of him and was proceeding leisurely, when he found somebody push him violently in the back and shout : " Go on, man ! " while at the same time standing on the tail of his greatcoat. Dalton turned sharply round livid with rage, and almost spitting with anger, hissed right into Captain Stubber's face: "Go on! That's right. Make a bloody door-mat of me!"

The original trenches were again occupied when the shelling ceased, and at 8 p.m. the Regiment was relieved by the 142nd French Infantry. We returned to billets at Begersburg, and next morning marched back well behind the line to rest and refit. Our share in the first battle of Ypres had come to an end.

During our stay at Begersburg we came across Com-mander Samson, the famous airman. He and his crew of bluejackets had a long naval gun mounted on a railway-truck. An engine and three or four wagons completed his train. This puff-puffed up and down a stretch of railway and shelled concentration areas behind the German lines. Samson had an aeroplane and did all his own 'spotting' in it. We were extremely impressed and wished he had several such guns instead of just one. The aeroplane spotting was something marvellous just then, especially when we recalled that two months, before, on Salisbury Plain, Colonel Cody had the last word in planes, and it looked like a contraption of matchwood and string.

There was a large lake round a private house near our billet. I discovered a boat with a pair of oars but no rowlocks. I found my spurs made excellent substitutes, but being somewhat short and thin in the neck, they both went overboard before long. Still, spurs were neither ornamental nor useful just then, and rowing in the early morning was good fun.

XV

THE morning of 21 November found us evacuating Begersburg in an attempt to reach the Brigade rendezvous one mile west of Ypres, preparatory to migrating south to peace and quietness. I can recall no details of our departure except that snow had fallen and the cold was bitter. There were myriads of spare horses to lead, and the narrow strip of *pavé* which did duty as a road was like Epsom High Street on Derby Day for congestion, while the language of the ' other ranks ' would have made a Hampstead Heath Bank Holiday crowd sit up and take notice.

Never mind. Ypres, now gutted, shell-torn and smouldering, was gradually left in the background. I was destined to return to it a score of times later on, and each time I approached the ghastly place with an empty, sinking feeling in my inside. Progress was slow, and as darkness fell that afternoon we were confronted with the problem of getting over the Mont des Cats on roads covered with a couple of inches of frozen snow. For the mounted men this was not so very difficult. They just dismounted and walked, leading their several horses. For the wagons, loaded to capacity and beyond, it was a different matter.

Bob Harrison rode on ahead of his transport and interviewed the Prior of the Mont des Cats monastery. All the ground on both sides of the hill right down to its base belonged to the monks. They let Bob and his convoy in at a gate well down on the north side, and he proceeded with comparative ease on a gravelled carriage-road over the summit and out at the base of the south side.

Headquarters, to which I was attached, were not so enterprising. We reached the base of the hill as night was falling and there we stuck. It seemed to be a case of every man for himself. No orders, no billets, just stand and freeze in the snow or go to Halifax. I was already half-frozen and hungry. So was Herbert. I made him fast to an iron post at the back of an *estaminet*, fed him, wrapped him up in his saddle-blanket and my own blanket, and left him to make the best of things for the time being. I had some money, so I wandered into the *estaminet* to see what I could find. It was full of people of another unit, all of them mere boys in appearance. There was an excellent fire in which Maconochies were warming. Coffee and rum were being served by a harassed landlady, and most of the troops already looked red-faced and jolly.

The most picturesque figure in the crowd was a fat young man, almost as broad as he was long, and resembling a stout buck navvy in khaki. He wore a dog collar and black tabs, so he must have been a padre of sorts. He was wild-eyed, roaring, and to all intents and purposes tight.

I was admitted into this jovial little circle, and was soon warm inside and out. I had no idea where the people of my own regiment had got to. Anyway, the evening wore on. We sang songs, led by the stentorian voice of the padre, who eventually became all sloppy and wanted to hug everybody. Finally we must all have flopped down to sleep just where we were. The next thing I remember is being kicked violently in the ribs and waking up with a start in the darkness. I banged my head hard on something as I sat up wondering where I was. At last I found a match and lit it; then the situation became clear. We had been sleeping on the stone floor. The poor lad next to me had an attack of cramp in the leg, hence the kicks. We were actually under the table, so my head had connected good and hard when I sprang up into a sitting position. I soothed my unfortunate bedfellow as best I could, and we lay down again and slept till morning.

More Maconochies, coffee, and rum were consumed for breakfast. The padre was a wonderful sight. So was poor old Herbert when I went out and found him. His whiskers were frozen into hard spikes like darning-needles, and he did his best to inform me, to the accompaniment of much jumping about and fretful neighing, that he was more than pleased to see me, and at the same time famished with hunger. The two blankets had kept his body and soul together, and after a good feed he felt like an entirely new horse, and was ready for anything.

I took leave of my hosts, and the regiment set off again up the hill in the direction of Hazebrouck. The going was worse, if anything, and walking more difficult than ever. At the rear of the long column I picked up George Hayes, a jovial shoeing-smith, and we trekked along together. George was to share many thrills with me in the next two or three months. Twice his horse fell with a thud and a grunt on the glassy road surface, and on each occasion jerked George off his balance, so that his heels slipped from under him and he measured his length on the ice beside his steed. But George was a grand character. He had made a solemn vow years before, on joining the service, never to swear or use bad language of any sort, and nothing could ever make him break it. He was never known to say anything more profane or obscene than : 'Suffering Moses!' George never could make up his mind as to when he had reached the limit of his capacity. When full to overflowing he would turn his cap round with its peak to the back, fold his arms across his mighty chest, and bellow forth sailors' songs in a voice like a foghorn. How often have I heard him inform all inhabitants of Flanders who happened to be within a mile of where he stood that : 'From Ushant to Pompey is sixty-five leagues!' A stouter fellow or more loyal comrade never served the King. He was a Hampshire man from the New Forest, and might have stepped straight out of the ranks of 'The White Company.'

In pitch darkness on the night of 22 November we billeted in farms round Borre, half a mile north of Hazebrouck. I can recall lodging Herbert in a cart-shed. This was the first time he had spent the night under a roof since he joined the Regiment. I found shelter in a cow-shed, and slept dry and warm on a bundle of hay.

Next day the Prince of Wales visited us and just walked round our billets. There was no parade that I can remember. We remained here a fortnight.

The surrounding country is flat and entirely given up to

agriculture, the chief crops being sugar beet, potatoes, and flax. It is all very low-lying, and intersected by deep ditches full of water in which the flax is soaked. The roads, apart from the main arterial highways, were of macadam, and between neglect, constant rain, and traffic, they were, just then, a foot deep in slush. The farm was filthy outside, although the interior of the house was spotless. There was an awful dunghill in the middle of the square formed by the house and outbuildings. Some of its contents must have reposed there since the middle ages. All available space in outhouses was filled with our horses ; wagons were parked in a field behind ; and the men distributed themselves in lofts, or wherever they could find a corner.

The owner of the farm was on active service. His wife, a short, round, decent little woman, did her best to carry on with the aid of a couple of slatternly maids, an old labourer, and a sort of village idiot. From morning till night she rated them in Flemish and got the necessary jobs done somehow. I knew no Flemish, and never could give my mind to learning the dreadful lingo. She was my first ' landlady,' and I admired her splendid spirit in carrying on against such odds. The troops, however good their intentions, were an awful nuisance to her. They could not realize what she was up against, or how tantalizing it must have been for her to have her work interrupted by their unending requests for all the trivial, childish things which seem so important to soldiers in billets. However, she bore it all with unfailing good humour.

The blood of generations of farmers runs in my veins. I sympathized with her, was able to help her in little things, and we grew very friendly. I think, during the fortnight of our stay, I was the only human being with whom she could converse freely on level terms. I appreciated this human touch tremendously. It was good to be able to talk of the things that are fundamental and vital, and to escape from the never-ending, futile clap-trap of the bulk of one's fellows. I generally sat up gossiping and drinking coffee with Madame in her kitchen far into the night, long after everybody else was asleep. Five o'clock next morning always found her spick-and-span and leading her bunch of servants a hell of a life. I was fortunate in meeting such excellent women while I was still young. Anyway, I have never forgotten my first landlady in Flanders, and I shall always see her standing on the threshold of the farm-house, as though she might be my own mother, and saying to me : " Au revoir, monsieur, et que le bon Dieu vous bénisse toujours," as I rode away never to return.

Madame had an aged mother who sat all day in an arm-chair in the chimney corner. She wore a snow-white, elaborately frilled, linen bonnet, a black satin dress covered with a stiff white apron, and a pair of tiny, shining, black shoes with silver buckles. Except that sometimes her eyes moved, she might have been a wax model. For days on end no one saw her move or heard her speak. Imagine my surprise, one afternoon, when I found her engaged in a lively conversation with Perry, the Doctor's servant. Perry sat in the opposite corner airing his master's shirt, and they were jabbering away in what sounded to me like Flemish. I made a point of seeing Perry afterwards and asking him what lingo he was talking. " Welsh," he informed me. " You know it's almost word for word like Flemish ! " He was quite serious, but I thought it absolute rot. I was positive there existed no resemblance between the two languages. But there it was. That precious pair, the wrinkled old Flemish woman and the chubby young Welshman, grew as thick as thieves. For years I sought the solution of this mystery, and it was only in 1929 that I got to the bottom of it. A Welsh headmaster of a London school, to whom I mentioned the matter, told me that in the St. Gowans Peninsula of Wales a number of Flemish weavers were settled in the reign of King Stephen. Their descendants still have little or no intercourse with the native Welsh, and though many of them have gone forth from there in all directions during the intervening space of eight hundred years, the stay-at-homes have preserved their original Flemish tongue. Perry came from St. Gowans and spoke to the old lady in the Flemish of his ancestors, though for all he knew he was speaking Welsh.

John Ayers, the Cook-Sergeant, now got into his stride

and provided hot meals daily. John was no artist, but the food he produced was devoured eagerly and pronounced excellent after what we had been used to in the Salient.

Two Frenchmen, reputed refugees from Lille, attached themselves to the cooks' department. They were jolly fellows, middle-aged, and between them they had not a bean. They would chop wood, light fires, wash up, and fetch water in return for their food. We christened one 'Louis.' He was a typical Frenchman, complete with Napoleon goatee beard. His chum, however, was something of a freak. He looked glum and long-faced, had a dud eye like a ball of suet, and spoke in a hollow voice. He was dubbed 'George Formby.'

One day a large grey draught-horse died of colic. A fatigue-party began to dig a hole in which to bury it. Just before heaving it in, George and Louis got a butcher's knife and cut themselves two huge rump steaks from the carcass of the unfortunate beast. They fried these in dixie-lids and devoured them with relish. They were amused at our appearance of disgust, and to prove to us that horse steak is good diet, as soon as they had finished their meal they started galloping round and round the field neighing like bronchos.

The troops were very badly off for clothing and boots. Supplies did not seem in any hurry to put this right. One needed good footgear for wading about in the cold mud, but days passed and no new ones came to hand. Jack Lane of the Machine-Gun Section actually had no boots at all. He got over the difficulty by binding two surcingle-pads on his feet and for quite a week he flip-flopped about with these contraptions. The men were highly amused and Jack got a good deal of fun and publicity out of the situation. The 'Heads,' particularly the R.S.M., did not like it. But it was a nice point, not provided for in the regulations, so they kept quiet, and in due course Jack was correctly booted again.

Splash Hall, a youngster slightly senior to me, had been running the Machine-Gun Section since the death of Doctor Holmes. He was an Acting Sergeant. Almost all his men were reservists, a very tough lot, but excellent soldiers. Splash was their superior in intelligence and education, and their equal in courage and experience in action, so he had the outfit well in hand. He was one of the best soldiers the regiment produced, but he suffered from one blighting drawback—he was young and untamed. So in due course a Sergeant-Major from Knightsbridge appeared on the scene and took over the M.G. Section.

Splash and his little outfit gave rollicking concerts in a farm not far from ours, A few of us often joined them, and jolly, though harmless, affairs they were. But the great ones frowned. Not the Commanding Officer. He had too much good sense for that. ' Why,' they wondered, ' did we not think of our position and come over to the Headquarters Sergeants' Mess to join the *élite* at bridge ? '

His Majesty the King visited the front at this time, and on 2 December came to Hazebrouck to inspect the 7th Cavalry Brigade. We turned out mounted and, as far as possible, clean, and formed up on a long ribbon of straight road outside the town somewhere. As the road was so narrow, the Brigade formed up in single rank. It was bitterly cold. I sat on Herbert somewhere in the long rank near the left flank of the Regiment. There was, as usual, a long wait. Herbert began to feel cold. He could not make head or tail of all this business, so he decided to mis- behave, anything to liven things up. ' Why on earth,' he must have thought to himself, as he flapped his ears back and forward, 'are all these hundreds of hefty horses standing in the cold on this miserable roadside like so many sheep ? ' All of a sudden he made a plunge forward. I checked him and gave him a piece of my mind. He stood motionless for a moment. Then he spun round about six times like lightning and dashed the rank all to bits. There- upon he and I were called some exceedingly pretty names by our neighbours, but we took very little notice, and soon Herbert gave it up and stood still. I was glad he did, not because of the share of attention we had attracted, we were used to that, but because just at his heels ran a ditch six feet wide and containing heaven knows how many fathoms of water and mud. A step back would have landed us both over our ears in the ditch. The prospect did not appeal to me. Still, I expect the sly old beggar realized the situation as well as I did.

At last the word reached us that the King had started right away at the other end of the line. We pull ourselves together, take up our dressing correctly, and all is still. Suddenly the silence is broken by a crash and some violent language a little to our left. It seems the Colonel of the Leicesters has allowed his fat cob to go to sleep under him as he sits in his place in front of his Regiment, and half a minute before the King reaches him they both fall down in a heap. It is just too funny. They sort themselves out, the Colonel mounts, and we put our faces straight just before His Majesty passes in front of us. Then come three cheers for the King, and so back to Borre and a mess-tin full of John Ayers' bully-beef stew.

Many of our reservists had grown quite picturesque beards during our month's mudlark round Ypres. These decorations were carefully trimmed and tended. There was keen rivalry between their possessors. It was generally admitted that Bill Canning's was the best specimen. He sported a silken, golden growth, which caused him in his brighter moments to resemble closely Franz Hals' 'Laughing Cavalier.' One day the Commanding Officer, Captain Stanley, asked him with a smile: "I suppose you *will* shave again one of these days?" The day was not far ahead. Next Sunday a church parade was ordered. For this function beards had to be shed.

We had our first pay-day here, too. I drew the sum of twenty francs (fourteen shillings) from our new Squadron Leader, Captain J. J. Astor, just arrived from home, where he had been recovering from wounds.

And then one morning, on 7 December, I said good-bye to Madame, and in torrents of rain the Brigade moved farther back. We moved only a short distance, but owing to one cause and another the trek took all day. The same evening we pulled up in the village of Ebblinghem. Not that we had the haziest idea where we had landed. It was still pouring heavens hard when someone showed me in with the aid of a flashlamp through a large farm gateway, and ordered me and my soaked companions to find shelter in the surrounding outbuildings. I rode through and across the farmyard in a straight line till Herbert stopped with his face against a barn wall. The darkness was like pitch. A civilian came out of the farm and helped us to find our bearings. He carried a hurricane lamp, by the light of which I spotted a stable-door. Inside was empty, so in went Herbert. I made him as snug as possible for the night and then retired to the barn, where I flopped down, soaked as I was, and slept soundly in the straw.

Ebblinghem was to be our rest billet for the next four months, until after the second battle of Ypres.

XVI

WHEN we woke up in our new billet on the morning of 8 December 1914, as soon as horses had been located and attended to, there began the always fascinating game of spying out the land. In the middle of a rainy winter like 1914 the village did not present too bright a prospect. I found myself with about twenty Troopers in the outbuildings of the old *estaminet* ' La Maison Commune.' Everything outside was smothered in mud. Within the house all floors and passages of dark flag-stones were shining after their early morning scrub. I blundered in, and soon, thanks to my small knowledge of French, was made a sort of honorary member of the family. The proprietor, I learned, was M. André Vanlerberghe, a very excellent man, prematurely aged, and subject to spells of forgetfulness and incapacity, as though he had had a stroke. He was a widower. His eldest son, a lad of twenty, was away on active service with the 27th Regiment of French Artillery. His eldest daughter, Anna, eighteen years of age, ran the family, the inn, and the farm, and ran them well. Young André, aged seventeen, did all the ploughing and other farm work, while Agnes and Jean, aged respectively fourteen and twelve, did nothing in particular except eat and giggle and grow.

Regimental Headquarters remained in and around Ebblinghem till May 1915. There were many excursions to the Salient during this period. Many a stout fellow went up from Ebblinghem never to return, and many a lass from the village wept bitterly and silently in consequence. The inhabitants, except for the one or two black sheep which are to be found in every flock, were extremely decent folk, and as the majority of our men were well-behaved we were on very cordial terms with them. In the villages immediately to the north and south the reverse seems to

have been the case. When one mentioned either of them
the Ebblinghemites would shake their heads and say:
" C'est un mauvais coin par-là."

The village seemed to be on the very borders of Flanders.
Everybody in and around it spoke excellent French, though
all could speak Flemish. They seemed to have no choice,
but used either language as the spirit moved them. In the
village to the south only a French patois was spoken, and
in those immediately to the north only Flemish, though
the schools carried on all lessons in French.

The first member of the Regiment astir on the morning of
8 December was John Ayers, our Sergeant-Cook.

It was about 5 a.m., and still pitch dark, when John took
his dixies from the G.S. wagon, filled them at the water-
cart, and made his way into an empty, windowless house on
the west side of the village square. Here, with the aid of a
lantern, he explored the two rooms on the ground floor.
The room on the right took his fancy. It had an open
fireplace with plenty of loose bricks, ideal for dixie-work,
and best of all, it contained one solitary article of furniture
which filled him with delight. This latter object was a huge
wooden chest about seven feet long, three wide and three
deep. Here, all in one piece, were table, chopping-block,
store-cupboard, seat, and couch. Another journey to the
wagon for some firewood, and soon the flames were leaping
round John's dixies and he was feeling at peace with the
world. He sat down on the big chest and proceeded to fill
and light his pipe. A slight movement within the box
beneath his seat startled him and at the same time fixed him
where he sat. Then came a violent bump. John jumped
into the air and then stood gazing spellbound as the lid was
slowly raised from within and a perfectly hideous face
leered out at him.

Neither spoke for some seconds. At last the occupant of
the chest emerged completely. John was undecided
whether to run or fell him with his meat-chopper. Then,
as the apparition moved across to warm its hands at the
fire, it paused, glared into John's face, pointed to its own
breast with a claw-like finger, and uttered the two words:
" Moi, malade." This broke the spell. The pair became

good friends and old ' Malade ' continued in possession of his sleeping quarters. It appears he had once been wealthy and still had rich relations in the neighbourhood, but he had drunk himself into a most appalling human wreck.

Meanwhile the rest of us washed and shaved and then made our way into the *estaminet* where we were made welcome by the family. Tables were placed at our disposal, tea, bacon, bread and jam came along from John Ayres, and very soon we were full enough to forget ourselves and transfer our attention to our surroundings.

On the east side of the village square stood the château where lived that elusive personage, M. le Maire, with a very fat, not so elusive daughter of eighteen or twenty. The officers of R.H.Q. were billeted in the château. They seemed to be very comfortable, except in one respect. Neither in the château nor outside it was anything in the nature of a lavatory, closet, or privy. Major Cowie got Tinker Bell to construct two portable wooden ones immediately, and had them placed in the grounds at the back. One was for the officers *anglais*, the other for M. le Maire and Mademoiselle. The latter young lady made a fierce scene with the misguided but well-meaning Major Cowie, and declared that rather than use the new-fangled contraption she would walk the six miles to Hazebrouck and pay a penny. I doubt, however, if even that was possible in 1914.

In a farm-house at the south end of the village lodged the senior N.C.O.s of R.H.Q. Here was a farm-house in a thousand. Everything, inside and out, was spotlessly clean. The house was surrounded by a moat twelve feet wide and crossed by a narrow iron drawbridge, the only approach. On the outer side of the bridge stood two gigantic dog-kennels, each housing a black dog of in-definite breed and about sixteen hands high. These two brutes subsisted on a diet of bread and milk and were used for turning a wheel which worked a churn in the dairy. The farmer, M. Dupont, was feeble and confined to the chimney-corner. His wife, just as old as he, was a live wire. From daylight to dark her sabots and her tongue clattered everywhere without ceasing. She seemed to keep going on innumerable small cups of black coffee, which she drank standing with a sweet stuck in her cheek, and still talking. She had talked the old man into the chimney-corner, and now she was attempting to nigger-drive the maid-of-all-work. Here she had no success. Cécile carried on calmly with her work and smiled as if she thought life and her mistress a huge joke. Her smile was more than a match for Madame.

At the 'Maison Commune' we were in clover. We had a good dry barn to sleep in, and the large *estaminet* in which to spend our leisure time. Restrictions on hours of opening had not yet been imposed. After three or four days here we were all new men. The war was a good twenty miles away. For the moment it was forgotten. The family treated us as part of itself, giving us the run of the house. I am glad to be able to say that no man of ours ever abused these good relations. In course of time Anna became like a sister to me, and a little mother to everyone else. The troops treated her with respect and she thought the world of them. Jean, too, might have been my young brother, so close pals did we become.

The men with me included Tinker Bell, Corporal Saddle-treemaker; George Hayes and Jock Ramage, Corporal Shoeing-smiths; Drivers Bill Canning, late London Fire Brigade; Gunner Cousins, late City Police; Jock Roy, Metropolitan Police; Ducky Tennison, Birmingham Police; Joe Easby of Yorkshire; Tim Kelly, Scots Greys and Glasgow tramways; and wee Jock Lorimer of the Greys. These were all excellent fellows. The respite and peace gave them a new lease of life. Every evening the old rafters of the 'Maison Commune' rang with our singing. George Hayes was much in request for 'Trafalgar Bay,' 'Drake's Drum,' and other naval numbers. Jock Ramage had a repertoire of daft ballads in lowland Scots dialect, of which one in particular, dealing with the exploits of Burke and Hare, always drew vigorous applause. Gunner Cousins rigged up a set of drums, and one way and another, we produced a good impression of the Trooping of the Colour. Tim Kelly established a dancing academy in the loft above the barn. He was a keen dancing-master and did wonders in making us proficient. The music was supplied by wee Jock Lorimer on a mouth-organ nearly as big as himself.

The Brigade was scattered about within a radius of five or six miles, with Brigade Headquarters at Hondeghem. We were under notice to rally at a predetermined point in a certain time. This time was lengthened or shortened according to the state of pressure in the line. When under very short notice we stood to with saddles packed and on.

After a week or so the Powers that were began to think out ways and means of curtailing our enjoyment and smartening 'us up. Closing time for *estaminets* was fixed for 8 p.m., Tinker Bell and I were ordered into the senior N.C.O.s' billet, to our unspeakable misery. Regimental Church Parades took place every Sunday at Staple, two miles away. Andy Kealey, a devout Catholic, who never missed early mass if there was a church within reasonable distance, was seen by the young R.S.M. to smile when the last-named imposition was mentioned. So to demonstrate to Andy and all of us that the R.S.M. is mightier than the Pope, he ordered him to parade with the mob every Sunday and march to Staple. Here Andy was permitted to fall out and return to billets under his own steam.

On 13 December a sudden jerk disturbed for a time the even tenor of our way. An attack was to be delivered by the 2nd Corps at Wytschaete. What a glorious hope! It was snowing hard and the whole of Flanders was a morass. Late in the afternoon I was suddenly ordered to take Herbert and go up to Berthen with Lord Newry to find billets, as it had been decided to move the Cavalry up into support next day. It was some three hours' ride, with snow falling thickly all the way. Arrived at Berthen, everything off the road was feet deep in mud. We lodged our horses in a tumble-down cart-shed and proceeded to business. I shall never forget going across a field to a farm-house a hundred yards off the main road, to inquire for room for horses. It took me nearly an hour to negotiate that field. The mud came up over my knees and threatened to take and keep my boots. When at last I reached the farm, I found half a dozen half-drowned artillerymen sitting round a fire in the open, drinking tea. They were amused at the sight I presented as well as at my query about billets. Anyhow, they gave me a drink of tea and back I waded.

When at length our job was completed I was starving and penniless, so Lord Newry gave me a few francs, and I found a pork-butcher who sold me two or three pork chops. Then I inflicted my presence on a hospitable shoe-maker, borrowed his frying-pan, and started in cooking my chops on his fire. In the end I had a good meal, and slept soundly all night on the old snob's floor.

Herbert had a bad night. He must have been quarrelling with his shed-mates. Next morning he looked tousled and had a nice piece of skin, about the size of a dollar, bitten out of his withers. Fortunately the saddle did not touch it. I soon made him comfortable. As the day was fine I tied him outside by himself, where I gave him a feed of corn, a piece of my mind, and left him a hefty bundle of hay to amuse himself with. The infantry attack we had come to support proved successful, so on 16 December we returned to Ebblinghem. Christmas was now in the offing and we proceeded peacefully to prepare for its celebration. Tinker Bell and I, though attached to the Sergeants' Mess for bed and food, made our headquarters during the day and evening in the 'Maison Commune.' Our horses were there, and so were our pals. Here, too, we received visits from old cronies in the outlying squadrons, particularly from 'D' Squadron, which lay in farms between us and Staple with its social centre in the 'Rat and Cat.'

The weather was vile, the country-side drab in the extreme, but we were exceedingly happy and appreciated what scant comfort we had. I had now no definite job. The Orderly Room Sergeant carried out all clerical duties. Soon he succeeded in foisting on to me the task of sorting and distributing the mail. Some job it was, too, with the Regiment full of new people and Christmas stuff beginning to arrive in lorry-loads. Still, it furnished an excuse for frequent visits to the Brigade Post Office at Hondeghem, which gave me the chance to take Herbert out alone and get the great chump used to all the things he had never seen before and which scared him stiff.

About this time a surprise was sprung on us in the shape of an order permitting batches of other ranks to proceed on seventy-two hours' leave to England. All the great ones went immediately. Before Christmas my turn came. I refused it, as I had no friends I particularly wanted to see in England. To me, Ireland was home, and to get there and back in seventy-two hours in mid-winter seemed pretty hopeless, if not quite impossible. I pointed out that the Scots Greys, many of whom were Cockneys, were granted an extra twenty-four hours to enable them to go to Scotland, and asked if a similar privilege might be extended to me. It was refused, so I dismissed the idea from my mind and got no leave till August 1915, when I took seventy-two hours and actually spent twenty-four of them at home. I had not been back a fortnight when the leave period was increased to seven days. Just my luck!

We had a rollicking Christmas. Turkeys and puddings arrived in plenty from Knightsbridge. The gentle art of helping oneself to such commodities on the way up had not yet reached the perfection of a year or two later. Every parcel from the Base bore the inscription in indelible pencil: 'Good luck to the boys, from Corporal Cartwright.' This made the old R.S.M. wild. Selby Cartwright was no pal of his. He had gone to the base with a batch of reinforcements, and being an adaptable sort of cove, had stuck there on a staff job and been promoted without any reference to the old man.

Drinks were plentiful. Lord Newry gave me, his fellow-Irishman, a bottle of whiskey. The sight of this caused Andy Kealey to dig out his family tree and try to prove his origin in the Green Isle. Visits were exchanged, and the whole village, troops and inhabitants, resembled one large, happy family. The people of Ebblinghem were good folk, as yet unspoilt by contact with all sorts and conditions of troops.

On Christmas Day closing time at the 'Maison Commune' was forgotten. At 10 p.m. we trooped the Colour once more to Gunner Cousins' drums and wee Jock Lorimer's mouth-organ. Old 'Malade' from John Ayers' box was loafing around picking up a drink here and there. When we were about to retire Joe Easby bought a bottle of rum, heaven knows why. For want of a better place he put it standing on the floor under his chair. When he stood up to go the bottle had vanished. We all searched, but could find no trace of it.

One of the drivers had fallen asleep in the midst of the jollification. We shook him and called him, but he would not wake up. A saddle was fetched and placed on his guts, the girth and surcingle made fast round him. Then we bore him in solemn procession to the barn, where we laid him down to sleep with his feet well home in the stirrups. Goodness knows what the poor lad thought or felt like next morning.

At dawn on Boxing morning John Ayers repaired to his cook-house as usual. He lit his fire, then banged on the old chest to rouse his friend ' Malade,' but got no response. He lifted the lid, and there lay the old boy, as dead as a door-nail, with Joe Easby's rum-bottle empty at his side. John was all of a dither for days, and the shock gave Joe quite a bad turn. Jock Roy and I had to take him in hand and keep an eye on him.

A hundred guests sat down to lunch in the 'Maison Commune' on the day of ' Malade's ' funeral, all in frock coats and heavy mourning, after seeing his miserable remains interred in the village churchyard.

During the whole month of January 1915 the Regiment remained in billets. Squadrons were busy getting new drafts into shape, and new material was gradually being introduced. The Practical Jokes Department showed us how to make hand-grenades from empty jam tins, and a number of N.C.O.s and men were trained in the manufacture and use of the new bombs. Great fun, this, for a while. Extra machine-gunners were trained. A group of snipers sprang into being.

Then on 27 January the Commander-in-Chief, Lord French, paid us a visit and inspected the Regiment. He was a popular C.-in-C., who inspired confidence and behaved just like one of ourselves. After the parade he made us a pretty speech.

We were now on our toes again. Though none of us suspected it, Ypres was calling, and meant to claim our attention in the very near future.

XVII

ON 3 February our 3rd Cavalry Division took over a sector of the line about Zwartelen from the French and held it for ten days. Then the other two Cavalry Divisions held the same sector for ten days each. Although the conditions in the trenches, which resembled drains, were pretty ghastly, and there was some foot trouble, our actual casualties during our six days in the front line were only two killed and four wounded. Our successors during the next three weeks were less fortunate. The nearness of the German trenches made it difficult and dangerous for the enemy to shell our position, but snipers were a pest. Mining was suspected, though how that operation could be carried out in the waterlogged ground beats me. The Germans were well supplied with trench-mortars, bombs, and Very lights, all of which were practically unknown on our side.

At 2 p.m. the troops went up by bus from Staple to the Hooge corner on the Menin Road. The relief took place without incident. The old L.G.O.C. buses, complete with driver and conductor, were a cheering sight. They had a tough time on the Flanders' roads, but what memories were revived on hearing the tinkle of the conductor's bell, and what chaff between conductor and 'fares' all the way along !

I was now given a definite job which lasted till the end of May. The limbered wagons were brigaded under Major L. E. Barry, and I was posted in charge of the 1st Life Guards' section of this new 'A' Echelon formation. By virtue of the seniority of my regiment I was senior N.C.O. of the outfit and had the good fortune to work directly with Major Barry during the next three months. I do not think there was ever a happier little formation anywhere during the course of the war. We worked like slaves, every afternoon loading rations, charcoal, sand-bags, barbed wire, ammunition, tools, and every possible commodity for feeding the troops and keeping the trenches safe and habitable. Every evening, after dusk, we set out for Lord Cavan's house beyond Zillebeke, going through Ypres and up the Menin Road to the railway crossing, then in to the right along the corduroy road, and round by the remains of Zillebeke church. It took what seemed hours to hand over our load. Then back we trekked over the same old route to our 'billet' at Poperinghe or Vlamertinghe, where we arrived exhausted about 3 a.m. Every yard of our route was shelled at some time or other during the twenty-four hours. Scores of dead horses lay alongside it in places, yet we never had a single casualty, man or horse, all the time.

'A' Echelon left Staple on the morning of 3 February and reached Poperinghe about 3 p.m. We went at once to draw rations and stores, and after dark proceeded up through Ypres and out on to the Menin Road. Here we halted while the troops passed us on foot. The machine-gun limbers left us and went up with them to Cavan's House. We others had to await their return and then get along, four limbers at a time, to the same destination. Each batch of four had to wait at Zillebeke church till the previous four had passed on the way down, owing to the state of the road.

Standing there on the creepy Menin Road, it seemed hours and hours before the order came which set us in movement. We had had nothing to eit or drink since morning; it was bitterly cold, and horses were restive. It was an eerie spot; shells were dropping round about; flares kept going up over the lines, and the rattle of rifle and machine-gun fire seemed just round the corner. I walked up and down with Herbert's reins over my arm and answered the same old question: " Who are you ? " a dozen times to the same fussy staff officers who were buzzing about like mosquitoes.

Suddenly I became aware that there was a solitary, dark, one-storied house alongside the road. I approached and knocked on the door. I scarcely expected an answer, but the door was soon opened by a middle-aged woman. I could not see much of her in the darkness. I asked her if she had any coffee, and without a word she disappeared into the depths of the building to return in a minute or two with a basin of good hot coffee. I drank this gratefully, gave her back the basin, and she closed the door and vanished as silently as she came. What a weird place for a woman to hang on to! Still, to her I suppose it meant home.

I was not left long to my meditations. The first four limbers were off and I with them. Though the air felt full of things uncanny, Herbert behaved like an angel. He was, however, on his toes all the way. The cracks of snipers' rifles round Zillebeke caused him to flap his ears back and forward, but I had to give him full marks for his conduct. Like many of my friends who were wild and woolly behind the line, he was a stout fellow in the vicinity of it. Each little convoy of four limbers then went back independently through Ypres. The whole echelon assembled outside the town and proceeded to a billet in a farm beyond Poperinghe.

What a farm it was! A dwelling-house full of refugees, about fifty men and women of all ages. I opened a door off the living-room and looked into the next apartment. Fully thirty men and women slept any old how on the floor. There was a good fire in the living-room and a pump which produced brown ' water.' This was the only source of water supply, though the surrounding fields were nearly all flooded. The farmyard was one large cesspool, the outbuildings foul. I tied Herbert up in a cart-shed, fed him and left him with a good supply of hay and a word of advice to behave himself.

The rum-ration was then issued and duly swallowed. Major Barry came to have a look round to see how we were fixed up for sleeping quarters and found Dan Elliott actually drinking water from the pump. " You ought to mix your rum with that stuff to disinfect it," said the Major. " That's all right, sir," replied Dan. " I've just prepared my innards for it by drinking my rum neat." We slept in some hay on the loft over the dwelling-house, just as we were, booted, spurred, and mud-caked, but realising we were in the Carlton compared with our comrades in the front line.

Next morning we were up and astir early. The farm precincts fairly stank. The refugees disappeared about their daily vocations in Poperinghe, and we waded out through the mud to find and tend our horses. Herbert's shed was empty. The rascal had broken his head-collar and cleared off. This was serious. Horses were killed in numbers daily in the Ypres area, and horse-lifting was practised pretty freely by ammunition columns. It was not wise to leave any horse anywhere unless well tied up and watched. Still, Herbert could not possibly realise that through his desertion he might easily find himself one of a team of six artillery horses in the next few hours. I went straight to the forage dump, whither I guessed his appetite might direct him, but there was no sign of him anywhere about the farm, so I went out on the road and scanned the surrounding country.

Half a mile away was a flooded field. In the middle of it were four horses romping about and splashing like porpoises. Needless to say, the ringleader was Herbert. I went straight to him with a nosebag of corn, and he gave himself up and came quietly. Being cross with him would have been mere waste of time. I just set to work thinking out ways and means of making the scoundrel secure for the night, and decided that while in our present billet he must be housed in an outhouse with a door which could be closed. That stopped his game.

There followed ten days of routine work. Always up and back over Ypres and Zillebeke every night. Often we had to crawl or simply stand on one side up to our axles in mud while heavier traffic held the crown of the road. Sometimes we found our usual route through Ypres blocked by fallen houses and had to make a groping detour in the dark through side-streets. More than once it was a case of galloping to dodge salvoes of shells falling at measured intervals along the road. Our shoeing-smith, Jock Ramage, had a busy and filthy time with the horses' feet.

Ypres was badly knocked about in February 1915. It was

shelled daily, but not with the same intensity as later in the year. The Cloth Hall stood up, a stark ruin, and the railway station received a daily dozen or so all to itself.

The civilians went calmly and stolidly about their business in the town, but they were mostly the poor devils, the *sans culottes*. All who possessed anything of value had collected what they could of their belongings and cleared out long since. Many shops were just left deserted, and the cellars full of wine presented a deadly temptation to stragglers from units in and around the Salient. I saw numbers of these slinking furtively through the streets at night like scared animals prowling for food. It was dreadful to think of British soldiers coming to this, but I had sufficient grasp of the situation to be able to say to myself on seeing one : ' There, but for the grace of God, go I.' The term ' shell-shock ' was as yet unknown in the vocabularly of the Royal Army Medical Corps, though the distemper was quite well known and called by various names, all equally sinister. Many a stout lad of the old regular army with nerves shattered through weeks and months of hell had no hope of sympathetic treatment. Dozens of them just tottered off into the blue and went to the devil.

One morning, coming back from Zillebeke in the dark, we were unable for a few minutes to get out of the Grande Place. As we stood by waiting for an opportunity to move on, I walked along the pavement towards the corner of the Rue au Beurre, exchanging a word here and there with the drivers. Suddenly out of a gloomy archway stepped a stalwart young Irish Guardsman. He had no equipment save his pack on his back. He looked wild-eyed and jumpy, but the sound of my ' brogue ' had stirred something deep down in the poor devil and he simply had to speak to me. To all appearances he was on the verge of madness. He greeted me with : " Hallo there, Townie ! What the divil are ye doin' here ? " I could get no sense out of him, and was grieved to think I could do absolutely nothing for him, much as I would have wished. Suddenly he said : " Would ye loike a nice watch, now ? " There and then he dumped his pack down on the pavement with a crash like broken crockery, opened it, and showed me it was chock-full of watches. "There y'are, now. Take yer pick," he said. My good genius in the shape of Major Barry saved the situation. He suddenly gave the order : " Mount ! " and away we went at a trot, leaving poor Paddy standing all alone in the wretched street with his loot. Heaven knows what was the end of him. There were many of his kind in Ypres just then.

The opportunity to loot was resisted by nearly everybody. Many, however, 'won' some little thing which appealed to them as a souvenir, while feeling that the complete destruction of everything was merely a matter of time. One of our drivers established a miniature *estaminet* in the locker of a G.S. wagon. His ambition was not so much to have a large stock as to possess bottles (full if possible) of many colours and shapes. He was one of my best friends, and many a good tot of Kummel or brandy came my way when my body and soul badly needed fortifying.

On the morning of 8 February, the Regiment in the line was relieved by the 1st Dragoons and marched back into Ypres, where it billeted in the Rue des Chiens. Things were quiet till 11 February, when a small party of 'D' Squadron got together with their rum ration in a large room where there was a piano. About 8.30 p.m. Frank Watkins was playing ' Somewhere a voice is calling,' and all were singing together, when the enemy started shelling the town with heavy howitzers. The concert carried on till presently a ' Jack Johnson ' landed straight into the house, which collapsed all about them. Six of the party were killed, eight wounded, and a few suffered badly from shock. Among the latter was Bertie Channon. Every stitch of clothing on him was torn to ribbons and yet he was not wounded. In a few days he went back home to return no more.

The 2nd Cavalry Division relieved ours on 12 February, and the Regiment returned to Ebblinghem by bus. We of the ' A ' Echelon collected the various impedimenta which formed our cargo, and trekked back after them by road through Abeele, Steenvorde, St. Sylvester, and Hondeghem to our former rest billets.

The Brigade limbers were now a small formation possessing an individuality of its own, and welded by hard and successful work into something like a good unit. Our Commanding Officer, Major Barry, was as our father. He knew us and our horses inside out. In all our work there was no fuss, but always a cheery word and a helping hand from everybody. We were all old friends now, and it was as well that this was so, for many more such trips to the Salient were yet to come and test every man and horse of us.

Back at Ebblinghem, Madame Dupont fussed around me like an old hen over one stray chick. She had missed me because I was the only *soldat anglais* who could stand up to her in conversation. And talking of hens, one day I heard her say in broken English to the R.S.M.: " When the English soldiers from my daughter's farm at Staple were in the trenches, my daughter's hens laid five-and-seventy more eggs every day ! " Small wonder ! The troops loved eggs in any shape or form, but especially did the Indian veterans appreciate them first thing in the morning well beaten up in rum and milk.

Anna had the flagstones of the ' Maison Commune ' shining and tons of beer in stock. Herbert's old stable was again at his disposal. Clippers had arrived from home, and soon he and his fellows were clipped trace high. For reasons of hygiene his mane was hogged and his tail cut to one hand's breadth above his hocks. I preferred him with full mane and tail, but needs must—so I gradually got used to him in his new tonsorial state. In two or three days' time he was very frisky and hitting the roads to Hazebrouck and Hondeghem like a two-year-old.

XVIII

WE enjoyed ten days of unbroken peace from 13 February to 23rd. The weather was wintry in the extreme, with much frost and some snow. Horses had a thinnish time. The barns in which they were housed were never intended for that purpose and soon became dilapidated. Walls of wattle and daub collapsed. Floors were deep in mud and filth. The unfortunate animals suffered from colds caused by the eternal draughts, and foot-trouble was frequent. Like true British soldiers, we hung empty corn-sacks over the gaping holes in the walls. The idea of using timber for this purpose seems never to have occurred to anybody, and as for building anything in the shape of a stable, it was simply out of the question.

Facilities for warming billets and drying clothing were absolutely lacking. During frost and snow one had to sleep in all one's clothes, including boots which were never dry, in order to keep warm. It is astonishing how little illness there was among the men. This immunity may have been due in no small measure to the feeling that any sort of existence twenty miles behind the line was preferable to trench life, and it was really worth while trying to keep going, as rest billets, for all their foulness, were really holiday resorts.

Troop Sergeants had a trying time, seeing that their forty horses and men might be scattered in groups of fours and fives in different farms a mile or so apart. Going round at night to issue the rum ration was a perilous job in more senses than one. Many a good sergeant started out at 8 p.m. in pitch darkness with the rum issue for his troop and the best of intentions, but failed to complete the round. Rum was rum in the first year of the war.

One dear old friend of mine very nearly lost his life on a

rum round. He had given much thought to matters connected with rum, and later on, when I became a Troop Sergeant, gave me some advice based on his researches in this direction. We both had a long enamel jug in which we drew each five pints to be issued out at the rate of eight to a pint. One night, as I started away cheerfully to dole out my supply, he said to me : " You ain't goin' to give it to 'em like that, are you ? " " Why not ? " I asked. " Come with me and I'll show you," said he. He conducted me to the village pump. Here he poured a pint of rum into his own water-bottle and filled up the jug with water to the original level. " There y'are," said he. " That's 'ow I gives it to 'em. Don't you realise, you ruddy fool, that they'll swear it's been watered, whether you water it or not ? " Having no personal use for a pint of rum, I did not follow his example, and though I'm afraid I went down in his estimation, we always remained good friends during the war and after.

Well, one fine frosty night my old friend started off round the outskirts of Staple with his long jug. He did not return to his billet, but there was nothing very extraordinary in that, so the troops went and dossed down to sleep at the usual time. That night the frost was extra severe. Next morning at daylight they found him lying on the dunghill in front of the farm-house.

He was stiff, and so far as they could see, dead. On closer investigation it was found that his heart still beat faintly. They took him inside, stripped him, rubbed him, wrapped him in blankets, and placed him in the chimney-corner. For two or three days his men tended him till he returned to full consciousness and life. The officers never knew, and soon my old friend was as merry and bright as ever.

On 23 February the Digging Department got hold of us and we sent out parties in all directions to dig, repair, and drain trenches for the next three weeks. We even found a party of one hundred men to go up and help to look after the horses of the 1st Cavalry Division during the time the latter were in the line at Zillebeke.

Haig's 1st Army saw fit to attack at Neuve Eglise on

L

10 March. Our digging and maid-of-all-work duties came
to a sudden end and we were ordered up to stand by in
case of need. We set out next day to the Brigade Rendezvous at La Kreule, ' A ' Echelon in rear of the mounted
men. Major Barry rode at the head of the latter formation,
I in rear. I was the last man of the column. The day was
fine and bright and the roads and fields timidly showing
signs of the approach of spring.

There is a windmill on the right side of the road half
a mile outside Hondeghem. This was working as we
approached, its immense sails swinging right over the road,
which at this point is sunk to a depth of ten or twelve feet.
The sides are pretty steep. Everything went fine till
Herbert caught sight of the working windmill. He just
pricked up his ears and walked quietly on till abreast of it.
Then a gigantic sail swished over our heads, and the next
thing I knew was that we were galloping hell for leather
across the ploughed field left of the road, away from the
mill and the rest of the Brigade. Fortunately for our
reputation we were right in rear and unseen, so we rejoined,
unnoticed by anyone who mattered, at a point where the
bank was less steep and the windmill well behind.

We arrived at La Motte au Bois and stood to all day in
the Forest of Nieppe. It was rumoured that Neuve Eglise
had fallen, and when darkness came we were ordered to
billet around Arrewage. Good billets they were, too. ' A '
Echelon broke up, limbers billeting with their Squadrons.
The machine-gun limbers moved in and settled down
quickly in an empty farm-house. Here Daddy Long and
Jack Lane discovered a tiny cottage quite empty of human
beings and containing a comfortable room with double
bed. They bagged this at once. Everything looked easy
for the night when the order came : " All limbers away at
once to Merville for rations and forage." It was a heavy
job for ten limbers to draw and distribute rations and
forage for 660 men and 660 horses. One limber can carry
four trusses of hay or ten sacks of corn.

Anyhow, we jogged on the three or four miles to Merville, and found mountains of supplies drawn up in lorries
by the roadside. There was no fatigue party, so we got

to work and first unloaded lorries. Then, under supervision of Quarterblokes, divided the lot into five portions
(R.H.Q. and four Squadrons). Then up with it on to the
limbers and away back to the distant farms where the
troops lay. Several journeys were necessary. A quarterbloke travelled with the squadron limbers on the first
journey so that the drivers could find the way alone on
subsequent journeys. We handled trusses of hay and 60-lb.
sacks of corn till our arms and backs ached. While working
we had to keep an eye on the teams of horses which were
restless with cold and standing about all day. One pair
slipped into the ditch and there was a merry dance getting
them out. Soon after midnight the last half-limber left
Merville with the last load for Jingo Brown's Squadron,
some three miles back. The driver was Jinky Jones of the
'Skins,' and I sat on the back, thankful that the job was over
and looking forward to some food and sleep.

Jingo Brown barked "Good night" to us as we
departed from his billet. We asked him the best way to
Regimental Headquarters, and without hesitation he
directed us, wrongly, of course. Off we went at a sharp
trot, and inside five minutes the road petered out and we
found ourselves in an orchard, apparently nowhere. What
was to be done now? Suddenly, a mile or so away to our
right, we heard voices raised in violent altercation—a
terrific row. We listened intently and were sure we recognised the voices of Jack Lane and Daddy Long. We
turned about, took the first road to our left, and in a few
minutes were home. All was peace and quiet, so we got
some sleep before morning.

Splash Hall, the Machine-Gun Sergeant, came across to
R.H.Q. about 6 a.m., and in course of conversation it
transpired that the rumpus Jinky and I had heard the night
before was due to a bit of claim-jumping on the part of a
very young officer and his servant. It seems they were in
late off some duty and stumbled upon the empty cottage
which had been claimed by Jack Lane and Daddy Long.
The two old soldiers, being away at Merville, and the
cottage being apparently untenanted, they moved in, the
officer into the bed, the servant on the floor. Jack and

Daddy were none too sweet-tempered on returning to their billet, and when they found it occupied they just saw red. The officer and his servant simply picked up their traps and ran. Splash had just heard the former telling his version of the affair to a senior officer. "One of them, a nasty, black old man, glared at me like a wild beast," he said, "grabbed me by the neck, and hurled me out of bed screaming: 'Come on, you! You suffering perisher! 'Op it!'" The other kicked my servant in the ribs, swore blood-curdling oaths, and as we retreated he lifted the jerry from under the bed and smashed it on the floor behind us.". "Why didn't you check them?" asked the senior officer with an amused look. "Check them!" replied the very young one. "I'd as soon try to check a whole Troop of Uhlans!" The very young officer, being a decent sort, and realizing he really had crashed in on the two veterans, said no more about it. He did, however, ask Splash Hall afterwards about the pair of worthies, and on being told they were reservists and policemen in civil life he nearly collapsed.

Our services were not required about Neuve Eglise, so on 14 March we trekked back to Ebblinghem. Here we put in some intensive training, now that the spring was advancing and roads and weather improving. Reinforcements in officers and other ranks joined us, and some oldish officers, as well as some young and daft ditto, were sent home.

On 12 April a re-shuffle took place in the billeting area. Our Regiment moved slightly east across the railway line with R.H.Q. in the château one kilometre east of Ebblinghem Station. This entailed quitting the old village, a move much regretted by us. The 'Maison Commune' would now be a fairish walk, and we would miss the chatter of Mme. Dupont and the smiles of Cécile.

The officers were actually lodged in the new château. Alongside it was a sort of home farm. Here other ranks and their horses found cover. I never knew who the owner of the château was, but the farm was in the hands of Mme. Dassonville, as nice an old lady as ever lived. She was a widow and sixtyish, the mother of a large family. All her sons were already either dead, or disabled in hospital, through the war, and all her daughters except one were married and away. There were two or three poor old workmen about, and a shepherd over one hundred years old still doing a day's work. Her daughter was about the most beautiful girl I ever saw in France.

The mother was a splendid old lady. She was obliged to attend personally to all important things about the farm. I am glad I was able to help her now and again. More than once I sat up all night with her watching a cow about to calve, and I shall never forget with what contentment we sat down in the chimney corner when the event was successfully over, and talked and drank a spot of coffee (with rum in mine), before toddling off for a couple of hours' sleep. I'm afraid if I had stayed long at Mme. Dassonville's place she would have come to regard me as a son. I admired her tremendously. In eight months of war she had lost her husband and two or three sons, but she continued to be calm and patient. Her great natural decency made a deep impression on me, and I was glad to be of service to her, if only in a small way. What would have become of France in the war without women of the stamp of Mme. Dassonville?

The men were quite happy in the new area during the fortnight we remained there. We were throwing off the effects of the beastly winter and beginning to feel fit and alert again. Every morning I got up soon after 5 a.m., ran the mile to Ebblinghem village, drank a cup of coffee with Anna, and ran back, arriving shortly after 6 a.m., just as the great ones were awakening from their slumbers. As they saw me come in they looked very knowing and were pretty certain I had been out all night. But I knew them well enough now to be able to ignore them and their remarks completely.

The only forge in the area was at Staple, a mile or so across the main railway line. One day Shoeing-Smith MacLean of the 6th Carabineers, arriving back hungry after shoeing horses all morning, reached the level-crossing just in time to have the gates closed in his teeth, with a train approaching two hundred yards away. Mac reined

back his mare and then flew over both gates in true Dick
Turpin style. Just the sort of stunt he had been waiting
for all his life. A great lad was Mac. A Canadian Scot of
the Tom Mix type. He was a source of delight to all who
understood him, and a thorn in the side of all the poor old
dodderers who did not.

General Kavanagh left our Brigade on 19 April to take
over the command of a division. Few generals were so
well liked. In action he spared nobody, himself included.
Out of action he just left us in peace. Stunt-merchants got
no encouragement or inspiration from him. His successor,
General Kennedy, was also popular, and was not slow to
comment in no very polished language on anything not
meeting with his approval. The troops liked him at once
for his soldierly bluntness. Their liking for Kavanagh was
rooted in respect and admiration, and I believe the humblest
Trooper in the old 7th Cavalry Brigade grieved at his
going.

XIX

I REMEMBER I was out with a few men and horses somewhere about Le Nieppe, on the St. Omer–Cassell road, on the morning of 23 April 1915. Goodness knows what we were doing. It was a beautiful spring morning. Suddenly a string of motor ambulances came tearing down the road from the north, and we pulled in to the right to give them plenty of room. They were racing all out. The two end cars slowed down just past us, then stopped on the edge of the road. The drivers and orderlies hopped out, and, pulling a Canadian soldier from the end ambulance, proceeded to carry him to the ditch, where they tipped him up and held him head down. The poor fellow was grey-green in the face. Yellow froth bubbled out of his mouth. He appeared to be in the condition of a drowning man, and they were trying to empty his lungs. More were treated in the same way, then put back, and the cars continued down the road hell for leather. These were a sample of the victims of the first gas attack launched by the Germans up at St. Julien at dawn that morning.

Here was a new departure which gave us serious food for thought. We hurried back to billets, and it was not long before the Regiment was called out, and up we went post-haste to Abeele, and from there to Godewaersvelde, where we stood to in reserve.

'A' Echelon was worked to death on this outing. In the daytime we had to keep pace with the mounted troops as they moved quickly from point to point in readiness to go into the line. Each limber had a definite load of ammunition and stores to drag about all day. At nightfall these were unloaded while we drew rations and forage for the unit, after which we loaded limbers again before getting any food or rest. Round and round and up and down this hilly area we went at a trot-out, every night in a different 'billet,' every day standing to in the open till we were suddenly rushed off in another direction. We moved, when we could move at all, at a fast trot, or even at a gallop. The roads were congested with every conceivable form of transport and mounted troops, including even Regiments of French Spahis straight from the Sahara. French transport and British did not mix well on a narrow road. How we cursed them all! This picnic lasted the better part of a week.

After dark on 26 April we rode up to Poperinghe. Here the horses were left in a field one mile outside the town, while the men proceeded on foot through Poperinghe and on up to Vlamertinghe. The limbers were left waiting on the roadside on the edge of Poperinghe. It was a beastly night, blowing a gale and raining in torrents. Hardly had the troops left us when the Germans began to shell Poperinghe with seventeen-inch shells. Our men must have been marching through at that very moment. We had not heard such terrific explosions before. The roar of the giant shell approaching the earth from a height of several miles made one stand and hold one's breath. Nothing happened till dawn. Horses and men of our little limber column were all soaked to the bone and starving. Then came orders to move up to Vlamertinghe. On the way we saw the results of the previous night's shelling. One enormous crater was in the middle of a side-street. Every house was shattered, the near ones to smithereens, those farther away roofless and windowless. One shell, one street! The inhabitants were all clearing out.

Up in Vlamertinghe all was quiet. It was, I remember, a raw, watery morning. We pulled into a field a quarter of a mile east of the town, unhitched horses, tied them to the wheels, and tried to get something to eat. The troops were in some large wooden huts on the east side of the same field. By noon we had horses and gear shipshape, and although there was much electricity in the atmosphere, we were not in possession of any information as to the state of things in front, so we just hung around and waited.

At about 2 p.m. Fritz began to shell the village. He sprayed them in bunches of six all over the place, and seemed to be working gradually round towards our field. When at last it was only too obvious we were for it, the order was given to get the horses out and across the road away from the shelled zone. As we unhitched the horses shells were actually falling in our midst. As each driver had two, and we had to cross a narrow bridge over the roadside ditch, a lively few minutes ensued. Being nearest the exit, the 2nd Life Guards and Leicesters were first across. Tim Kelly was having some bother with his pair, Charlie and Harry. I had Herbert untied and was going to Tim's assistance when another salvo landed alongside us, and a piece of metal of considerable size, judging by the noise it made, hummed through the couple of yards' space between us. Then, with horses plunging and kicking, we were just crossing the little bridge, when a dud struck in the ditch at the edge of the culvert. Herbert nearly jumped over the moon, while Tim used such language to Charlie and Harry as must have made them blush. Anyway, we got out into safety just as the next six shells fell right into the huts. Looking back over our shoulders we saw some of them going up into the air.

Fortunately for the regiment, the only direct hit on a hut was on one with only four men in it, three of whom were killed and one wounded. One of those killed was my old gymnastic instructor, McFeeley. He had left us on the reserve about 1912 and gone to Australia. Here he was quite comfortable, and became a Sergeant-Major in the Australian Forces at the outbreak of the war. He came with the Aussies to Egypt. From there he travelled home to England and joined us at Ebblinghem on 23 April. Thus he came right from the far side of the world to rejoin his old regiment, only to be killed immediately in a miserable hut in Vlamertinghe. There was much sorrow over Mack's death. He was a fine fellow, no finer perhaps than those who were killed with him, but he had been a landmark in the Regiment in pre-war days, where his fencing, strong-man stunts, and jolly personality had made him popular. His brother, whom I particularly liked, was terribly affected by this sad business. I think it should be forbidden for brothers to serve together in the same unit. I came across the same sort of thing more than once.

When the shelling ceased the whole Brigade moved across the road to a field half a mile south, where we spent another nasty night in the open, standing up, frozen, hungry, swearing volubly. Then followed five more days of musical chairs round the Flanders villages. Days of terrific work for us of ' A ' Echelon after everybody else was finished. Each day we stood to in reserve at some point of concentration, and finally on 2 May we went back and billeted in St. Jans-ter-Biezen.

This village was miserable but still inhabited, and it was possible to purchase liquid refreshment there. ' A ' Echelon was not slow to avail itself of this amenity. We had a good hot meal, and after an hour in a warm *estaminet*, being very weary, we retired to our field on the east edge of the village. Here we had some straw and wagon-covers. There was every prospect of a night's sleep.

On arriving home, warm and contented, with no thought in our minds but a good night's rest, we were surprised to observe just inside our gate a very smart carriage, such as wealthy men used to drive to town in before the advent of the motor car. Its inside was comfortably upholstered and lit up by candles. We tip-toed across, peered cautiously through a window, and beheld one Sparks, the Veterinary Officer's groom, lying buried deep in cushions, smoking his pipe and reading a book. Sparks was quite a good sort, if something of a recluse, and we withdrew silently and unnoticed to see if we could play some trick on him. The sight of him in such luxurious surroundings was too much for us. We now noticed that the field sloped steeply away from where the carriage stood, down to a large pond at the bottom. This solved our problem. Back we crawled to the carriage. Hands on spokes, shoulders to the back, and at the word ' Heave ! ' we launched friend Sparks down the slope at breakneck speed. He, of course, was absolutely unprepared and helpless, and when next he had time to survey his surroundings he found himself in the middle of the pond with his smart conveyance up to the axles. We left him to his fate and went off to sleep. That carriage careering down the hill had been a fine and soothing sight, and a fitting end to the first quiet evening we had had for some time.

Next morning bacon was sizzling in dixie-lids and we were stamping round putting the final touches to horses and harness and trying to get warm, when the R.S.M. stalked into our field, summoned us all to him, and addressed us as follows: " The Mayoh of this town reports that last night his carriage was wantonly pushed into the pond and wrecked by the troops in this field. I want the person or persons concerned to step forward and own up now." No movement or reply on our part. " Very well, then," he continued, " if nobody owns up I'll have a guard in full marching order mounted on the carriage to-night from 6 p.m. to 6 a.m. and every night while we're heah." With that he pranced off and we got down to the business of breakfast. Should we own up? No fear! Why shouldn't we have a bit of fun? And what was the use of the old carriage, anyway? Besides, it was still a long way to 6 p.m. So we sat tight. The promised guard never mounted, for that afternoon we marched up again to Ypres, stood to all night till 6 a.m., and then came back to decent billets in Herzeele, where we arrived about noon. Here 'A' Echelon was momentarily dissolved, returning to Squadrons, whilst George Hayes, Tim Kelly, and myself turned in with Regimental Headquarters.

There were comfortable farms with spacious dry barns in and around Herzeele. At last the troops were able to have a wash and to sleep with boots off. George, Tim, and I decided to rig up an open-air shelter in an adjacent field and to sleep in the open. The weather was fine and sunny in the daytime. A clear stream flowed ten yards from our bivvy and we were soon spick-and-span.

Here George Hayes found the first louse we saw in the war. It was a surprise, and at first George felt embarrassed. On organizing a proper search, however, it was discovered that we all had some. Tim, being an older soldier than George and myself, simply remarked when shown the first specimen : " Och mon, it's a puir body that canna keep a few o' they wee beasties ! "

A very namby-pamby young soldier on R.H.Q. who was somewhat near-sighted now came forward and said to Tim : " By Jove, I've been worried at night by those things, but I thought at first the bally things were hay seeds that had got down my back."—" Hay seeds ! " exclaimed Tim contemptuously. " Aye, hay seeds ' avec ' legs ! " And thus there joined us a constant companion, who for the next three years was to defy all our efforts to dislodge him from our persons. Not that we did not try hard enough. Not only were all billets lousy in the end, but the very ground and grass of the fields were infested, so that the best one could hope for was temporary relief.

Having washed and fed, we proceeded in the afternoon to take stock of our position. Our bivvy was on the right bank of a little stream, one hundred yards east of the T in Arret, South of the Herzeele–Wormhoudt road (Haze-brouck 5a map). On the right of our field ran a railway line, alongside it the main road. One hundred yards along this road to the left was a cross-roads in whose N E. corner stood an *estaminet*. Not so bad !

Six o'clock that evening saw the three of us seated round a small table just inside the *estaminet* door, and placed so that when the door opened we were behind it. We wanted beer, and were pained when the landlady said she had none. She was, however, an enterprising woman, for realizing that the arrival of troops meant a demand for liquid refreshment of some sort, she had bottled several casks of wine and had the full bottles built up from floor to ceiling against the wall behind her counter. This would enable her to meet the rush without running to and from her cellar.

George Hayes was disgusted, despising as he did all Froggy drink. Tim and I, however, persuaded him that we might at least try a bottle of wine. George drank several glasses at one gulp, pulled wry faces, and spat on the floor ; but soon he was visibly mellowing, so we entreated him to go slow, and we had quite a pleasant time. The house filled up with soldiers of many units. At 8 p.m. (closing time), our little table had empty bottles all over it, all under it, and all round it. The place was still full at 8.30 p.m. George Hayes had long since turned his cap round with peak to the back and was singing ' Sons of the Sea ' in full blast, with everybody present going all out on the chorus. Tim Kelly had just finished an argument with a 21st Lancer by informing him : " The Royal Scots Greys, 2nd Dragoons, second to none, that's my old regiment. Why, you poor fish, if you were one more number down the Army List you'd be in the ruddy A.S.C. ! " when the door opened and in strode the R.S.M. He walked straight up to the counter without looking to the right or left. In a twinkling the three of us slipped from behind the door and out through it, pulling it behind us while his back was still turned. Then we remembered no more till we woke up in our bivvy next morning in full marching order and with mighty thick heads.

How we had got there we had not the least idea, but there we were. In our amazement we went after breakfast to inspect the only route by which we could have got back. Sure enough we had crossed the road and railway, nego- tiated a fair-sized ditch, got through a small hole in a hedge, and all that without stumbling or getting a scratch. We had not been seen. Nobody knew anything about the matter, but we were wise enough not to try any more wine evenings.

Next evening we had a walk round and visited some of our old friends. A party went up to Ypres and dug trenches all night, returning like drowned rats early on the morning of 6 May. On the evening of 7 May we rode back to our old billets near Ebblinghem. I said ' Good-night ' to Major Barry about 3 a.m. as we separated at Staple cross- roads to go to our respective farms. I led my little gang along to the château, and was soon sipping coffee and hearing all the latest farm news from my dear old landlady, Mme. Dassonville.

XX

DURING our absence the good folk in and around Ebblinghem had been roused to a pitch of enthusiasm by the sight of Territorial Army units marching up to the Ypres sector. I did not see the Terriers myself, but was given a glowing account of them by the villagers. Battalion after battalion had marched up past the railway station in the direction of Hazebrouck. The men, in shirt-sleeves, with full pack, looked cheerful and sturdy. British stock rose to a giddy height, and French veterans of 1870 predicted early victory, with the Kaiser, very much the worse for wear, hanging from a lamp-post in Unter den Linden.

We were allowed one whole day in rest billets. Midday on 9 May saw the regiment off up again to Vlamertinghe by bus, while 'A' Echelon trekked up in the usual way, and that evening took up its abode in a field on the right of the Pop.-Vlam. road just outside the latter village. The field stank and was a mud bath. Horses were tied up to wheel-lines and men slept where they could in the open. I made my bed with Rubber Reeves in the slush beneath the Maltese cart. Sleep was important. For the next fortnight we never managed longer than from about 2 a.m. to 7 a.m. daily, and this was always interrupted by shelling of the village and surrounding fields at dawn.

We were the hewers of wood and drawers of water for the troops of the Brigade in the line. Our mornings were spent trying to attend to our horses and gear, and keep them in shape. Afternoons found us visiting all sorts of dumps in the neighbourhood, where we drew and loaded up with every conceivable kind of material, as well as rations and forage. We were lucky if we got back to our field loaded by 6 p.m. Between that hour and darkness we had to get hold of something to eat. Nightfall saw us wending our way out on to the old familiar roads, through Ypres, up to Halte, and finishing somewhere round Zillebeke. At this period Ypres was being shelled severely, and the roads beyond were absolute hell, but in all our nocturnal journeyings up and back during the six weeks since February we never had a single casualty.

On returning to our field in the early hours of the morning, we had our rum ration and a drink of hot tea, before groping our way to our mud-beds for a few hours' sleep. I was fortunate in having on our outfit a Driver named Belsey, a good fellow and a teetotaller. I gave him sole charge of the rum. He was a rare good lad and did his job so well that all had complete confidence in him and there never was a grumble or ' rum-scandal ' of any kind.

Keeping our horses fit was a whole-time occupation. George Hayes, our shoeing-smith on this occasion, did the work of half a dozen. The wear and tear on shoes in that awful country was terrific. The drivers, too, were devoted to their horses, and no trouble was too much for them. Horses came first all the time, as was right and proper. We were desperately anxious about them on the lines at night, lest they should get loose and stray. Stray horses were picked up by neighbouring units and spirited away like lightning.

Herbert, bored by the drab surroundings, and attracted by the forage dump, refused absolutely to remain tied up at night. No head-collar was strong enough to hold him after he discovered he could smash it with an upward jerk of his head. For a night or two I got no sleep worrying about the rascal. Then I thought of a plan. I reinforced his head-collar by tying a built-up rope round his neck with a non-slipping knot, and then on the end of his head-rope I tied a full thousand-round box of ammunition. The other handle of the box I fastened to a picketing-peg driven well home in the ground. Now he would have to lift the box of ammunition before putting any strain on the peg. This took the snap out of his jerks, and the built-up rope was too much for him to break. With the aid of a good ration of hay I thought I now had him pinned down to a point. Night after night, however, he pulled up the peg, visited his pals, and finally the forage-dump, all the time with the thousand rounds on the end of his head-rope, like a ship dragging her anchor. Anyhow, he could not scamper off now, and in the morning he could be traced in the mud.

Danny Maher of the 'Skins' had a little black horse, reputed to have come from Lord Derby's stables, and a general favourite. One day Danny discovered the animal was not eating, so he came to George Hayes and myself and reported with a very long face. On examining the horse we discovered a nasty abscess on the angle of the jaw, caused probably by filth getting into a small scratch. George and I held a hurried consultation and decided not to send it away to the Veterinary Section, where it would be kept for weeks, if not for ever, but to operate there and then ourselves. George cleaned, sharpened, and boiled his jack-knife. Danny held the horse's head while we shaved round the spot. One swift stab and the abscess was open and draining. We plugged the wound and in a few hours the horse was eating as usual. Frequent dressings effected a complete cure in a couple of days. We had no more casualties, but we had to keep our activities to ourselves, not daring even to tell Major Barry. Operations by amateurs were not looked upon with favour.

On our first night coming back through Ypres it was noticed that a shell had played havoc in a music shop, and two drivers of the 2nd Life Guards bagged a large cabinet gramophone, which they brought 'home' in their empty limber. They also won a selection of records. A gramophone concert was announced for the following evening. As soon as all was ready for the journey up, we took our tea in our hands and crossed over to where the gramophone stood, a foot deep in mud, beside a hedge. When all were assembled a Trooper of the 2nd Life Guards, whose name I never knew, but whom I shall never forget because of his resemblance to D'Artagnan, stood by in his shirt-sleeves, and announced that the concert would begin with the William Tell Overture. He wound up the box, put on the record, and when it had spun round to normal speed, applied the needle to the outer edge. Not a note of music resulted, nothing but the scratch of the needle on the revolving disc could be heard. Consternation and some chaff among the audience. Again and again D'Artagnan tried to start the thing, but with no result. Then a mud-stained driver stepped forward, placed the needle in the centre of the record, and behold, the thing played. Marvellous discovery ! None of us had ever heard of a record beginning in the centre and working out to the edge. The concert went off with gusto. The records were nearly all of classical music, and the troops listened in profound silence. We repeated the programme on several evenings until word came from Major Barry to mount and turn out.

When a vocal record was being played we often joined in and sang with it. One driver, Aubrey Foster of the Blues, had a fine bass voice and was the backbone of our choir. He was wounded later on, and when in hospital in England deputized at a concert for some vocalist who failed to put in an appearance. Some big musical noise heard him, and when next I met Aubrey, in 1922, he had just returned from singing in grand opera in Leipzig.

A sad thing happened on the morning of 9 May, when the Regiment came back from the front line for three days to the reserve. Just before the relief was completed a very ancient, red-nosed Corporal of Dragoons, answering to the name of Flash, got hold of some spare rum. By the time the troops were moving down the communication-trench he was lying helplessly drunk. Corporal Angus MacTodd, always a good Samaritan without a thought for himself, hid old Flash till everybody had passed on, then hoisted him with all his gear on to his back and carried him the whole way to the end of the long trench without a rest. When they emerged Mac was exhausted, so he flung Flash's carcass on the ground and flopped down beside it, dead beat. Some busybody noticed them and fetched the doctor. ' Both drunk,' was his verdict after a sniff at Flash. Mac woke up at this, but was promptly placed under arrest. Flash was dead to the world, so a motor ambulance arrived on the scene and he was chucked in. The ambulance started off with a jerk and flung him out, cutting his head open on a stone. He went right back to hospital, where he was treated as a wounded man, eventually reached

M

England, and no charge was ever brought against him. Poor Mac, however, was tried, broke, and sentenced to a long term of imprisonment. Before he could be removed to durance vile the regiment went back into the front line. The big German attack of 13 May was launched; Mac distinguished himself on that occasion, was reinstated in his rank, and had his conviction quashed.

The troops were in a bad way in the front line, and, as I afterwards heard, in a bad position. At 5 a.m. on 13 May the Germans began plastering them with heavy shells and minenwerfer, and continued the strafe all day. The trenches held by the 7th Cavalry Brigade were blown to bits and our Regiment suffered over a hundred casualties. The whole Cavalry Division had a thin time that day, but as I was not in the beastly mess I am not going to dwell upon it. Handfuls of men here and there did some excellent work. George Hindenburg distinguished himself and was awarded a well-deserved D.C.M. Others, including a very snappy Captain, if all accounts are true, did not. Many good men were lost, among them my old friends Ted Castle and Victor Burton. We should never again hear 'Martha.' For days we felt the shadow of this disaster hanging over us all, but we carried on, working harder than ever, till the Division was relieved on 21 May. Some of our dead were still lying about unburied when the regiment went back up to the same sector in July.

At about 9 p.m., after finishing our last fatigue and picking up our loads, we of the limber column set off back to Ebblinghem. When we were a mile or so down the road Major Barry discovered he had forgotten his water-bottle back in the farm beside our field. His servant, Gathercole, went back for it and found that the old field had just been shelled to pieces, and a column of Artillery with mules, just moved in, blown to smithereens. We felt this shelling would come in the end and were thankful we had missed it. Our good luck held right through.

At Staple I parted from Major Barry in the very early morning, and we separated to make for our respective billets. It was my final parting with this most excellent officer, though at the moment I did not suspect it. It was also my last trip in charge of the limber outfit, and though I used to see all my old drivers from time to time, I was never to work with them again. It was all too good to last.

Finally, about 4 a.m. on a glorious May morning, the same old trio, George Hayes, Tim Kelly, and myself rode in through the gate of Mme. Dassonville's farm, watered and fed our weary horses, and left them comfortable before going scouting round for food for ourselves. We were ravenous and thirsty. We made a bee-line for John Ayers' cook-house and found that worthy asleep with a half-full rum jar at his head. This was spirited away outside, together with some cold ham and bread. John never moved. Then we did a silly thing. Instead of walking down to the village, where smoke rising from the chimneys told us that Anna was astir and would be glad to give us coffee to drink with our food, we sat down where we were and started eating and washing down our food with neat rum. All the big-wigs on Regimental Headquarters were still sound asleep and would remain so till 8 a.m. Most probably they had had a strenuous night at bridge.

At 5 a.m. we cleared off to the end of the field in which the wagon-lines were and went to sleep in the ditch. We woke up at about 8 a.m., feeling like boiled owls and hating being back again among our old friends. They, too, hated the sight of all three of us.

Next day a draft of some hundred and fifty other ranks, including Jim Fleming and Charlie Wright, arrived from Knightsbridge, and the powers set about re-forming the regiment. I ran across the R.S.M., and he nearly brought about my collapse by greeting me with a cheery " Good morning ! " But that was only the prelude. He stopped and immediately asked me : " I suppose you know you're transferred to ' D ' Squadron from to-day ? " No, I didn't. How could I ? " Well," he went on, "you are. You'd better get along there after dinner." I was delighted, but afraid to show it. Like lightning the question flashed through my mind : ' How about Herbert ? ' It could not matter where I went away from Headquarters, but I didn't fancy leaving Herbert behind, so I asked the R.S.M. : " May I take my horse with me ? " " I'll see," he answered.

After dinner I collected my belongings and my horse and rode out from R.H.Q. with a light heart to 'D' Squadron, which lay just round the corner in Mme. Brock's farm. 'Thank heaven,' I thought. 'At last I am back among the ranks, where I always wanted to be from the beginning.' I was overjoyed. But there was a snag in it. When Orders were published that afternoon they contained this interesting paragraph :

'No. 2829 A/Sergt. R. A. Lloyd is transferred to "D" Squadron for duty IN THE RANK OF CORPORAL.'

That was a pretty dirty bit of work. I had come to Flanders wearing three chevrons in October 1914. Right through the second Battle of Ypres I had done a Sergeant's job in charge of sixty horses for several weeks in and around the Salient, without the slightest mishap. I had also managed to keep out of trouble of any kind. Now I was going as a corporal to serve in a Troop whose Sergeant was junior to me on the regimental roll of N.C.O.s, and whose second Sergeant was actually a corporal of another regiment. However, I was clear of all those gentry on R.H.Q. at last, so I just took my jack-knife and cut off one chevron, after which I possessed my soul in patience.

XXI

I REPORTED to 'D' Squadron on the afternoon of
24 May. Mme. Brock's farm, in which my new home
lay, is marked on the Hazebrouck map at the elbow of
the road from Château to Lynde on the left-hand side.
The Squadron had just filled up its gaps in the ranks with
men from the new draft.

I had not handed in my revolver and was not asked for
it. I carried it afterwards on a belt beneath my jacket, as
my rank of Corporal did not entitle me to that weapon.

Barney Rudd, the Sergeant-Major, and Bob Harrison,
the Quarterbloke of 'D' Squadron, received me kindly.
Being both Yorkshiremen they said little. I was not long
in sensing the family atmosphere of the Squadron, and after
the first few days of heart-ache at the loss of my third
stripe, I gradually became imbued with the feeling of peace
and decency which reigned all round me. In my command
of a section of seven men I felt free and happy. The
Troop Officer, Lieutenant Jacques de Pret, a Belgian, was
everything a British officer should be, and we in No. 2
Troop thanked heaven for him. The Troop Sergeant,
Jim Fleming, was the same stout fellow. He could not
help the absurd position in which he and I had been placed.
Bogey Giles, second Sergeant, was always a sort of Santa
Claus to me. I was admitted at once to full membership
of the little community of the Troop of forty men, and,
making my shake-down in a corner of the field, I slept
happily once again a yard or two behind the heels of the
Troop's horses. These were tied on a breast-line and were
all fit, shining, and happy in the glorious May weather
which had just set in.

I could not very well tie Herbert in his proper place in
the Troop. As a stranger, especially one with a strong
character and will of his own, he would have had trouble

with the other horses. I tied him alone, a little on one side, and allowed him to break the ice between himself and his new acquaintances gradually.

My section of seven men seemed pleased at having me for their section leader. They all knew me since the far-off days on Salisbury Plain, were mostly Irishmen, and—blood is thicker than water. Good fellows they were, and I owe them much for their good comradeship and encouragement at that time when I sometimes felt bitter about many things. The section comprised the following : Trooper Cook of Aylesbury, the only Lifeguardsman in the Troop besides Jim Fleming and myself. Troopers Daly, Irwin, Vietch, and Tate of the Inniskilling Dragoons, the first three being Irishmen and Tate a Tynesider. Trooper Richard Brockwell, 1st King's Dragoon Guards and Bermondsey ; and, lastly, Trooper Bill Brewer of the Queen's Bays and Birmingham. All except Cook and myself had served in Africa and India, whilst Brockwell had served through the Boer War. Their average age was about twenty-seven. Cook was a trained bomber, Daly a sniper, Brockwell the Troop Cook, and Brewer looked after the pioneer pack plus pack-horse. They were all hard as nails, keen soldiers, very humorous in their mixture of back-chat, and during all my association with them I never saw a break in their cheerfulness. We all called one another by our Christian names, and taking things all round didn't care a rap for anybody. Our only thought was the welfare of the section, men and horses, and the Lord help anybody who attempted any liberties with us or our gear.

The horses were interesting and, on the whole, a good lot, all except Brockwell's, which was then suffering from debility, and looked poorer than it actually was owing to its strange colour—yellow, with small brown spots, just as if they had been burnt into the coat with the tip of a red-hot poker. Brockwell looked after it all he knew, called it Richard after himself, and it was the one worry on his mind. Sandy Tate rode a black polo pony, a most delightful rogue, who shared in, and enjoyed, many pranks with Sandy and could almost talk. He was roughly half Herbert's size.

Our food was good and satisfying. Bob Harrison as Quarterbloke, and Brockwell as cook, saw to that. I had a talk with Bob as to my own status in the regiment. I sometimes felt in the beginning like throwing in my stripes and reverting to Trooper. He was quite sympathetic. He advised me to keep quiet and carry on, doing my best in the capacity in which I happened to find myself. " Things will right themselves in time," he said. They did.

I never entered Mme. Brock's farm-house. She was a fearsome personage, short, stocky, dark, not over-washed, loud-voiced. Bogey Giles and Brockwell had crossed swords with her on a matter of firewood and been badly discomfited. We gave the place a wide berth.

For five days I remained a guest of Mme. Brock. Then the Regiment was moved back to another billeting area at Campagne. I hastily took leave of Mme. Dassonville and the Vanlerberghe family, after which I marched out in the ranks without a care in the world. Next day the Brigade went up from Campagne to the front line at Ypres for ten days. One man to every four horses remained behind in billets. I was left behind to carry out the duties of Sanitary Corporal. Of my new duties, beyond the dimensions of a latrine ($3' \times 2' \times 1'$), I knew absolutely nothing, nor did I feel elated at the honour thus conferred on me. I was allotted a sanitary squad consisting of two men, Troopers Ship of the 'Skins,' and Macdonald of the Carabineers. What these two worthies did not know about the business was not worth knowing. I believe now that I was returned to the Squadron with a bad name and instructions to be given a rough time, and that my new appointment was part of a little scheme for dressing me down. This did not dawn on me till afterwards when I saw the same trick played on others. I was still very green.

During the ten days when the troops were at Ypres those of us who remained behind had an easy time. There was plenty of work in connection with the horses, but weather was glorious, the countryside at its summer best, and we felt as if we were on holiday. The Squadron lay all in one field, half a mile south of the canal. Arques was twenty minutes' walk, Ebblinghem four miles distant. Many of us visited the old place of an evening, without official permission, of course. Our return to camp was fraught with danger, inasmuch as there were only two bridges over the canal, one in our own village and therefore out of the question, the other a mile along to the east, at Wardreques. Here a corporal's guard of French Territorials had a post. At night a French sentry, with loaded rifle plus bayonet, walked the bridge, which, being a narrow structure, was impossible to cross unseen by him. It would have been madness to try to rush past him, so we tried guile and were always successful. Some of the sentries were easygoing and let anybody in khaki pass without question. One, however, was inclined to be 'regimental.' He was known as old Boney, and was a tough problem to get past.

One horrible night I was returning on a bicycle from Ebblinghem and reached the bridge in torrents of rain. As luck would have it, old Boney was on sentry. At first I thought the coast was clear, and was thinking the rain had washed him out of it, when, half-way across I was pulled up with a long French bayonet at my chest and a shout of " Halte là ! " Off I got and said : " Anglais." No good. Boney demanded a pass. I had none. Very well, he must ask me to come with him to the guardroom. 'That's torn it !' I thought. 'Once in there and I'm for it.' Then I said in French : " Right ho. That's quite simple. The Corporal of the guard knows me." " On verra," said Boney, as he hobbled along behind me with rifle at the high port. He knocked at the guard-room door. I had half a mind then to jump on my bike and make a getaway. A voice from within asked who was there. " Here is somebody who says he is an Anglais," shouted my captor. " He has no pass and he wants to cross the bridge. He says you know him. What's to be done ? " " Let's see him," said the Corporal. The door was opened, and the Corporal, whom I had never seen in my life, and who was just getting into bed, gave me a look and with a grin said : " Good enough. I know him. Let him pass." A stout fellow ! I quickly said good night and made tracks, thanking my guardian-angel.

A small group of scallywags from the Regiment were stopped on the bridge by Boney a few nights later and got away very neatly. When asked for a pass, one Perry, the Doctor's servant, produced an unused field service post-card from his pocket and solemnly showed it to the Frenchman, who, seeing the crown and other mystic signs in a corner, was duly impressed and let the gang proceed.

With the troops away, and the *estaminets* closing at 8 p.m., time sometimes hung heavily. Thus the beautiful summer evenings often found us at a loose end. There was absolutely nothing to be done.

Just outside the village of Campagne was a farm in which the Veterinary Officer was billeted. In a field alongside stood an enormous cherry tree laden with ripe fruit and about thirty yards behind the dwelling-house. One evening, over a quiet drink, with Freddy Whittle and Spivvy Dutton, it was proposed that the three of us might stroll round to the farm after dark and get a few cherries. Good idea ! It would be dark about 10 p.m., so we agreed to meet at that time and toddle round there. When we met Spivvy had four nosebags with him, evidently intending to do himself well. As the house lay a little back from the road we decided to enter by the main gate and approach the tree without making a sound. By this hour the farmer and his family would be in bed and asleep.

All went off as planned, and we found ourselves beneath the tree. It was the largest cherry tree I have ever seen. The lower branches, heavy with fruit, hung down within our reach. All we had to do was simply fill our bags and walk away as we came. But this was much too dull for Spivvy, who was a policeman and weighed sixteen stone. He insisted on climbing the tree. All the best cherries were, according to him, higher up. Before Freddie and I could start dissuading him, he had already made some progress, and was up in the branches puffing and plunging like a great bear. Up and up he went and had reached a fairish height when suddenly the ringing of a bell in the farm-house gave Freddie and me a turn. Evidently the farmer had an alarm rigged up in case of a raid such as ours. Dogs began to bark. Soon people were shouting, and like a ton of bricks Spivvy hit the ground at our feet. He picked himself up, took one look towards the house, and then, leaving his cap and the nosebags on the ground, made a bolt straight up the field away from the farm. Without a second's hesitation Freddie Whittle followed him at top speed, leaving me standing. Fortunately it was fairly dark. In despair I scooped Spivvy's cap and the nosebags together and started off after my two comrades, just as people and dogs were emerging from the house. I ran like the wind, not knowing in the least what lay at the top end of the field, as we had not reconnoitred it.

Suddenly a tall, close whitethorn hedge loomed up ahead. There was no sign of a gap, but Spivvy, without slackening his pace, just did a header through the top where the bushes were thinnest, and landed safely on all fours in the field beyond. Freddie, five yards behind, being somewhat short, made a terrific spring for the hole just made by Spivvy and I saw him shoot head first through it, at least so I thought, as I panted along a good ten yards behind him. Imagine my surprise on reaching the fence to hear smothered oaths and splashings from the far side, and to find poor Freddie hanging head downwards suspended by his spurs from a small branch. I shook him off into the ditch below, threw the cap and bags after him, retired a few yards for a take-off, and shot safely through myself. The pursuit had apparently given up. We arrived 'home' without mishap, and although the raid was duly reported and questions asked, nothing ever came of it. We had quite a good haul of cherries, but the escapade might easily have ended in disaster, due entirely to the original monkey in a policeman who couldn't resist climbing a tree.

The troops returned from their spell at Ypres on 7 June. Two people of my Troop were among the killed, Corporal Billy Bodell of the 'Skins,' a good fellow, and a Trooper whose name I forget. I now had plenty to do in the sanitary line, and was much chivvied by the new Medical Officer, Captain Anderson (Major Cowie having been hit up at Ypres). I was gradually becoming an authority on various makes of latrine, grease-traps, and incinerators. The M.O. kept everlastingly rounding me up. Every man has his weak spot, I suppose. His was incinerators.

Now something happened which was to cause much grousing and gnashing of teeth right till the end of the war. Something which was sufficient to drive long-suffering men to despair. A Saddler Corporal named Cullen of the 7th Black Horse, attached to our Squadron, went home on leave. He returned equipped with brushes, polishes, burnisher, and chamois-leather. With these devil's implements he polished his saddle and other gear till it all fairly sparkled. This, of course, he did on the quiet. Then, judging the moment carefully, he hung up the lot just inside the gate of our field where it would catch the Captain's eye as he entered. It did catch his eye, and held it. The Squadron Leader went off at once and fetched the Colonel from down the road to inspect the baubles. Cullen was sent for, blushed and smirked, and was nearly awarded a V.C. The net result was that a supply of cleaning kit was obtained from Knightsbridge and the reign of spit and polish began.

We remained for a month in Campagne, and although there was all the time a party of 100 men in the line about Neuve Eglise and Sailley, and there was much wrath over the attempts to make us 'posh up,' we enjoyed peace and good weather, which put us all in good trim after the beastly long winter.

My section went forth every evening as a section and explored the country inns. About half a mile behind Wardrecques we discovered one whose landlady was an Irishwoman from Dublin. Her French husband was in some hospital, and likely to remain there for keeps, with shrapnel in his back. We were sorry for her, as he must have been a decent fellow. She was surrounded by mother-in-law and a mob of sisters-in-law, who all obviously hated her, and whom she was powerless to kick out. They resented her talking to us either in English or French, so in order not to embarrass her we soon avoided the place.

On 15 July we moved slightly back to a woebegone village, Quiestede. Here Major Barry left the Regiment to serve elsewhere for the rest of the war, but he never forgot us of the old 'A' Echelon any more than we forgot him.

XXII

IN my important capacity as Sanitary Corporal I was the last person to leave the Squadron field at Campagne. I was trotting merrily along accompanied by my two precious underlings, Ship and Macdonald, to join up in rear of the Squadron for the march to the new billeting area at Quiestede. Just before we caught up my attention was drawn to somebody struggling and swearing in the language of Falls Road, Belfast, down a side-lane. Very likely some poor soldier in trouble with a pack-horse, I thought, so sending my companions on ahead, I turned down the lane to give a hand.

Here I found the famous Shtot-Shaw of the Skins. It seems some genius had found a means for making use of Horace, the Squadron mule. A pack had been made up for him with a spare saddle and two roomy wicker baskets, and it was intended that in the side-panniers refreshments for the officers should be carried. Shtot-Shaw had been selected to lead the mule. At the first trot the baskets had slipped round, one on to its back, the other under its belly, causing Horace to execute some very picturesque kicking. When I came on the scene Shtot-Shaw was making frantic but futile efforts to right the pack, with his own horse and the mule making rings round him in the narrow lane. I took and held his horse, advising him to unload the baskets before readjusting them. This he did, and to my amazement I noticed that their sole contents were one dirty shirt and an old dilapidated accordion.

After much struggling the pack was made fast and off we set at a fast trot to catch up the regiment. By this time the whole Brigade had linked up and was strung out along the road, with our regiment in front. We proceeded, still trotting fast, to pass the 2nd Life Guards and ' K ' Battery, R.H.A. Every now and then a wag shouted to us:

"Where are you three off to?" This produced much laughter among the troops, and Shaw always replied something appropriate in the language of his native Ulster. At last we caught sight of the rear of the regiment, just as it turned into a field. On the road outside stood the new Brigadier-General, Kennedy, watching the units ride in. As we drew level I saluted and gave Shtot-Shaw, still red-faced and foul-mouthed, the command, "Eyes right!" The General looked amused and perplexed and shouted to me: "What bloody commando is this?" I shouted back: "'D' Squadron, 1st Life Guards' officers' mess mule, sir." The General waved us on, obviously much tickled. I only hope he did not follow it up later to cadge a drink.

The whole regiment lay together in one large, bare field behind the village of Quiestede. The field was lousy and surrounded by a deep ditch full of filthy water. The Indian Native Cavalry had been our predecessors on this pitch, and the 'Skins' felt sore about having to sleep on the same ground. It was definitely an unhealthy camping site, but there is always a silver lining to the darkest cloud, and here too there were compensations. Not far away, at Roquetoire, lay an Indian Brigade containing the 'Skins' and 17th Lancers. Naturally the Skins went over to visit their old regiment. Here they made the interesting discovery that the units in the Indian Cavalry Brigade were actually equipped with bits and stirrup-irons of solid nickel. I'm afraid many of these priceless articles found their way back to our Troop with the return of the visitors. I won a pair of stirrup-irons, but unfortunately no bit could be found wide enough to fit Herbert. The advent of these articles reduced our cleaning to a minimum.

I was having much trouble with my horse's mouth. That was Herbert's one fault, he had a mouth as hard as a rock, and he *would* pull. Since coming to the ranks he had done more drill, and I found to my disgust that nothing I did would prevent the curb-chain from galling him, or the cheek-pieces of the bit from chafing the sides of his mouth till he bled. Everybody was quick to notice this and criticize it as though it was my fault, but nobody suggested a remedy. I was thoroughly disgusted with myself till one day I 'found' a beautiful snaffle of good width. Bang went Herbert's bit into the ditch, and for the remainder of the campaign I rode him on a snaffle and he had no more mouth trouble. I had plenty of trouble over it myself, though. All sorts and conditions of officers pulled up to look at the awful sight. When asked why Herbert affected a snaffle, I explained as courteously as possible, but was never understood. Several times I was ordered to get a bit. I always said : "Very good, sir," but never did anything about it. Often I saw senior officers shake their heads as much as to say : "Good Heavens ! A troop-horse with a snaffle ! Whatever is the army coming to ?" Funny trait in the English character, that. They reasoned : "I've got to ride my horse on a bit, so why shouldn't you ? Never mind if it injures the animal. It's doing the right thing, and that's all that matters."

Then one Monday morning, 26 July, at dawn, Barney Rudd came to my bivvy and hauled me out. "Get a move on, young fellow," he said. "The regiment is ordered up to the Salient by bus to-day. You've got to take some limbers up by road and start at once." All dressed up as I was, even to my spurs, I was soon out, and watered and fed Herbert while I collected my kit, packed my saddle, and scrounged some breakfast off Brockwell, the Troop cook. When all was ready I rode round to Regimental Head-quarters in the village for orders. I felt thoroughly disgusted and disheartened, and cursed myself fervently for not having thrown in my rank. I had been sent back to the Squadron and now had a Section of my own, and here they were monkeying about with me again. Why could I not go up to Ypres with my Section instead of leaving them to somebody else at the critical moment and going off on some miserable side-show ? The limbers were bound to be a wash-out now that Major Barry had left us.

On reporting at R.H.Q., the R.S.M. gave me orders to go with two limbers to Elverdinghe and report to the Commanding Officer, Colonel Stanley, when I arrived. Soon my two miserable limbers made an appearance and we proceeded leisurely as far as Ebblinghem, where we stopped and had a second breakfast. Then away up along the same old roads. At Abeele the tall, dark girl in the red blouse, who lived in the large house of red brick on a hill to the right just past the level crossing, came out and waved to us. This always happened whenever we passed through Abeele in the daytime. I never knew who she was or anything about her.

We reached the château grounds ahead of the troops and had a look round before they arrived. A corner of the big stone château had been lopped off by a shell. The village was miserable, stinking, and empty. When at length I was able to report, Colonel Stanley ordered me to peg down in a neighbouring field in which was a field kitchen belonging to a French battery of heavy guns. The French Quarter-bloke, a man of colossal size, expressed delight at meeting me, lifted me in his arms like a child, and before I could break away, kissed me on both cheeks. Considering that I then weighed over fourteen stone it will be gathered that he was a hefty fellow. I was his honoured guest and he gave me the best his store and kitchen could produce.

That night it rained hard and we were swamped. I had to report at the château again next morning, and getting there before anybody in particular was up and about, surprised a Scotsman of the Greys in the act of cutting oil-paintings from their frames with a jack-knife. He had two or three already rolled up. Still, it was no business of mine. In the adjoining chapel there were signs of vandalism, and even the graves in the vaults beneath had been prised open. Thus this particular line of business was not confined to one side only.

As the day advanced I got going. My four drivers and I were employed on fatigues of every description till the regiment returned to Quiestede on 5 August. Once in quest of timber for trench revetting I had to visit a forest north of Poperinghe in the neighbourhood of a Trappist Monastery. Here I spent an interesting day watching the monks at work.

Joe Green of the Blues had two limbers from his unit and there were also two from the N. Somersets. We worked independently. After the second day we were moved back to a little farm a mile south of Elverdinghe, and were quite comfortable here when we had a chance. There was a fine apple tree in our field beside the farm-house. Although it was only the beginning of August, the tree had been almost completely stripped of apples by the troops. One very fine afternoon a very old lady came out from the farm and strolled slowly round the tree. It was probably her first outing for a twelvemonth. As she looked up into the branches I heard her mutter to herself in surprise : " Il n'y a pas beaucoup de pommes cette année." Small wonder !

After a monotonous spell of labour we packed up and returned to Quiestede on 5 August. Almost immediately we moved billets further back to Delette, just outside the interesting old town of Therouanne, once the capital of France. 'D' Squadron bivouacked in a fresh, clean field alongside the River Lys. R.H.Q. lay at Coyeque, the next village farther back.

Our Squadron spent a happy month at Delette. Weather was excellent. Life was free-and-easy. The summer had arrived in earnest, and the clean turf of the field felt good to sleep on. Now the troops began going steadily on leave. I told Barney Rudd, the S.S.M., I had not had a spell of leave, and he promised to see the Squadron Leader about it. Our field sloped down from the Delette–Coyeque road to the river. Across the road ran the ' Harry Tate Railway ' with one train in the morning and one in the afternoon. The village of Delette was quiet and clean. Near it lay ' K ' Battery, R.H.A. Our Squadron and the Battery became good friends and visits were frequently exchanged. The Squadron carried out training on most days, and very enjoyable it must have been in that rolling country dotted here and there with woods. To my unutter-able disgust, I was excluded from these operations, having to remain in camp to get on with my sanitary duties.

It was now that I got to know Richard Brockwell, our Troop cook, really well. He was a splendid cook, who worked at his job from dawn to dark. Nothing was too much bother for him. He was not content with just doing his job and getting it over. He actually did his level best always and under all conditions, and cooking for forty men in the open air can be hard, dirty, exhausting, and thankless toil. Brockwell made friends with an old shepherd in a cottage just down the road. Every evening he used to make himself spick-and-span before visiting this old man in his home. They sat with a drink of something, smoking and talking, goodness knows how. I have no doubt Brockwell was able to give the old shepherd an occasional tot of rum or packet of tobacco, and I know that our Troop always had flour, fresh vegetables, and sometimes even fresh meat, when the others were down to bare rations.

Brocky, as we called him, soon built a good oven, and encouraged by Mr. de Pret and Jim Fleming, and helped by myself when the troops were out in the mornings, he produced a dinner which would be hard to beat. He had, however, set his heart on making boiled jam-roll, and to this end had got his wife to send him some pudding-cloths from Bermondsey. There was rejoicing when they arrived. That morning Brocky made the required dough, and rolled it out with a bottle on a large, flat tree-stump. I opened a tin of jam and spread it on the circular cake of flat pastry. Immediately every wasp in the world settled on the jam, and we stood there helpless and gaping, not knowing what to do. We waited till all had settled, then rapidly rolled the pastry up, thus swamping all the wasps in the jam. We now unrolled it again, tipped all wasps deftly and quickly with a knife-point into a waiting pail of water, then rolled the pudding up, tied it in the cloth, and put it to boil in the dixy. This process was repeated till sufficient jam-rolls were made, and we must have reduced the wasp population of Picardy considerably in our efforts. Very excellent jam-rolls they were, and the other Troops envied us our luck.

Brockwell's wife sent him a weekly consignment of black shag tobacco and cigarette-papers. From these he made cigarettes with a kick in them, and at daybreak always smoked one as he lit his fires. A fire in the early morning always attracts people, especially a cook's fire, and Brocky always had some early visitors, mostly, I am afraid,

N

attracted by the chance of a cup of tea or one of his famous hand-made, he-man cigarettes. One inveterate cigarette-cadger was my colleague, Ship, of the sanitary squad. Brocky determined to cure him. So he saved up half a dozen very juicy fag-ends and from them manufactured a perfectly harmless-looking cigarette that would kill a mule. Comrade Ship duly rolled along, and in the ordinary way was presented with the horrible fag. After a couple of draws he began to fidget and change colour. Soon he departed and was violently sick. The cure was complete. Brocky also cured the tea-cadgers by serving them all liberally one morning and then informing them after it was drunk that by order of the Medical Officer he had put salts into it. The effect was marvellous, though, of course, there was not a grain of salts in the tea. The sanitary squad petitioned him not to repeat this trick.

Brocky still had his old spotted horse, Richard, who, in spite of all his care, was suffering from debility and looked wretched. One morning an order came for all horses proposed for casting to be paraded before the General at a certain hour. Brocky had to get dressed and take his old mount on parade. He returned looking dejected, donned his cooking rig-out, and got on with his job in silence. Jim Fleming asked him: "How did you get on, Brocky?" —"When my turn came to ride past the General," was the reply, "he shouted, ''Alt!' looked first at the old 'orse, then at me, and said: 'My Gawd! Wot an 'orrible creature!' I wasn't sure whether he meant me or the old moke." Anyhow, as a result the poor old horse disappeared and Brocky had a new one.

My old friend, Driver Dapper Smith, was in sore straits at Delette. His duties included looking after a pair of heavy draught-horses. One of these was a fine old upstanding bay, named Longboat, who, like thousands of his type, did his work till he dropped, and was not noticed. The other was a massive light grey. A real beauty. He was fat and sleek and shining. Every morning Dapper drove his pair to the Brigade ration dump, and straightway the grey became the centre of an admiring crowd of staff officers, who thumped him in the ribs, slapped him on the back and neck, and fussed over him like a crowd of old dames round a fat Persian cat. None of these horse-enthusiasts dreamt that at 5 a.m. every morning Dapper found the grey horse smothered in mud and filth from ears to tail. As a matter of fact getting him clean and keeping him so were gradually wearing poor Smith's nerves. We others, realizing the awful job he had, wondered how he managed it.

One glorious morning I awoke at four o'clock and got up to have a look round. Larks were just tuning up over the neighbouring fields, and in the silvery Lys trout were jumping briskly before the heat of the day set in. Just the sort of setting that held one spellbound at the sheer beauty of the peaceful country-side at dawn. Suddenly I was roused from my meditations by the noise of a barn door opening, and immediately Dapper came out leading the famous grey. He was no grey now, but thickly coated with filth, in which he had been wallowing. Smith's face was like a thundercloud. I slipped behind a bush and watched. He allowed the horse to graze, leading him quietly nearer and nearer to the river bank at a spot where there was a large, deep pool. The simple, unsuspecting animal was soon nibbling grass by the water's edge when Dapper, holding a lengthened head-rope in his hand, stepped quickly back a few paces, then rushed at the horse and with a terrific push in the flank sent it flying into the river. Down under it went, then its head emerged snorting like a hippo as it struck out for the shallow water farther down-stream. Dapper stood on the bank manipulating the long head-rope and giving vent to his feelings in a spate of blood-curdling language. " Yer perishin' mudlark ! " I heard him hiss. " If I was a moneyed man I'd buy yer aht of the ruddy Service, I would, and shoot yer ! " At length the animal waded ashore, shook itself, and was tied to a tree so that it could not lie down and roll. Smith rubbed all the water out of its coat with a button-stick, and soon it was sleek and silvery and shining and fit to be patted by a duchess.

Dapper Smith was always a popular fellow, and while we were at Delette his turn came to go home on seventy-two hours' leave. The rumour was put round that he was going to get married. Be that as it may, when the day arrived the Squadron turned out to give him a royal send-off. Armed with jam tins, turnips, and every imaginable species of rotten vegetable, we lined the hedge as the Harry Tate train came slowly past. Dapper put his head out of the window to make a few parting remarks, and he at once became the centre of a hurricane of greengrocery. He withdrew into the carriage, put his fingers to his nose, and was gone, leaving us cheering him like madmen.

Barney Rudd now informed me that I was due to go on leave after Smith. This meant that, bar accidents, I should be away in three days' time. It was August and the weather was splendid. I made up my mind to go home to Ireland whatever happened. I knew I must not chance over-staying my leave, because if a man returned late off leave the Squadron would miss a turn. This was precisely the old schoolmarm's trick of keeping in the whole class because one child had blotted its copybook. Anyhow, we thought it mean, as it punished the innocent for the guilty, and might come particularly hard on some poor devil and his family if in the meantime all leave was suddenly stopped.

On the appointed day I set off on the local Harry Tate line accompanied by Dan Elliott of the Skins, one of my old limber-drivers. We reached Boulogne in the evening and put up in a large building like a brewery. Next morning we walked down to where the leave-boat lay in readiness. We had our leave-warrants stamped at an office on the quay, and were waiting for the word to go on board, when a tall, elderly officer wearing chaplain's tabs approached me, and, seeing my cap badge, asked me if I could give him any information concerning a Trooper Abrahams of ours who had been reported missing. Like a flash there came into my mind a letter Paddy Irwin had received from a friend in hospital, in which was written: 'I was buried by the shell that killed Abrahams.' So without hesitation I answered: "Yes, sir. He was killed on 13 May." He asked me how I knew, made some notes, and then took my name and number. I didn't like this, somehow. However, the boat was off immediately, and realizing my long-awaited leave had started, I had not a care in the world.

Arrived in London, I found out to my great joy that I just had time to catch the Irish boat-train. Saying a hurried good-bye to Dan, I made a dash and caught the express. Everything went smoothly, and at 11 p.m. that night I found myself in Waterford, where I made the staggering discovery that there was not another slow train in the direction I required till the following morning. That looked like throwing twelve hours of my precious seventy-two away there and then. However, I had a walk round, and a friendly citizen of Waterford advised me to try the goods' sidings. Away I ambled across a maze of lines, and eventually ran across a goods train with steam up and its nose facing the right direction. There could be no mistake about it, this was my train.

The guard was nowhere to be seen, so I climbed into the guard's van, sat down, holding my rifle between my knees, and waited for him. The engine gave a screech, and was starting to wheeze out on its way, when the guard came running, puffing, and talking to himself, and jumped into the van. On seeing me in possession he nearly jumped out again, and was clearly at a loss as to how to handle the situation. It was no joke to board his train just as it started and to find his own private den occupied by a six-foot soldier in full war-paint. The more so as he had quite obviously been drinking pretty hard for some days. " Can you give me a lift as far as Durrow ? " I asked him. He started at the sound of my voice, sucked some porter with the help of a grimy hand from his large, pendulous, black moustache, and grunted : " All right." Durrow was forty miles from Waterford, and I calculated it would take the old ' Goods ' three hours to do the journey, so I lay down with my rifle by my side on an iron bench and shut my eyes, but did not go to sleep.

My presence seemed to exercise a peculiar fascination on Mr. Guard. He sat down on the opposite side of the van and stared hard at me. Every now and then he stood up, turned his back to me, and muttered to himself in a hoarse whisper I could distinctly hear : " Holy Jaysus, I'm afeard o' me loife ! " At about 2.30 a.m., in pitch darkness, he yelled to me : " We're just outside Durrow now ! " The train was crawling. I don't know whether it stopped or not. Mumbling a word of thanks, I jumped on to the platform, cleared off across the road, and entered a large wood through which I had to walk in inky blackness, but on rides and paths I had often trod in the old days, for the best part of two hours. It was an eerie walk, as such walks in Irish woods can be, but I was almost home, so I kept plodding. Our house stood on top of a small hill, which I scaled on my hands and knees, so as not to make a row and rouse first the dogs and then the household. It was now about 4 a.m. and a Saturday morning. There were no local trains to Waterford on Sundays, so I had figured out that I should have to depart again that same evening without spending a night at home.

The dogs made no sound as I approached the house, picked up a handful of sand, and threw it at father's window. He soon popped out his head, and as he had no idea I was coming, must have thought he was dreaming. I warned him not to wake the others, but it was no use. Next moment mother had the front door opened and her arms were around me. The first question she asked on recovering her breath was : " When do you go back ? " I could not bear to say what I thought, so I replied : " To-morrow morning."

There was no going back to bed for her or father now. She sent me upstairs to my old room with instructions to strip carefully and throw my clothes, tightly rolled in a bundle, through the window into the garden, the farther the better. I then had a wash down, changed completely into civilian clothes, and rejoined the family below, where tea was now ready. Dawn broke to find us all sitting round the old table, with mother trying to hide her excitement, father watching me very hard when he thought I was not looking, and saying little, and my younger brother and sisters all rather in awe of their big brother whom they had not seen for two years. There was one gap in the family circle, as the brother next to me in age had enlisted on reaching the age of eighteen and was away with the 2nd Royal Dublin Fusiliers.

I spent a quiet day. Mother saw to that. Before lunch

I just went for an hour's stroll down to the village with my father to stretch my legs and look up old friends. The postmaster, a Crimean veteran, held my hand in an iron grip and asked with sympathy : " How much furlough have ye, then, young fellah ? " On being told seventy-two hours, he exclaimed : " The Lord save us ! Sure ye haven't time to get the smell av the powdher off ye ! " Then down to the strand to see old Jack Vale, Indian Mutiny veteran. Standing over six feet tall, and as broad and straight as a man of thirty, this fine old lad had been a driver in the Bengal Horse Artillery before 1857, and was still fit enough for a full day's work. He used to boast : " I never soldiered in the Queen's service. I belonged to the army of the old Company."

Later I discussed with my father ways and means of getting back. The Cork–Waterford fast train did not stop anywhere in our neighbourhood, although it ran, on Sundays. Waterford was forty miles away, and there were no local trains on Sunday mornings. The only possible solution was to cycle to Waterford. I borrowed, therefore, a bicycle off the curate, a hefty young man.

After a peaceful day and night among my own folk, which did me untold good, and helped to adjust my bearings on life in general, I set out shortly before 7 a.m. on Sunday morning to cycle the forty miles to Waterford and catch the boat-train there at 11.30 a.m. I had never done any great amount of cycling and the roads were none too good. Besides, I had my rifle and other gear tied on to my machine, and before I got far I realized I had set myself a strenuous task. One sight I shall never forget—the great beauty of the Comeragh Mountains in the morning sunshine, as I pedalled my way alongside them for a couple of miles.

I reached Waterford Station ten minutes before the train was due. I was leg-weary and horribly lonely now. I handed over the stout curate's bicycle for return by rail, then found the station water-tap, filled my enamel mug with a mixture of water and some whisky mother had given me, sat down on a seat and sipped it till the train came in. Once seated in the railway carriage, I realized my leave was now to all intents and purposes over, and all too quickly, and I was once more in the grip of the machine against which there was no use struggling.

Back at Delette everything was just as usual. I don't know if Herbert missed me or not. He was not demonstrative, except in presence of a full nose-bag. The Irish contingent in the Troop were all anxious for news from home. All I could tell them was that Guinness' Brewery was still in the same place, and working. I had noticed a subtle undercurrent of unrest among the people at home, but I kept that to myself. Much blood was to be shed all over the country-side before I set foot in Ireland again.

XXIII

TOWARDS the middle of September 1915 the stage was being set for the battle of Loos. The two other Brigades (6th and 8th) of our Cavalry Division moved up to take part. They came into action as Infantry and the 6th Cavalry Brigade entered and held the village of Loos on 26 September. My old friend, Frank Wootton of the Blues, did good work with the 8th Brigade, and was awarded the Military Medal. Another old friend, Percy Scott of my own Regiment, who had volunteered for service with the Pigeon Squad on Divisional Headquarters, although to begin with he didn't know a pigeon from an emu, also did very good work, at least he told me so. I wonder whether he was the lad who sent the famous message. The yarn is somewhat threadbare, but will bear telling again.

The General and Staff of the Division, so the story goes, were anxiously waiting in the Headquarters' dug-out for news of the attack. An hour passed without a message of any kind. Two hours, and eventually three hours elapsed, and still silence. Not a runner, not a telephone message, absolutely no news. The General had by this time drawn many pretty sketches on his blotting-pad, and his Staff were wondering when he would explode, when suddenly a signaller rushed into the dug-out carrying under his arm a pigeon which had just arrived in the loft. General and Staff rose and rushed him. Here was news at last! When they had removed the message and opened it out they were fairly winded on reading : ' I'm fed up holding this damn pigeon. Here goes ! '

Our 7th Cavalry Brigade was sent off in another direction, up to the North of Cassel, where we scampered about and stood around nearly freezing to death at night, doing nothing, in the open. After a splendid summer the weather was beginning to break, and a long, dreary, wet autumn and winter were setting in. I forget how long we pottered about in this delectable area, perhaps a week, till one evening, in torrents of rain, we arrived back at the village of Buysschere, just north of the Forest of Clair-marais. The Interpreters had been sent back ahead of the troops to secure billets for the officers and themselves, and fields and firewood for the troops.

On reaching our allotted field the cooks fell out to draw firewood, prior to preparing a hot meal. Our Squadron supply of wood consisted of one tree-trunk which had just been fished out of a pond where it had probably lain since the Waterloo campaign. This was too much for our Squadron Leader. He fired the Squadron Interpreter on the spot, and Bob Harrison suggested I should take over the 'supply' part of old Bon Sonty's job. I stepped into the breach at once, and for the next six months had the time of my life. It did me no good in the long run, as it was just one more sideshow which took me away from my normal duties as Corporal in charge of a section of men. Anyhow, I moved with Herbert to Squadron Headquarters, where I worked daily with Bob Harrison. The ensuing months, up to the time of old Bob's departure for England, form about the happiest period of my soldiering.

A good meal and a comfortable night's sleep made us feel new men again when we woke up on our first morning in Buysschere. Horses and gear were quickly put in order, and we had the afternoon free to do as we liked. The Squadron Leader of 'B' Squadron, lying in a recently cut corn-field next to ours, must have had a bad night. Not only did he keep his 160 men grooming horses and cleaning kit all morning, from 8 a.m. till 1 p.m., but at 2 p.m. that afternoon he lined them up at a yard interval on the edge of the large corn-field and then marched them to and fro for a couple of hours, picking up stray ears of corn. We of 'D' Squadron could not believe this possible. In the ordinary course of events we rarely came across 'B' Squadron. Giving up their siesta, our men collected and peered at this glorious sight through the intervening hedge, not knowing what to make of it. One or two scallywags were about to hurl appropriate jibes through the hedge, but the saner ones, perceiving the prospect of a first-class row, persuaded them to keep quiet, and soon we all cleared off and left our neighbours to their gleaning.

Our next move was back into the grounds of a distillery, once a monastery, between Renescure and Arques. Here we remained a fortnight or so, and the first week, being wet and stormy, had a miserable existence, sleeping in a muddy field which got worse every day in the driving torrents of rain. The excursion up behind Cassel had been a nightmare for cooks, working as they did with dixies in the open in foul weather; and Brockwell, our Troop Cook, with twenty years' service and two campaigns to his credit, had gone through a trying time. Now, at the distillery, he stood out in the open all day, soaked to the skin, with the cold rain running through him into his boots, trying to keep a fire going and cook hot meals in a quagmire. But he stuck it without a word of complaint, and we always had our meals on time. After some days of this, I saw Brockwell one morning struggling round his dixies in the downpour, and looking like a drowned rat, when the Medical Officer, Captain Anderson, came along and spoke to him. As Brockwell answered the M.O. gave him a look, ordered him to stop work at once, and come along to his billet. Brocky didn't want to go, but the M.O. insisted, so he handed over and went along. That was the last we saw of Brockwell. He caught a chesty cold up around Cassel, carried on working for weeks under the awful conditions, and developed pneumonia. He died in the hospital in Arques within a few days. In my time I have met many heroes, both decorated and plain, but if I were asked who was the finest fellow I knew in the war, I should unhesitatingly say: 'Richard Brockwell.' His death gave the Troop a shock, and although Arques was only just round the corner we heard nothing of it till weeks afterwards.

The weather now turned suddenly fine. A sort of Indian summer set in. Bob Harrison and I got into our stride and scoured the country-side in search of clover, straw, bran, brewer's grains, and linseed for the horses, and potatoes, vegetables, and beer for the troops. Bob received a weekly allowance in money from the Field Cashier for this purpose, and I did my best, with the French at my command, to help him to make the most of it.

One day we discovered a field of second-crop clover all ready to be cut. We bought it as it stood. A scythe and hay-rake were procured in Arques, and with Percy Richardson, Dapper Smith, and Harry Pudney, we spent two glorious days cutting and carting the clover. Bob, in his shirtsleeves, swung the scythe as only a long-limbed Yorkshireman could. He was, for the moment, back again over a space of twenty years, doing the job he was born to do, and it gave him a new lease of life. Percy, a fellow Yorkshireman, relieved him at the mowing. Then I took a hand. Dapper and Harry, thinking we were, all three, barmy to work so hard, raked and loaded the clover, supplying much light-hearted patter in the vernacular of Peckham Rye.

Then, in the evenings, Bob and I would saunter into Arques, ostensibly to buy potatoes, but actually to sit in a cool garden at the back of a little *estaminet*, sipping leisurely long glasses of alleged whisky and soda, and yarning about great feats with the scythe performed long ago on the meadows of Yorkshire and Westmeath.

The fine spell of weather came to a sudden end and with it our farming experiences. Immediately we were ordered away back into the depths of Picardy. As usual our march was accompanied by plenty of rain, and one dark October night we arrived, wet, cold, and hungry, in a village at the back of beyond, Verchocq by name. When this hole was mentioned later on to inhabitants of Ebblinghem, they shrugged their shoulders and said: " Ah, c'est tout à fait la campagne par là." It was too ! Paddy Irwin and I tried to sleep that night in a long farmer's cart in a shed without sides. Next morning we woke up mutinous and frozen to the marrow.

For the next six months this stinking village was the rest billet of our Squadron and ' A ' Squadron. Regimental Headquarters lay further along at Rumilly, with ' B ' Squadron at Aix en Ergny. ' B ' Squadron Leader lived two miles away from his Squadron, so that every evening in all weathers his Sergeant-Major and Quarterbloke had to tramp to his billet between 6 and 8 p.m., to report even when there was nothing to report, and to ask for orders even when there were none.

All sorts of detachments went up to all parts of the front and performed all sorts of jobs during this period. The horses remained in Verchocq, and the ensuing winter of rain, cold, discomfort, and general all-round uselessness nearly broke our hearts. I was better off than my comrades, being out alone all day and every day buying supplies, often riding three horses daily between dawn and dark. For the others it must have been almost unbearable.

There now appeared frequently in Regimental Orders a paragraph asking for applications for commissions in the Artillery. Jim Fleming and I made application every time the order appeared. Our applications never got farther than the Orderly Room waste-paper basket. It was ordained that no regular Lifeguardsman should be given a commission, so there the matter remained. We just had to grin and carry on.

Bob Harrison and Barney Rudd soon got permission to take over and convert into a Sergeants' Mess an empty bungalow in the middle of the village. Just before this happened, the N.C.O.s of the Regiment were adjusted in their proper places on paper, and I became a Sergeant again, so I at once moved into residence in the new mess with Barney and Bob and Farrier Ted Pettit. An ancient transport driver, one Archibald Murray, was appointed cook, I rode into Fruges and returned with two barrels of beer, and the Sergeants' Mess was a going concern. The bungalow was absolutely devoid of furniture, but a good lady, Madame Soudain, proprietress of an *estaminet*, lent me lamps, tables, chairs, crockery, linen, and refused to take a cent for them. She was a good soul, and one of the few decent people in the village. The troops were miserably housed, and the horses had soon kicked the barns in which they stood to the level of bird-cages.

Many units in back areas contrived to stage an occasional fire, accidental of course. The 2nd Life Guards were quite famous for their fires. More than once we all turned out to admire the red glow in the night sky, marking a conflagration in one of their billets. It did not require a professional fire-bug, complete with taper and tray, to start one of these. A cigarette-end thrown down carelessly, or a candle left burning unattended, was sufficient to reduce the average French farm to ashes in quick time. More by good luck than good management we had only one such fire during our sojourn in France, and that took place in Jim Fleming's billet in Verchocq not long after we moved in there.

It was about 11 p.m. when the alarm was given, and by that time all outbuildings of the farmstead were blazing merrily. The troops on the spot promptly rescued horses and belongings, but the barn was like a furnace in no time, and it was feared that the flames would shortly reach the dwelling-house.

Charlie Wright, Archibald Murray, and a few of us residing at the other end of the village recalled having seen a small house half-way down the main street with a red door on which were the words, ' *Pompe à Incendie*.' that is, ' Fire Engine.' We ran to this place and burst in the door just as the fussy old *garde champêtre* (village policeman) arrived on the scene. He raised Cain because we had not waited for him to open the door in the proper manner, and then tried to restrain us till he had noted down in his log-book the exact time of departure of the engine. They do these things thoroughly in France. We pushed him aside, seized the drag-ropes, and with a mighty heave and a cheer had the old engine out in the street and away at a run. The poor old engine had not seen the open air for upwards of fifty years, and took some pulling. Charlie and I were about to give in after the first hundred yards, but catching sight of old Archibald Murray pulling and snorting in front of us, in spite of his poor old feet, like a thoroughbred Clydesdale, we buckled to once more and eventually brought the engine to a standstill outside the burning building.

How we swore and cussed in our despair when we discovered that in our mad rush up the street every bolt, nut, screw, and all detachable gadgets had dropped off into the road! Nothing remained of the engine except four wheels, the bare tank, and the two drag-ropes, so we left it and became spectators.   Except for what could be coaxed out of a wheezy old pump in the farmyard, there was no water available.   It was impossible to form bucket-chains. The one hope of saving the dwelling-house seemed to lie in demolishing that part of the loft over the gateway connecting the house with the outhouses.   Frank Askey took a felling-axe and shinned up on to the roof.   Here he proceeded to enjoy himself, sending timber and tiles flying in all directions, till it became obvious to us spectators that another wallop or two would precipitate the remains of the structure, plus Frank Askey, on to the ground beneath.   Our Sergeant-Major, Barney Rudd, realizing the seriousness of the situation for Askey, stepped in below him and shouted up : " Get down, you damn fool ! You'll kill yourself ! " Frank swung his axe once more.   The remaining tiles on that part of the roof described curves in the air, and one fair-sized specimen landed square on the top of old Barney's head and knocked him clean out.   I ran and lifted the old lad, and bathing his cranium with cold water brought him to.   Apart from an egg-like bump on top of his skull he was none the worse.

Askey, wondering if he had slain the Sergeant-Major, quickly scrambled down and disappeared.   But he had done good work.   The gap in the roof was now complete and though the outbuildings were gutted, the dwelling-house was unharmed.   I don't know what became of the *Pompe à Incendie*.   We left it where it stood, with the *garde champêtre* and some oldest inhabitants jabbering and gesticulating round it, and cleared off back to bed.

Very soon, at the beginning of December, our Sergeant-Major, Barney Rudd, went home to England for discharge on completion of twenty-two years' service.   His departure left us with a sinking feeling which became not a whit more buoyant when we learned his successor was to be George Hindy from ' B ' Squadron.   George was in many ways an excellent fellow, but we doubted, with some justification, whether any good could come out of ' B ' Squadron. George's greatest fault was that he was a ' Yes man.'   If the

Squadron Leader said : " That black horse must be white-washed at once," George would have said : " Very good, sir," and had the white-washing done. He was also a bridge fiend, and the introduction of bridge into the mess destroyed the family feeling which had always existed between us. Nobody has any right to sit and play bridge in a room where others have to spend their evenings. We ought to have laid violent hands on the bridge-merchants and chucked them out.

I continued to work happily and busily with Bob Harrison. He and I shared a room in the mess, Bob in a bed, I on the floor. Our horses were housed just outside in a cartshed.

Christmas was now drawing near, and we were praying that we might be left alone in peace till it was over. Existence in the village was very drab and monotonous, the surrounding country uninteresting, and the weather and ground too bad to allow training. Time, especially in the evenings, hung heavily. Our Squadron Leader provided us with a large hut, to act as concert-hall and canteen. I added the office of canteen-manager to my other duties. Tim Kelly, Ally Brooks, Bullet Nisbet, Trumpeter Godwin, and Trooper Sims, formed and trained a Squadron band, and very good it was in time. Our Squadron Leader procured the necessary instruments from England. Joe Burnham, a genial Corporal in Charlie Wright's Troop took on the big drum, and the side-drum was played by Shtot-Shaw.

A little later a cinema projector and films, all from the same source, made their appearance, and for a while the troops were amused. Combined cinema shows and concerts were given, to which the C.O. and other senior officers were invited. These were good shows, well attended, and went down well for a time. The band did yeoman service. When Ally Brooks met a tune he could not play, he just held his cornet to his lips and puffed his cheeks in and out as he thought fit. Bullet Nisbet was applauded for his euphonium solos, ' Nazareth ' and ' Love in Idleness.' Godwin arranged and conducted some pretty pieces for two or three instruments. I particularly remember 'Sweet and Low.' Tim Kelly's trombone solos were blasting affairs.

Vocalists were also in evidence. Alex Bamberry, a wee Scot, made us hold our sides as he sang ' Sergeant Donald Dougal.' Jocks Griffin and MacLeod, who really could sing, rendered as duets ragtime numbers such as ' The ghost of the violin,' and ' The ragtime navvy.' You could hear a pin drop while these two sang ' Bonny Scotland,' ' Annie Laurie,' and ' The wee bit land.' Dusty Millar of the ' Skins ' gave a fine impersonation of Charles Austin in 'Drink,' giving as an encore ' The Spaniard who blighted my life.' A terrific wag, named Zillwood, of our own Regiment, entertained by telling stories which nobody but himself could possibly put over.

Then there were choruses with band accompaniment. Nobody ever knew more than one verse of any song. No Englishman ever does.

Last but not least came the French ditty : ' Après la guerre finit,' which was not, as many people supposed, a product of the Great War. The Stationmaster of Lille, a refugee at Ebblinghem, told me that song was sung in the Waterloo campaign, and he believed even back in Marlborough's wars. Strange how it should spring up again after a hundred years. The British soldier does not change much throughout the centuries.

Within a day or two of Christmas it was decided that I should proceed to Boulogne, per Harry Tate railway, to purchase and bring back a cargo of Christmas fare and a hired piano. I asked for Sims to come with me and lend a hand, but was refused. He would have made all the difference in the world, but the suggestion was turned down.

I set out by the morning train and reached Boulogne the same afternoon. Here I met Dusty Parsons of the Royal Dragoons, going home on leave and taking home some belongings of his C.O., Colonel O'Neill, who had been killed. We made for a modest hotel near the harbour, where we fed. Then we walked out to see how the land lay. I was glad we did so, as I had little time to waste in the morning, and could do no shopping that night, all markets

o

being closed. We located the markets, went to a cinema, returned, and after supper and a bottle of champagne, retired to bed.

Next morning early, Dusty departed for England, and I crossed the bridge towards the markets. It was raining and blowing a howling gale. At the vegetable market I bought over a hundredweight of Brussels sprouts. These I had put in a huge sack I had brought for the purpose, and I then looked round for somebody to carry them to the station. Not a soul could I see in the shape of a man, except one lanky youth. I approached him and offered him a couple of francs to carry the sack to the train. He agreed, so I heaved them on to his back, and he tottered away with knees knocking sparks out of each other. When he had gone ten yards a squall of wind blew across the market-place, caught old Lanky and the sprouts, and hurled them both into the gutter. He rose with all the strength knocked out of him. He couldn't go another yard. There was nothing for it but to hump the sack on my own back and trudge off to the station with it myself. This was, besides being waste of valuable time, a risky business, in case I met a Red-cap, or a young officer who would raise hell if a Sergeant of the Life Guards should pass him without saluting, even from beneath a mountainous sack of Brussels sprouts.

However, I dumped my load without incident and hurried back to the fish-market. Here I bought some baskets of good whiting. The hefty fishwife offered to see them taken to the station for me. That was a blessing. Then I bought apples, oranges, some joints of meat, and finally, after a fierce bout of bargaining, succeeded in hiring an old piano from a Hebrew furniture dealer.

At last the old Harry Tate steamed out of Boulogne station with me and all my purchases on board in the guard's van. I think it took seven hours to do the twenty-five miles to Verchocq, where a crowd awaited me, and conveyed me and my wares in triumph to billets.

Our Squadron, at any rate, had a good Christmas. There was plenty of good cheer. We forgot for the moment our daft existence, and concentrated on enjoying ourselves. In company with the other Sergeants of the Squadron I had a photo taken on the château doorstep. That is the only war photograph I ever had done. It is now a valued possession.

Some days after the festivities had died down I was ordered to appear at the regimental Orderly Room at Rumilly. No reason for this honour had been given me, so I proceeded along the road examining my conscience, but could find no flaw in it. I was marched in immediately I arrived. The Colonel sat in his chair, beside him the Adjutant, behind him stood my old friend, the Orderly-Room Sergeant. All three, and the R.S.M., who had marched me in, looked as cheerful as if they were about to be hanged. The C.O. picked up a scrap of paper and barked: " What do you mean by giving information concerning regimental matters to people who have nothing to do with the regiment ? You are aware, I suppose, that if you have any such information, this is the place to give it ? " I racked my brains but could not make out what he was driving at. Then he went on : " It seems you told some person at Boulogne when you went on leave last August, that Abrahams was killed on 13 May. How did you know he was killed ? You weren't there." It flashed on me now what had happened. Somebody had rapped the Orderly Room on the knuckles for not making certain of the nature of casualties before reporting them. Everybody in ' D ' Squadron knew Abrahams was dead. The Orderly Room must have had a strange way of compiling casualty lists. ·I saw now that anything I might say would be waste of words, so I dried up and stood there like a stuffed dummy. Silence gave them no cue, and at last the C.O. spluttered : " Don't you dare ever to do that sort of thing again. Go away ! " Away I went, cursing to myself. When I got back to Bob Harrison I gave vent to my feelings. He calmed me down and advised me to forget it. I had one consolation, however. Abrahams' people now knew the worst, and would not spend months, and perhaps years, hoping against hope.

Shortly after this little *rencontre*, my old friend, the Orderly-Room Sergeant, departed for the base at Rouen, where he remained till the end of the war. Patsy Hyland, the clerk at the 3rd Echelon, Rouen, had got a commission, the only one a 'regular' of our regiment managed to get. The Orderly-Room Sergeant went down to fill Patsy's place. He liked Rouen. And to think they burned poor Joan of Arc there !

About the end of January, Bob Harrison completed twenty-two years' service and left for home. We arranged to give him a good send-off. As he had to proceed down to the base one night, we had supper and a drink or two before he went. Bob was already dressed for the journey, and at the end of the little feast we hoisted him up on our shoulders and carried him round the room singing : 'For he's a jolly good fellow.' Then we stood still, holding him aloft while we sang 'Auld lang syne.' Bob had his back to the wall during the singing, and when we stood aside to let him down, he remained hanging up. It appears a very large nail had penetrated his British warm coat and held him in suspension. Carefully we lowered him to the floor. There was a three-cornered rent in his coat, which he kept as a precious souvenir. Then the time came for dear old Bob to depart, and with heavy hearts we saw him go. With him went all that was best in the old 1st Life Guards, but his spirit stayed with us. In spite of everything 'D' Squadron had always something of the family about it, and always remained faithful to the memory of the two men who had moulded it—Barney Rudd and Bob Harrison.

To my great surprise I was asked to take Bob Harrison's place ('Acting' of course) as Squadron Quartermaster Sergeant. I knew this could only be a stop-gap till somebody with sufficient seniority could be unearthed. I accepted, and was now Quarterbloke, Interpreter, and Canteen Manager. Everything except what I wanted to be, and ought to have been—a plain, common, or garden duty-sergeant in a Troop.

XXIV

MY duties as Acting Squadron Quartermaster Sergeant were pettifogging rather than difficult. I carried them out for about two months in the beginning of 1916. They consisted in drawing and distributing rations and forage for the Squadron, indenting for, and issuing pay, articles of clothing and equipment, and the upkeep of the stores, which formed the marching cargoes of limbers and G.S. wagons. In addition I had charge of the transport staff and horses on Squadron Headquarters. Extra to these duties I fulfilled the roles of Interpreter and Canteen Manager, but these were not by any means burdensome.

Every morning at the ration dump I met many of my old friends, including Andy Kealey, now Quarterbloke of ' A ' Squadron, and dear old John Ayers, the Sergeant Cook. The Quartermaster, Captain Yeatman, a fine old soldier who minded his own business and wore a decoration for gallantry in the Boer War, seemed charmed with me and my work. After a week or so he informed me that I was a capable Quarterbloke, and said it would give him great pleasure to recommend me for extra pay at the munificent rate of sixpence *per diem*, while functioning in that capacity. Anyway, I had, one way and another, a busy time, and the addition of the extra sixpence to my already princely wage in no way troubled my conscience.

Through my Interpreter's job of buying forage I came to know nearly every farmer and brewer within a radius of twenty miles. Some of them were jolly interesting folk, too.

On the top of the downs a battalion of navvies, composed of tough, red-faced, white-haired old men, was engaged on digging a reserve line of trenches. Every. fortnight, when pay-day came round, they disappeared for a week. On pay-day, and for two or three days after, we passed them in small groups sound asleep in the ditches by the roadside. Their Commanding Officer must have been a hound. He had a row of wooden crosses erected along the top of the hill beside the trenches, and many times as we passed by we saw a dozen or more of the unfortunate old men tied up to them with arms outstretched. This was the most disgusting sight I saw in the whole of my army service. I met several of the old lads here and there in the neighbouring *estaminets*, and good fellows they were, though terribly disillusioned and fed-up. Many of them had seen service in various small wars twenty years back. Not a few were old sailors who presented some wonderful model sailing-ships in bottles to the patrons of their favourite *estaminets*. Some time later I heard they were sent away digging in the front area and suffered heavy casualties.

The French people could no more make head or tail of the navvies than could their precious C.O. Many times I was asked : " Pourquoi est-ce qu'on les appelle les navets ? " ' Navets ' pronounced something like ' Navvy ' is French for turnips.

Meanwhile all went serenely and squalidly in the village of Verchocq. A strong party from the Regiment served for a spell in the Hohenzollern Redoubt, and there were digging and other expeditions to Vermelles and Sailley. In my role of A.S.Q.M.S. I took no part in these but remained behind on my usual routine.

Most of the natives of Verchocq were typical of the grasping French peasant. They were out to make what they could out of the Troops. Consequently they had no scruples about selling rum. In spite of all that the authorities could do, it was always possible to purchase any amount of vile spirit, which could only have a pernicious effect. In the straggling mile of village there were some ten *estaminets* and two private houses, the ' Jockey Club ' and ' Cavalry Club,' where the stuff could be obtained. One honest proprietress of an *estaminet*, Mme. Soudain, refused, or practically refused, to sell rum.

Mme. Soudain was an energetic, if somewhat corpulent lady, with a sense of humour, and several hives of bees in the garden behind her house. Every year she manufactured a good quantity of mead. Great stuff it was, too, this favourite beverage of our Anglo-Saxon ancestors. The first day she produced it she gave a small glass to Shtot-Shaw, then acting as cook in George Boylan's Troop, with cook-house in her yard. Shaw sipped it, drained it, smacked his lips, and in his very best French spluttered: "Kesky say, Madame?" All agog with laughter, the good hostess replied: "Hidromelle." Shaw was unable to grasp the name in full, but the middle syllable, pronounced 'drum,' stuck in his mind. He at once rounded up his pals, Baluchi Appleyard, Sammy Dowd, Bullet Nisbet, and beamingly informed them he had located a grand new drink. The trio listened attentively to Shaw's glowing description, then with one voice asked: "What's it called?" "Drummer-boy!" replied Shaw. "Garn! Yer pullin' our legs," says Bullet. "No, I ain't," answers Shaw indignantly. "Come along and I'll show you." So in walked the bright quartette. Shaw banged on the counter and called proudly: "Cat Dummer-boys, sivvou play, Madame." Madame understood at once, and with a smile as broad as a barn-door proceeded to serve them. Shaw's stock rose up beyond measure. The modern Trooper, however, having neither the capacity nor the carrying-power of the ancient Viking, some of us were obliged to advise the good lady to soft pedal a bit with the hidromelle.

Two miles outside the village, on the top of the hill near Rollez, Madame Cuvillier kept a modest *estaminet*. Charlie Wright, Jim Fleming, and I walked up there every evening whenever possible, had some supper, which very often consisted of roast veal, potatoes, and mountains of good salad, with a bottle of decent wine. We then gossiped awhile with Madame (whom Charlie called Mrs. Cooper), and her family, then walked back to Verchocq to call the roll before going to bed.

The horrid winter still held us in its grip. The sheer filth of our surroundings baffles description. The Troops were bored beyond words. Only once in a while did something happen to cheer them up and set them smiling

for a day or two. There were also signs that the officers of
the Squadron were feeling the strain.

A powerfully-built Lifeguardsman, Archie Goodall, once
went with his Squadron transport to draw rations and
forage. Archie could carry quite comfortably on his head
two trusses of hay or four sacks of corn. The Supply
Officer looked on in amazement, then said to the R.S.M.,
who was standing alongside: " I'd like to have that man
down at Railhead. It takes four of my men to handle one
truss of hay. He'd be a host in himself." " I've no doubt
you could have him if you asked the C.O.," replied the
R.S.M., mindful of some of Archie's little tricks.

Next day Archie Goodall accompanied the supply lorries
back to Railhead, where he lived in luxury, slept in a real
bed, and every day astonished natives and Troops alike
with his strong-man act. Three months passed before it
dawned on him that he was being exploited as a sort of
human crane. Then all the thrill went out of the job, and
he asked to be returned to his Regiment. We were to have
a few more laughs over Archie before the end of the war.

One evening Jim Fleming was informed that a young
officer was due to arrive from Knightsbridge and ordered
to find a groom and a servant for him from his Troop.
On calling for volunteers he was answered by two Troopers
of the 'Skins.' They were appointed on the spot, and detailed
to proceed to the billet allotted to their new master and put
everything in readiness for his arrival. Among other
things they had to prepare a bath for him. That evening
Jim went along to the billet to see how the two worthies
were progressing. He came back to the Sergeants' Mess at
a run and fetched me along to see them. We stood outside
the window and watched. It seems both had celebrated
their appointment by getting exceedingly drunk. The
room was bare except for a large rubber bath full of water
in the middle. In the bath, splashing like a stranded whale,
and quite powerless to get out, lay the groom fully dressed.
The floor was inches deep in water; the walls splashed
almost to the ceiling. In one corner sat the other worthy,
absolutely unable to move, holding his sides and rolling
with laughter. It all made a weird picture I shall never

forget. Jim and I walked off and left them to make the
best of it. Very likely the young officer failed to
materialize. Anyway, we heard no more about the matter.

There were by this time several young Lifeguardsmen
in the Squadron. They had joined us in small batches at
different times and were quietly absorbed into the Troops,
where a certain amount of wastage continually went on
from one cause or another. George Boylan had several in
his Troop, and they, being long and young and hungry,
tried the none-too-sweet temper of the Troop Cook,
S. H. Shaw, rather sorely at times. Shaw was a good
cook. Normally he would be up at daybreak, and now that
the year was advancing and spring well on the way, he
was out soon after daybreak and cooked breakfast in the
open. Tea was made, and when there was bacon it was
cut in slices and fried in a dixie-lid. To turn the slices
Shaw had a pointed stick like a conductor's baton. As he
squatted beside the dixie-lid doling out the bacon on the
point of his stick a crowd of young rookies usually stood
by waiting, with large slices of French bread, to make a
rush for the bacon fat. Shaw scorned these growing lads
with all the scorn of which an old soldier is capable. One
morning, just as he was lifting out the last rasher, a long
youth leaned across him from behind and dropped a huge
slab of bread into the hot fat, which splashed into Shaw's
face. Without standing up he poised his stick, stuck it
into the slab of bread, and hurled it over his shoulder on to
the filthy yard. Then he stood up, and, taking a running
kick at the lid, sent it and the fat flying. Whereupon he
calmly walked off whistling with his hands in his pockets.

Soon afterwards there appeared on the door of Shaw's
cook-house the following notice :

'THEM BLOKES WHAT COMES FOR EARLY MORNING
TEA TO-MORROW WILL GET A RUDDY SHOCK.

Signed S. H. S.'

Knowing Shaw for the redoubtable individual he was,
nobody turned up, so we never found out what the
intended shock was.

It was not always possible for me to accompany

the wagons to the ration-dump every morning. One of the other Quarterblokes would see to anything important, and Dapper Smith, Percy Richardson, Peter Swain, or Harry Pudney were alert enough to be able to look after the interests of the Squadron. I always had to be present when the wagons returned about noon in order to see to the daily distribution.

One day when I was unable to go with them I was awaiting the return of the wagons, and was surprised when they came round the corner of the village street to notice a stranger sitting on the box beside the driver. As they came nearer and I was able to see them distinctly, it gave me a shock to discover that the passenger was my old sparring partner, George Beasneys.

After my little one-man strike back in August 1914, he had returned to take over a Troop in 'C' Squadron. There he reigned about two or three days. He became Musketry Instructor, and had managed to hold that job down till now, when he was sent out to take the place of Bob Harrison as Quarterbloke of 'D' Squadron. Everybody stood aghast. The Lifeguardsmen knew him of old, and the Dragoons had not forgotten him since the Knightsbridge days. Anyway, here was George, successor to Bob Harrison, which meant that my term as Acting Quarterbloke was now at an end.

I was glad to see the arrival of anybody to relieve me of my temporary job. I still wanted to get back among the men in a Troop. Before many days my wish was granted, and I found myself second Sergeant to Charlie Wright, in his Troop. That was a move in the right direction at last.

XXV

NUMBER 4 Troop, 'D' Squadron, with Charlie Wright as Troop Sergeant, to which I was now posted, was as good a Troop as one could wish to belong to. The four Corporals were Jock Morrison and Chris Dean of the 1st Life Guards, and Joe Burnham and Bill Warren of the 1st King's Dragoon Guards. Half the men were Dragoons, the rest Lifeguardsmen. The former included some great characters, such as Tom Cradden, Jock Faid, and George Ford of the 'Skins.' Our own men were a good type of youngster enlisted for the 'duration.' There was one old Lifeguardsman, Willie Smith, a very humorous customer and one of the best soldiers I ever met. Smith had been a Corporal three times, and as there were no less than four Smiths in the Troop, went by the name of 'Gypsy.' The others were nicknamed 'Dusty,' 'Shady,' and 'Leatherlip' respectively. The horses were a good bunch, and, thanks to Charlie's good sense and tactful handling, the Troop practically ran itself. The only dud anywhere about was an officer, Second-Lieutenant Bellwether, a wealthy, middle-aged Colonial, who owned millions of sheep in some far-distant corner of Australia. This old lad thought of everything in terms of sheep, regarded us all, except Charlie Wright, as sheep, and was, in fact, the world's woolliest sheep himself. We could not stand him, and he knew it. Charlie had him absolutely tied up and harmless, so there was little he could do in the way of making our lives miserable.

I was very happy in my change. It was refreshing to work once more among the cannon-fodder. We were billeted in a farm owned by a fussy little man, M. Blancpain, known to Charlie Wright as Mr. Whitbread. The spring was advancing in all its green splendour over the country-side. Cavalry training began now in earnest.

Every day was spent on schemes among the quiet country lanes and leafy villages of the district. To begin with, this training was a most welcome occupation. Eventually it palled. We had done all these exercises so many times before that the troops grew impatient at the monotonous uselessness of our existence. Hard, hungry work all day, with idle evenings in drab, lousy billets, brought on the inevitable outbreak of drunkenness. Our rations were scandalously short. Beasneys, our new Quarterbloke, may have been responsible, I don't know; but I have actually seen Shady Smith, the Troop Cook, draw as a day's rations for forty men two pound-tins of bully beef, four or five potatoes, one small onion, and a few biscuits. This had to be supplemented by scrounging in an area already scrounged to the limit. Anyway, a certain section of the men reacted to these conditions by getting drunk as frequently as possible.

Charlie and I had trouble with one or two members of our own Troop. If a man was arrested and awarded Field Punishment No. 1 or No. 2, he became a prisoner, and at night slept snugly in the Squadron Guard-room, while his more sober comrades did sentry-go over him all night. We could see no glimmer of sense in this practice, so we found an attic in M. Blancpain's house and, with a stout padlock and chain, converted it into our own private 'clink.' All drunken men of our Troop, when caught, were thrown in here and left till sober, sometimes for a full forty-eight hours. Old Bellwether never knew about it. We hoodwinked him easily enough. One day, however, we had a narrow escape. A Divisional General happened to ride through the village, and as he passed our billet three inmates of our clink removed each a tile from the roof, poked their heads out, and gaped down on the great man with a drunken leer. Apparently they were not noticed.

There were also some exciting moments about 8 p.m. when the *estaminets* were supposed to close. One evening Charlie had to take off his jacket in order to chastise a loud-voiced young soldier who was shouting some cutting things about sergeants in general. The resulting scrap was short and sharp. Charlie laid his man out inside two minutes, with a couple of ribs broken. He then ran him along in a villager's pony-trap to the Field Ambulance, where he deposited him, recommending him to say he had been kicked by a horse. We heard nothing further about this lad. He belonged to the Scots Greys and may have been posted to his own unit on discharge from hospital.

The 'Jockey Club' was a source of much annoyance to us. This establishment was a tumble-down, thatched cabin standing back from the main road about two hundred yards from our billet, and inhabited by a gipsy-looking fellow with his wife and numerous progeny. The latter were all more or less naked infants, except the eldest, a girl of fifteen who looked twenty-five. The father led a mysterious existence. As father of seven children and upwards he was exempt from military service. He always had rum for sale. It was particularly vile stuff, and he had a knack of skinning our fellows of their money and then throwing them out into the road. Charlie and I kept a close watch on him but never actually caught him out.

One night when we were returning from a visit to another Squadron, and it was about midnight, we were startled by a loud report somewhere at our end of the village. A minute later a soldier passed us running like mad towards the château. He ran so fast that we failed to stop him or recognize him, so we walked on past our billet towards the 'Jockey Club' to investigate. On the grass outside the door stood the proprietor holding an old muzzle-loader about six feet long and still smoking. As we approached him I kicked something in the grass and found it to be a soldier's cap. The man was wildly excited and kept jumping about and shouting : " Wallie Château ! " We calmed him down and discovered eventually that he had previously warned Wallie Mawson, an officer's servant from the château, to keep away from the Club, as he suspected him of designs on his daughter. Though he had seen no sign of Wallie for some time after this warning, he had reason to suspect that he was paying secret visits at a late hour. So on this particular night he dug out his old fowling-piece, loaded it, and went into ambush in a front room with a broken window. Sure enough, about midnight along came Wallie. Out poked the long barrel through the broken pane. Bang! Wallie's cap was blown off his head, and he turned and beat it like a hare. It was a near thing. However, all's well that ends well, so we just laughed, said good night, and departed.

Another evening at roll-call, two of our lads, McTavish of the Carbs and Scott of the 'Skins,' failed to answer their names. We decided to give them a while in which to turn up, but as they were still not forthcoming, we thought a visit to the 'Jockey Club' might throw some light on their whereabouts. We went round very quietly, tip-toed to the front door, and tried the latch. It made a noise but did not open. We could hear a scuffling inside, so we ran quickly round to the back and grabbed Mac as he bolted out. He was promptly booted in the pants and ordered to make straight for his billet. Then we entered the house and with the aid of an electric torch proceeded to explore the interior in the hope of unearthing Scott. The place was empty, except for the two bedrooms. In one slept about fourteen youngsters, all in the same bed. In the other the old couple lay serenely side by side and leered up at us. We were beaten, so we sheepishly wished them a most polite good night and withdrew. On arriving back at our billet we found Scott there before us, but only just. Later in the year Scott was wounded on the Somme, left for home, and we saw him in the Troop no more.

Twenty years later, on Christmas Eve, 1936, I happened to be walking past South Wimbledon Station, and on reaching the 196 bus terminus a conductor looked hard at me, then approached me and we shook hands. It was Harry Scott. He looked just the same old packet, and in the few minutes before his bus started again for Camberwell Green we had an interesting talk about old times. Suddenly he said: "Do you remember the night you and Charlie Wright raided the 'Jockey Club' and nabbed McTavish?" —"Yes," I answered. "We expected to find you there too."—"I *was* there," he said proudly, "but you couldn't have found me in a thousand years. I heard you arrive at the front door, ran to the bedroom, jumped straight into the bed, and lay doggo between the old man and the old woman!" For twenty years he had waited to tell me of this brilliant move, and I had to acknowledge it was a win for him. We had a laugh together, and before parting wished each other the compliments of the season, feeling a good deal the happier for our chance meeting.

Then one day, when all signs of winter had vanished and summer was upon us, fatigue parties were recalled from the line, and the Regiment marched back to Merlimont on the coast for training. It rained cats and dogs the whole way. It was still pouring in torrents when we reached the coast, but as soon as horses were tied up, Jim Fleming, George Beasneys, and I, the sight of the sea being too much for us, stripped off our clothes, covered them up in the dunes, sprinted the fifty yards across the sands, and plunged into the water. I was last off the mark, and my speed was not increased by the laughter which overcame me on seeing George some yards ahead. He was not normal about the knees. Other parts of his anatomy were not built on orthodox lines either. We all felt better for our swim, in spite of having to dress in the pelting rain. Next day, and for the remainder of our sojourn, the weather was boiling hot. This was pleasant till horses began to develop sand-colic, so after a short spell of bathing horses and light training we trekked back again to Verchocq.

Training was carried out on the broad sands at Merlimont. Troop and Squadron drill combined with bathing would soon have had the horses very fit if they had not been tethered in a field where, instead of grass or soil, there was a foot of sand, which in a very short time brought on sand-colic. Every morning at an early hour we formed line with our backs to the dunes and galloped barebacked into the sea till the water reached the horses' shoulders.

George Boylan, Troop Sergeant of No. 3 Troop, was home on a musketry course at Hayling Island at this period. His second Sergeant, Ally Brooks of the 7th Black Horse, ran the Troop and rode George's horse. Ally's legs were short and round, and the horse, a handsome red chestnut of sixteen hands, was given to doing unexpected and original things. One morning he would gallop dutifully to the water's edge and then stop dead, allowing Ally to go on, describing a series of graceful curves through the air before landing with a loud flop in the water some yards ahead. Another time he would gallop in a few yards, then pretend to be frightened and jump six feet into the air over a line of tiny, white-crested wavelets, again shooting poor old Ally on ahead into the briny. Everybody except Brooks found these antics extremely funny, and the horse appeared to get a real thrill out of it.

I could never understand why, when King George V came to France that year and held his great review of the troops, this horse, out of all the thousands available, was chosen for His Majesty to ride. It certainly was a handsome animal, and with George Boylan on its back behaved perfectly; but it had had no schooling like the few remaining old Life Guards' horses. There was consternation throughout the Empire when it was learned that the King had been thrown, but we in 'D' Squadron were not surprised.

On returning to our permanent billeting-area we found some signs of excitement among the villagers. An enterprising Corporal had been left behind there with a couple of men in charge of regimental gear during our absence. This trio soon ran short of money, and they were in a desperate plight till the Corporal devised a plan for raising the wind. He got hold of a signallers' helio tripod, mounted on it the square wooden base of an ancient gramophone of the horn variety, taking care to leave the hole for the winding-handle in front, and covering this with a square of black cloth, he proceeded from house to house in the village 'photographing' family groups at ten francs a time, and collecting a deposit, if not the whole ten francs, on the spot. Thanks to the extreme simplicity of the villagers and his own cool cheek, this lad did a roaring trade. Our return found him at his wit's end. His clients were growing impatient and demanding either the photographs or their money back. Anyway, he dodged them by 'going sick,' which he accomplished so successfully that he was home in England within a fortnight. I never heard what was the ultimate end of the cameraman, but he was a likely lad and should have gone far.

Again we dawdled around Verchocq for a week or two, during which Lord Tweedmouth of the Blues organized a magnificent boxing tournament.   The war played havoc with Army Boxing, and consequently with British Amateur Boxing.   Dozens of first-rate men were lost or maimed. Early in October, 1914, we had lost Sergeant Johnny Arthurs of the Skins, who in 1912 had won the light, middle, and heavy-weight titles in India all in the same week.

Then we were suddenly ordered to pack up and trek down to St. Riquier in the Abbeville area for intensive field training.   Here we bivouacked in a large field just outside the town.   A stone over the door of one of the out-houses of an adjacent farm bore the following inscription in old French : ' Joan of Arc spent the night of 16th June as a captive in this stable on her way to Rouen, Anno 1430.' The town of St. Riquier was either in advance of or behind the times, for in a very fine *estaminet* one could see the ' other ranks ' of an evening sitting openly regaling them-selves on whisky and soda.   Here we scampered all day about the rolling country-side, and rumours began to be spread abroad concerning a certain ' gap.'

While here Jim Fleming, Charlie Wright, and myself made the acquaintance of a prosperous miller who was an exceptionally good fellow.   His only son was an airman, and he had one daughter of nineteen, a tall, dark, intelligent girl who was always cheerful and did the work of two or three men about the mill and fields.   We passed many pleasant evenings at his place.   He was glad of our company, and was one of the very few Frenchmen we admired and respected.   In his mill-stream were some magnificent trout. Next summer, 1917, on passing that way again, we called on him.   His house was full of officers, and he was sick and tired of the whole lot.   Mademoiselle was not in.   We ambled off to the turnip-field, where we discovered her doing her job of hoeing in line with the farm-hands.   She was pleased to see us and was still the same stout soul of a year ago.

A sudden order sent us trekking back to Verchocq. Here we spent just a few days collecting sundry odds and

ends of gear, and towards the middle of June moved away
suddenly to the Somme area.   I'm afraid our precipitate
departure proved a shock to some of the *estaminet*-owners.
Many of the men, being old and valued clients, were given
credit.   They paid their debts on pay-day.   Our sudden
move out took place on the day before that on which we
were usually paid.   The order came at 8 a.m. and we were
off at 9 a.m.   On the doorstep of her *estaminet* stood Martha,
a long-faced, very scraggy landlady, looking exceedingly
glum and waving a sheet of white paper in her hand.   The
paper bore the score of a small circle of thirsty clients, who
were quite powerless to settle the matter.   I mentioned that
I thought this hard luck on Martha, but Jim Fleming took
the matter philosophically, saying it was only a levelling-up
of ill-gotten gains, and he added: " In any case, when the
trumpet sounds 'Boot and Saddle' all soldiers' debts are
automatically cancelled."

The Brigade rallied at Fressin, where we stayed the night.
Charlie Wright knew the place, having previously spent a
month there as Instructor to the Yorkshire Dragoons.   He
and I put up with his old landlady, and knowing we were
bound for the 'gap,' arranged a huge spread in her
estaminet, to which we invited all Sergeants of the Squadron.
A grand binge it was, too.   At about 10 p.m. three French
Interpreters came along and demanded a room for the
night.   Charlie and I had bagged the only spare one, so we
just told them to beat it.   This they did with a bad grace
but with sound sense, so we sat down and carried on.   The
party broke up after midnight.   Some of our guests, being
pretty well primed and in a strange village, found difficulty
in locating their quarters.   One gave it up and slept near
the pump in the *estaminet* yard.   Another, after walking
round and round a small apple tree several times, and
finally concluding he was lost in the jungle, flopped down
and slept till morning on a lettuce-bed.   Charlie and I saw
him still there next morning when we awoke and looked
through our window.

By a series of night marches we now worked our way
up to Bonnay, close to the little town of Corbie.   Beautiful
weather made these night marches quite pleasant.   We

walked a good deal, leading our horses, and all felt wonderfully fit and ready for anything. Then, during the last two night marches, it rained hard, and the roads became full of converging traffic of all kinds. Eventually we reached the outskirts of Bonnay, and in torrents of rain tied our horses in groups among the trees, while the men lay down and slept anywhere they could find among the horses. I woke up to find myself lying in a broad pool of water. All around me was a scene of wet, tousled misery. Soon all were roused, and breakfast and the ensuing fine day helped to put things right. But the rain and traffic had turned our wood, which was in a marsh beside a canal, into a mud-bath, which never dried all the time we were there.

XXVI

THE story of the Battle of the Somme has been told and re-told to such an extent that the volume of ink spilled in its telling must be almost as great as the volume of blood spilled over the whole area. So far as the Cavalry is concerned there is nothing much to be told. We trained all we knew for the impending battle in our normal role, while our chiefs talked of a ' gap ' through which we were to be rushed as cavalry when the enemy line was pierced by artillery and infantry. Looking back now I cannot recall many signs of faith in this scheme on the part of the ' other ranks.' Not that we were not prepared, and even glad at the prospect of a chance, to play our part. We were determined, should the opportunity actually arise, to put up a good show. Every man of us, however, had taken some part in trench warfare as infantry, and in many sectors no-man's-land was as familiar to us as our own billets. We considered ourselves more than a match for Fritz, and had proved it in the past. But we realized he was a fine soldier, brave and tenacious, especially in defence, who would not give way without ' having a go.' His industry in digging and building lines of defence put the British soldier, and especially those in authority, to shame. Thus we smiled at the optimistic blitherings of our superiors, and moved up to the undertaking without any particular feelings of either elation or misgiving.

The ensuing weeks proved that the men in the ranks were right. The ' gap ' did not materialize. The infantry (the P.B.I.), who in the first few days cheered us as we rode up to our kicking-off point, soon ignored us completely, if they did not actually jeer at us, and before very long they saw us, as cavalry, no more.

Day after day we crawled about in the stinking mud

back at Bonnay, while horses became soft and ill through
inactivity and foul conditions. The thrill of the mad
gallop through was not to be. Neither did we have
the satisfaction of ' going over the top ' as infantry. As the
days wore on, and right through the battle, we of the
Cavalry left our horses in back areas and worked night
after night, and very often day and night, on pick-and-
shovel jobs about the line, such as trench-digging, road-
making, wiring, water-carrying, burying, whilst occasionally we took over a portion of the line and held it for
a time in order to relieve the infantry. Our Horse Artillery
left us and went up to take its place beside the field
batteries, where it did valuable work.

The bones of many cavalrymen lie in the chalk of the
Somme battle-fields. But our men were not killed in the
excitement of the attack, nor in putting up a desperate
resistance to counter-attacks. For the most part they
perished under shell-fire in lousy bivouacs just behind the
line, or out in no-man's-land at night while manipulating
picks, shovels, or reels of barbed wire. And all detested
the whole daft business.

Our worthy Troop Officer called our Troop together on
the evening of 30 June 1916, and proceeded to deliver to
us an inspiring speech. He began : " Boys, it's the eve of
Waterloo ! " Jock Morrison exploded, and covered his
mouth with his hand like a schoolboy. I'm afraid we were
an unappreciative audience. That same night Charlie
Wright, who had developed fever after our forty-eight
hours' soaking, had to report sick, and was sent down the
line, eventually reaching England. Bellwether's face was
a sight next morning at dawn when he heard of Charlie's
departure. Without Charlie Wright he knew he was a lost
sheep. He had no longer any use for Waterloo, but tore
his hair helplessly and repeated to himself : " Sergeant
Wright gone ! Whatever shall we do ? " Jock Morrison
whispered to me : " He means whatever shall *he* do ? " and
Jock was right. We were all sorry to lose Charlie, but
agreed he would have been a fool to go into the battle ill
as he was. However, I had the Troop solid behind me. I
knew Jock Morrison and the others would back me to the

last, so we decided that, apart from Bellwether, we were not so badly off.

The bombardment of 1 July saw us saddled up and standing-to at dawn. There followed several hours on our toes. In the evening we were still waiting for something to turn up, when our Troop Officer came along, called us together, and proceeded to form a bombing section from the Troop. Jock Morrison was our chief bomber, but being now acting as second Sergeant, he could not budge. Eventually the section was formed under Joe Burnham, and ordered to be in readiness to move up to the line at short notice. This threw some light on the prospects of the ' gap ' and served to show us how matters really stood.

Two or three days of inactivity at Bonnay followed. Then, after the capture of La Boiselle on 3 July, the idea of the ' gap ' seems to have been abandoned. Immediately a party of forty men under Sergeant Fred Lidster were sent up with picks and shovels to fill in shell-holes after the infantry had advanced, so as to make some sort of level track for the advancing field-guns. A nasty, hungry job it was, too, and typical of all such undertakings. The party was ' nobody's child ' and had to scrounge rations and a place to sleep where it could, after being shelled again and again off the ground where they tried to work.

On 5 July I was sent up to La Boiselle, then a chalky scar on the hill-side, with about forty men to carry out any fatigues that might be given us. Lieutenant ' Dinky ' Geard was in charge of our party, which was part of a large detachment from the Brigade under a Major of the Leicesters, a fine fellow whom we all knew well and admired, though I cannot recall his name. We reached the huge mine-crater in the afternoon and flopped down in the grass beside a freshly-dug, deep communication-trench. No orders came to us for a time. Mr. Geard, being young and just out from home, wanted work, and on asking the Major if there was anything we could do, was advised to ' get down to it ' and possess his soul in patience, as work would find us in due time. Next morning at daybreak it did. Our men were allotted to some deep dugouts in which Stokes' mortar shells and hand-grenades were stored. Standing on the dugout steps they passed these commodities up all day long without a break, till arms and backs ached. Then just before nightfall we got back to our bivouac beside the communication-trench. And this is where the Leicester Major proved himself a soldier. We were all dead beat, but somehow he had contrived to find and have ready for us the best hot meal of stew we had eaten for weeks. That night the men were ordered to sleep on the bottom of the deep trench, in case of shelling. I slept outside on the grass, and before trying to sleep watched, fascinated, the bombardment just ahead, which shook the earth and lit up the sky in one broad continuous flash. Soon all were sound asleep.

Around midnight gas-gongs up towards Contalmaison began to ring. In a minute or two they were sounding back at La Boiselle. I got up and found it was no false alarm. A thin, yellowish cloud was drifting about the neighbourhood. The Major ordered me to rouse all men out of the trench and to see they had their gas-helmets on. The box-respirator had not yet come into being. We were equipped with grey flannel bags for slipping over our heads, with eye-pieces and rubber mouth-piece. These had to be tucked securely beneath shirt or jacket, and were then pretty effective. What a job it was getting the men up out of the trench! Many had to be slung out half asleep. When all were out and helmeted I heard a man coughing and spluttering close to me. It proved to be Gypsy Smith. He had his gas-helmet on, but as he always slept in the open wearing nothing except a thin singlet, he had clean forgotten about tucking in the helmet ends. So he went on breathing gas, spluttering, and cursing, till we put him right. He seemed none the worse afterwards, and had his leg pulled for some time.

The gas dispersed in half an hour or so, and we were allowed to stand down and go to sleep again. It came across twice again before morning, and I shall never forget the job I had to shift the men out of the trench on both occasions. They cursed me in their semi-dazed state and refused to budge till literally kicked out of it. Eventually I had them out with helmets on. We had no casualties. Next morning they were apologetic and grateful. Fortunately no shells dropped near us, and after a week's hard toil we returned to our horses at Bonnay.

Here we attempted to make our horses comfortable, and to give them sufficient exercise daily in the mud of the morass. Jim Fleming and I grieved over the departure of Charlie Wright, but proceeded to make the best of things. Every evening when possible we walked into Corbie, where we procured something to eat and drink. We also bought any vegetables we could find for our Troops, and discovered an excellent brand of onion hitherto unknown to us. It was elongated, like a rugby football, bright pink in colour, and very mild in flavour. We ate these out of our hands like apples.

Before long we moved back. For the next few weeks we trekked up and down and across the back areas of the Somme, spending a second spell round Corbie, till we knew the whole country-side and every hamlet in it like a book. One bedraggled village, whose name I never knew, was a landmark somewhere between Amiens and Corbie. At one end of its one street stood a house of two storeys with high, whitewashed gable. Its owner must have been a barber, for high up on the white gable some British soldier had painted the following legend in black letters a foot high :

'HAIR CUT
Bond Street or Boston Style

DRY SHAMPOO
(If not Itchy-koo)'

A dozen times I rode through that rotten village, and always the old house with its message caused us to smile. I wonder if it is still there.

I got along fairly well with Bellwether, but there was no love lost between us. Charlie Wright had been diplomatic enough to humour him and make a fuss of him. I just ignored him, apart from the bare necessities of our daily intercourse. Very soon George Haywood arrived and took over the Troop, relieving me of direct contact with him.

One day when in cheerful mood the old chap offered me an attractive job on his ranch. I just smiled and thanked him. I discovered later on that he had made both Charlie Wright and George Haywood the same offer, so it was as well I did not take him too seriously.

George Haywood differed from Charlie Wright in being less of a diplomat, more reserved, and possessing an acid wit. He resembled him in that he was very capable, an excellent Troop Sergeant, and a loyal friend. Not long after joining us, I forget where, we actually returned once more to Verchocq, our last sojourn there. We bivouacked in a field on the bank of the River Aa. For some days weather was ideal, and we enjoyed a rest after our aimless flutterings of the past two months. Old acquaintances were renewed, and Martha and others recovered their outstanding debts.

Old man Bellwether now became difficult to get on with. He was peevish and continually trying to make trouble. In this he failed absolutely, because he rubbed George Haywood up the wrong way, and without his aid he could not accomplish much in the way of a 'strafe.' One morning the old lad attempted a spot of bother by pretending he smelled rum off Jock Morrison. George Haywood laughed at him and then proceeded to tell him a few home truths concerning strong drink in general and the nightly consumption of whisky at the château in particular. He stamped off in a towering rage.

A day or two afterwards, while our Troop was at 'Stables' in the field beside the river, I finished grooming my horse, old Herbert, and started to clean and put my saddle in order. Mr. Bellwether, who was close by, and whose duty it was to see each horse and pass it as clean before its owner stopped grooming, immediately saw red. He called me out, and though the thing had been a daily occurrence, asked what the hell I meant by leaving off grooming before I had his permission. I replied very quietly that I had always done the same and that tradition allowed the second Sergeant to do so. He went straight up in the air. George Haywood manœuvred him well away from the men and I followed. When we were well out of earshot George let fly and told him in plain language what we all thought of him. The old man wilted under George's eloquence. There was no need for me to say a word. Finally he just dried up and walked away in the direction of the château. George and I kept our mouths shut when we returned to the Troop, and for the rest of the day expected some sort of retaliation. Nothing happened. Bellwether departed for England next day and we never saw him again.

One day, without any warning, the weather broke. In a few hours our field by the river became a swamp, and we expected to be washed away. We stood two days of this deluge before orders were received to move away to the high ground behind the Sergeants' Mess. It took us another two days to rescue our gear from the mud and dry it. Then we quitted Verchocq for good, and we were not sorry, as we had been hanging on in that area for so many months that we could scarcely look the inhabitants in the face any longer.

A veteran Dragoon, Trooper Wellbelove, went home on leave from Verchocq. He was the Medical Officer's servant, and a thoroughly good fellow. The Doctor, Major Cowie, was very much admired by the troops because of his devotion to duty and his unfailing presence among them in times of stress in the line. He had been wounded at Ypres and gone home. In his spare time out of the line Major Cowie was never idle. In his young days he had been a good boxer and all-round athlete. Now that he was no longer so young, he turned his attention to geology, and reaped a rich harvest of fossils in the many disused sandpits in the back areas. These trophies he had stowed away, intending to get them home at the first opportunity. When Wellbelove's leave was granted he called at Headquarters and asked to be given a parcel to take home for Major Cowie. To his surprise he was handed out a sixty-pound corn sack full of hard material and weighing about a hundredweight. Being a loyal fellow, and having no idea as to what the sack contained, he humped it away, panting and cursing, but had no opportunity to satisfy his curiosity regarding its contents till he was actually on the leave-boat out in the Channel. Here he untied it, and made the staggering discovery that he had been humping a sack of stones of various sizes and shapes. Overboard he chucked the lot, feeling that he had been served a particularly dirty trick. Major Cowie's disappointment at the loss of his treasures may be imagined, but poor old Wellbelove had just cause for his indignation.

Our new move took us up again to the Somme, where we concentrated as a Division on the slopes of the valleys around the town of Daours. Very likely the idea of the ' gap ' had been revived. Anyway, here we remained for weeks while the rain beat us and our horses into the mud. Rations were scandalously scarce, and conditions the worst we had known since Ypres. There was absolutely nothing to do except to wallow, and starve, and curse, till at length we were mercifully relieved from our misery and sent back again to Picardy, where we settled down in the straggling village of Cavron St. Martin, close to the town of Hesdin.

XXVII

IT was in the month of September 1916 when we settled down to rest-billets in Cavron. 'D' Squadron had the entire village to itself. Our Troop was billeted in a house in the village on the road to Montreuil. Our hosts in the farm-house were the most weird specimens it had been our lot to encounter. The presiding genius was Madame, a lady of about forty, who never washed, never combed her hair, never swept or cleaned anything, and as far as we could see, never slept. She devoted all her time to the cultivation of tobacco, and a marvellous crop it looked just when we arrived. It had been gathered and was in process of being sorted out and hung up to cure. The good lady did all this herself and let all else look after itself. She had an *estaminet* of sorts which was run by a refugee from Arras. This establishment never brought in a cent except for drinks sold to the troops. The whole place was so filthy that even the villagers could not face up to it. Madame had a daughter of eighteen, a tall, well-built lass, inclined to talk and be sociable. She had, however, inherited her mother's dislike of cleanliness, and although she went to mass on Sundays dressed like a duchess, she was dirty beyond description. Sometimes she served drinks in the *estaminet*, and on one occasion as she bent over our table I was able to observe that her hair, which was unusually long and thick, was crawling with lice, and held together with eggs of these insects. We were not long in giving the *estaminet* a wide berth. There was one son, a boy of twelve, who sat all day like an imp in the chimney-corner, stole his mother's best golden leaves of tobacco, rolled a leaf into a cigar, and smoked them one after another all day and half the night. He must have had an inside and lungs of copper. None of us could tackle these raw smokes without suffering unpleasant after-effects.

On the far side of the road dwelt an old couple in a small dilapidated cottage with some spacious outbuildings, in which we had most of our horses stabled. The old man had served as a soldier in the 1870 campaign, and once showed me his medal with the black ribbon. The old lady affected to be of superior stock and to have seen better days. Our landlady and her family referred to the old pair as " Ces sacrés bourgeois," while the two old 'uns retaliated with " Cette vermine-là," which we considered about met the case. Besides his war-medal and his wife's gentility, the old soldier was terribly proud of a huge golden pumpkin which grew on the edge of his little garden. It was a remarkable vegetable, but the old lad had never given it any attention beyond his admiration. In his pride he reminded me of the man who possessed the large plum described by the famous French writer whose name I cannot recall.

The village and its surroundings being quite new to us, and up to our advent untenanted by troops, we had the usual interesting day or two spying out the land. The *estaminet*-keepers were new to red-caps and their regulations, so that at first it was possible to get a drink up to 10 p.m. The best *estaminet* stood on a hill to which a winding road led gradually up. A few yards outside its back door there was a sheer drop of a hundred feet to the main road below. One evening I received a welcome visit from my old friend, Tim Kelly, so in company with three or four of the old hands we proceeded along to this hostelry for a drink and a chat. As usual with any company in which Tim happened to be, we lost count of the time. The good landlady was ignorant of the wiles of red-caps, and at about 9.30 p.m., when two of these gentry visited the place and knocked at the front door, those of us who knew the lie of the land slipped quietly into an inner room, while poor Tim, being ignorant of the geography of the place, rushed out through the back door in headlong flight, and went straight over the edge of the precipice. A second later he was on the road below, none the worse for his plunge, as his fall had been broken by sundry shrubs on the cliff face, but very shaken and angry and venting his rage in blood-curdling oaths and threats. When the coast was clear, we others hurried out to find poor Tim's remains, but half-way down his language reached up and put us at our ease, and when we joined him we all laughed till we could laugh no more.

There was another *estaminet* in Cavron which displayed a variety of bottles on shelves behind the counter in the bar. This place of refreshment found its own little coterie of *habitués*, and one evening at closing-time, a certain soldier of George Boylan's Troop, being penniless and not over scrupulous, stole a highly coloured bottle from the shelf behind the counter during the absence of the lady from the bar, and tucking it under his jacket, carried it off to drink at his leisure in his billet. In the middle of the night his comrades were awakened by his groans, and on looking at him they saw that he was writhing in agony and frothing at the mouth. The Medical Officer was fetched, and put matters right with a stomach-pump, but the patient was groggy for days. On examining the bottle it was found to contain a bleaching liquid used for washing clothes and sold under the name of ' Javello.' The label bore this name in large letters, but it conveyed nothing to our light-fingered friend.

George Beasneys had the time of his life at Cavron. It was not long before the men of the Squadron were in a bad way for riding-pants, but that did not seem to worry George. He seemed to be absolutely reckless and to bear a charmed life.

George Haywood went away for a time from Cavron and left me in charge of the Troop. I had a hot time with the Medical Officer, Captain Anderson. On weekly inspection he invariably found some of my men lousy. He used to strafe me good and strong and bark at me: " When are you going to get these men clean ? " A very silly question, I thought, but with the aid of the other men we eventually made some progress in de-lousing all those lads except one. He was the very limit. His name was Brown, he came from the West of England, and was well-educated and of good family, but of all the useless soldiers I have ever met, he was the worst. Otherwise he was a very decent young lad, enlisted for the ' duration.' When he had driven me to the verge of despair I spoke about him one day to Mr. Peat, the new Troop Officer. He promised to consult the Squadron Leader. A day or two later the Adjutant visited out billet and asked me to bring Brown up before him. His very first question took Brown's breath away and left me gasping. It was: "Brown, would you like to take a commission?" When he was able to speak again Brown answered that he would. He was off within a week, and the M.O. left me in peace.

No more was heard of Brown, till one day in 1919 I was crossing Trafalgar Square, when I heard my name called loudly behind me. On stopping and looking round I was amazed to see a spick and span young Staff-Captain running towards me with hand outstretched. It was none other than my old friend. He seemed to have acquired no 'side' at all, was very pleased to see me, and looked as presentable a Staff Officer as one could wish for.

We were not allowed to linger very many days around Cavron before a party of us went up to dig in front of Albert. We set out in the early morning, and as I paraded the troops in the half-light I noticed a man of my own Troop carrying a sack over his shoulder. I asked him what it contained, and was told "rations." I went and felt the sack and found, to my complete astonishment, the old 1870 veteran's pet pumpkin. Heaven only knows what was the fellow's motive in scrounging this monstrosity, with which he could do absolutely nothing useful, and which weighed half a hundredweight. He must have shed it on the way up, for on arriving at Albert the sack and its contents had disappeared.

Up around Albert we were located in huts outside the town, and at night we carried out wiring and digging fatigues in and around the front line.

This spell of work lasted but a short time, but our spell back at Cavron was not of long duration. In November a large party from the Brigade paraded at 4 a.m. one morning and went up by train to the Beaumont Hamel area. Practically the whole of my Troop came up with me, and on parading them in the dark I discovered that two worthies were missing from their places. I entered the *estaminet*, that being the likeliest place to locate them, and, sure enough, there they were. They had roused the old refugee, and sent him out to find some eggs. In his absence they had gone behind the bar and filled their waterbottles with the landlady's rum. They were just waiting for the eggs when I found them. I got them out and in their places, and again I noticed a man of my Troop with a sack on his shoulder. My question as to its contents drew the usual reply : " Rations." On investigating I found it to be full of chickens, which the man, a great fellow, and terrific chicken-scrounger when he got going, had collected in the course of the night. I kept my mouth shut, and in due course we marched away.

Our destination was a field in front of the village of Englebelmer. It was full of shell-holes and covered with a thin coat of snow above several inches of mud. The men proceeded to inhabit the shell-holes, which they covered with scrounged wagon tarpaulins, while the N.C.O.s, numbering about nine, took up their abode in a small tin hut about eight feet square on the edge of the field. Here was misery indeed. Immediately we got in, Jock Macdonald and I set out for the village to see if we could discover a canteen. We were weary and hungry, and, approaching the village, asked a soldier if he knew of one there. He directed us into a farm-yard and down some steps into a cellar. We followed out his directions, and on arriving underground flashed a torch round about. We spotted a solitary soldier sitting asleep with his head in his hands on a case of whisky. We woke the poor devil up and asked : " Is this the canteen ? " " Yus," he answered. " That's right. I'm the canteen. But it's an officers' canteen, see ? I've got nothing but whisky. There's a big general canteen up on the corner of the main street." We thanked him and proceeded up the road. There was a canteen where he sent us, and I bought a large bottle of cherry brandy and some tins of tongue. Bread there was none, but we had a few biscuits. A good meal followed on our return, though the cherry brandy proved too rich for some of our little group and they were violently sick in the night. During the meal there was a banging on the tin wall of our hut. I heard my name called, and on going out found the chicken-merchant looking very pleased with himself, though covered from head to foot with mud. He had brought me a chicken from his private store. The unfortunate fowl had been plucked and trussed in the shell-hole, then boiled, goodness knows how, with his fellows, in a petrol tin. It tasted of petrol and was as hard as rubber; but I accepted it and thanked him profusely. I knew my fellow-Irishman would have been deeply insulted had I refused his gift. We kept the chicken till next day, and then made a combined assault on it till nothing remained but the bones.

Next morning, and for many following mornings, the troops went up on road-making jobs about Hamel. Their miserable quarters must have made an appeal to some of the senior officers, for next day, before I could set out on fatigue, Major Ricardo of the Blues came along to find me. He said to me: "You're an expert on canteens, aren't you?" I answered that I had run one, so he asked me if I would care to start one here for the Brigade. I agreed, and in half an hour we were off into Albert with a G.S. wagon, where at the Expeditionary Force Canteen the Major bought supplies of all kinds to the value of about five thousand francs. The only accommodation available to house these wares was an ordinary bell tent, which the Major secured and brought along.

On reaching our field the Major left me with the tent, the stores, and his blessing, and, promising to send me an assistant, hurried off to his own quarters. We had the tent pitched and the stores stacked inside by noon. There was scarcely room to move a hand within. Across the tent-door I rigged up a sort of counter, and then laced the door so that only one client could put his nose or hand in at a time. I made out a short price list, to which I added the words: 'Opening at 2 p.m.,' and hung it outside on the front of the tent. A Brigade of navvies in the vicinity got wind of the fact that I was going to sell black shag tobacco at a ridiculous price. Other bargains were duly boosted, and when we looked through the crack of the tent-door, at 1.30 p.m., we beheld a queue of soldiers two deep and half

Q

a mile long. This startled us somewhat, but we opened at the advertised time and carried on. We soon sold out of several commodities, but there was a stream of customers till after dark, and when the last client left the tent-door my assistant and I drew a deep breath and looked round in our tent. We had sold out completely. We were knee-deep in mud, in which were embedded French notes of every denomination, and the tent-pole was leaning back from the door at an angle of 45 degrees. What a rush it had been ! Our reputation as a going concern was established. We decided we had done enough for that day, so my assistant went to bed on the counter and I departed to sleep in the tin hut. During the night, and every night while we were there, we were smartly shelled, but nobody was ever hit.

The following morning we rescued all our paper money from the mud and counted our takings. There was no need to take stock. There was no stock left. The G.S. wagon was at my disposal, so off I went to Albert to restock, and as I had now some idea of the commodities likely to be in demand by our own men I was very welcome on my return. I stocked cigarettes, bottled beer, cake, chocolate, and tobacco. The canteen was a blessing to the troops, and we were grateful to Major Ricardo for starting it. In a week's time I was in a position to repay him the amount of his original outlay. We bought all goods at the E.F. Canteen at a discount of 5 per cent. There were no *sous* or halfpennies to be had, so anything which came to an odd halfpenny was put up to the next penny. Matches, for example, were supposed to be sold at two boxes for three-halfpence, but had to be put up to a penny a box. With our complete daily selling out we made a considerable profit. The venture opened my eyes to some of the aspects of shopkeeping.

On refunding Major Ricardo his money, I asked that somebody should take over the daily profits and make an occasional audit. This was for my own protection. A young officer of the 2nd Life Guards kindly took this task on, and we continued to flourish. I had found that there was a silly order in the area which forbade any soldier, except the drivers, riding in any army vehicle. In order to circumvent the redcaps on the road to Albert, I drew up a pass on a square of cardboard in writing capable of being read at a distance of several yards. My managing director, the young officer, kindly signed this and got an official stamp of some kind on it. So when the redcap on duty stopped me daily I held up this imposing document to him for inspection and was signalled to carry on.

After three weeks of canteen-managing I had grown so sick of it all that when the Sergeant-Major sent for me and told me I was due to go home on seven days' leave I jumped at the idea and proceeded to take steps to hand over my charge. The Quartermaster of the 2nd Life Guards, being Quartermaster to the Brigade fatigue party, now came along and took over books and cash. My friend, Sergeant Bob Barber of 'B' Squadron, was appointed to take my place. As I handed over to him, I made a special point of impressing on him the importance of my large cardboard pass. He did not seem impressed. The first day, on going to Albert, he left it behind. The redcap duly pulled him up for riding in the wagon. A heated scene ensued, Bob was reported, and collected a severe reprimand, and all before I had been gone twenty-four hours. The profits must have been considerable when the canteen was wound up a few weeks later.

XXVIII

THE chance of going home on leave for seven days, coming quite unexpectedly as it now did, was almost too good to be true. I had actually had one whole day at home in the last three years, two of which I had spent on active service. To say that I was elated at the prospect would be putting it too mildly. In our present capacity we were simply wasting time and good men's lives for no tangible result. We were shelled at work and shelled at rest every night, and although our casualties up to the time of my departure had been slight, I knew it was only a question of time before we caught it hot and strong.

I soon discovered that I was to have a fellow-traveller in the shape of a Sergeant of ' B ' Squadron—Dan Freeman of the ' Skins.' He was a good lad who had strayed into ' B ' Squadron in some unaccountable way, and in spite of that strange atmosphere, had contrived to hold his own with a bit to spare. He had plenty of guts and was afraid of nobody, not even of his Squadron Leader. One Friday, while we were at Corbie on the Somme, the said Squadron Leader sat on a truss of hay beside a large pile of forage and paid the Squadron out. Dan Freeman happened to be away somewhere on duty. He returned hot and bothered half a minute after the pay-out was finished, caught the Squadron Quarterbloke's eye and asked whether he would kindly explain his lateness to the Captain and ask him to let him have some money. The Quarterbloke didn't like bearding the lion, and said in a whisper : " I'm afraid it's no use. The Squadron Leader has finished paying out." " Oh, ask him," said Dan. Then came a squeaky voice from the other side of the pile of hay : " What's that ? What's that ? " " Sergeant Freeman, sir. He's just arrived, sir. He wants to know if you'll pay him, sir ? " stammered the Quarterbloke. " Certainly not ! " was the reply hissed back from behind the forage. Dan turned away mumbling to himself: " Would you believe it ? The . . . ! . . . ! . . ." " What's that ? What's that ? " squeaked the voice from behind the hay. "Bring him here ! I'll pay him ! I'll pay him ! " So Dan was duly paid. But what a business !

Dan and I reported for our leave-warrants at the orderly room at 6 p.m. It was pitch dark. The duck-boards outside the office were slippery, and on coming out Dan, in his excitement, slipped off into the mud, which was so deep that for a moment all I could see of him was his hand holding the green warrant. Anyhow, we fetched him up on dry land again, and were ordered to make the best of our way to Acheux, where we would find a train. We had only a very hazy idea of the whereabouts of this town, having never been near it, all our operations taking place on the other side of Englebelmer. On inquiry we found it lay a good five to six miles away to the west of our lines. There was no good purpose to be served by hanging about in the darkness and mud, so we trudged to the main road and started along it in the direction away from the line. The going was bad, and we were beginning to curse it when some empty ration lorries overtook us. We held them up, begged a lift, and the rest was easy.

There is no point in describing our journey to London. Enough to say that we reached the Strand Corner House almost exactly twenty-four hours after leaving Englebelmer. Covered with mud as we were, the attendant refused to take our British Warms or anything else we possessed in the cloak-room, so we just sat down in the restaurant, threw our kit on the floor beside us, and ordered a good meal. I had just enough time to catch the Irish boat train from Euston, and Dan was off to Leicester. Our waitress paid great attention to us, and informed us her young man was ' over there.' His name, she said, was Smith, and he was serving in the Infantry. We scratched our heads, kept our faces straight, and looked very wise, but could not place him, to our great regret.

We parted company, with a good lining in our insides, and I forget all details of the rest of my journey home till

I actually arrived. Since my last leave my father had left Ireland and come over to Birmingham, where he had secured a post, and was waiting till he could find suitable accommodation to bring over my mother and the rest of my family. Meantime, mother had moved down into County Cork, to a little town where she had spent her girlhood, and where she had a few good friends. This town happened to be an important stronghold of the Irish Republican Army in the rebellion of the same year, and when I got out of the train there I was amazed to see the railway station sandbagged and wired, and men of an English unit with rifles and machine-guns holding the place. Mother met me, and as we strolled along together everything else in the town seemed quite peaceful.

I spent five very restful days at home, during which I wandered freely all over the place. I took care to have no communication with the English soldiers, kept my mouth shut, and my eyes and ears open. What I saw and heard gave me many a twinge, and I had good cause to believe that pretty nearly everybody was to some extent crazy.

During my five days' sojourn, never once, in spite of the state of tension round about, was I or my uniform insulted by anybody. Many young men from the town, drawn from all classes and creeds, had served or were still serving with the British Expeditionary Force. But I did receive one insult which stung badly, rankled for a long time afterwards, and came from a totally unexpected direction. When the day came for my departure (I had decided to spend the two remaining days of my leave with my father in Birmingham), I said good-bye to mother in the house, and then strolled along to the railway station by myself. I passed through the sandbagged entrance, showed my pass to the individual in charge, and was allowed up on to the platform. I had about five minutes to wait for my train and was the only person to be seen anywhere about. Suddenly there came out of a door at the other end of the long platform and over which was suspended the sign ' Buffet ' a damsel of about seventeen. She tripped along to me like a fairy, smiled her most bewitching smile, and, in the accents of Mayfair, lisped : " Would you like a naice cup of tea?" A sudden wave of fury swept through me. My face must have shown what I felt, for the damsel gave a little startled cry and bolted back to her buffet like a scared rabbit.

Hell! What did she take me for? Did she think that because I was dressed in the uniform of the British Army I must be some miserable conscript from Peckham Rye, going about in fear of his life, and thankful for the ministrations of this butterfly, who fancied herself doing war-work in enemy country? Five minutes ago I had been with my mother, in whose veins not a drop of English blood flowed, and who was worth a whole shipload of this young lady and her kind. My blood boiled, and from that moment my sympathy was entirely on the side of my country.

Over in Birmingham I found my father working like a nigger, and with prospects of making good in his new surroundings. We spent two very happy days together, and I met many very good people, who, like himself, had left the old country for various reasons, but mostly for political ones. In my present frame of mind I put down all this silly topsy-turvydom to English stupidity and misgovernment.

I thought the Englishwomen in London, who saw men away at Victoria, were a pretty depraved crowd, but they were little woolly lambs compared with the sweethearts and wives of Birmingham. Between one thing and another, I was not exactly sorry when I got aboard the cross-channel steamer in company with Dan Freeman and felt myself under control again, and with a prospect of something to do which would keep me from thinking too much and getting into mischief. On landing we proceeded to the rest-camp. Here everybody in authority disclaimed all knowledge of our working-party up at Englebelmer, which had been given some daft temporary title, so next morning we were simply put on a train for Cavron St. Martin, where we arrived, to everybody's surprise, just in time for dinner.

Very soon the troops returned from the forward area. Christmas was not far away, so we settled down peacefully to prepare for it. Something happened to George Beasneys just at this time, I forget exactly what, but I can recall another short, successful spell in the role of Acting Squadron Q.M.S.

My friend, George Haywood, was laid up about this time with some form of influenza. It appeared to affect his back and limbs, and he was in a bad way for some time. Fortunately Beasneys had returned and I was back in the Troop. It was precious little I could do for the ill man. He lay in a small room on a wire-netting bed of home manufacture. There was no fire-place, and so cold was it that his breath froze on the ceiling of the room and hung down in icicles. For days poor old George was quite unable to move. In his place I should have gone crazy. In the end he made a good recovery, but I'm afraid he paid for it later on with rheumatism.

Christmas 1917 passed, and then we were moved away back to within a mile of the coast, our Squadron being all in one village and our own Troop housed in a brickfield. Here we had attached to us for a while a very slim, youthful Lieutenant. To the troops he was ' Strip ' because of his likeness in length and thickness to a hotchkiss-gun strip of twenty-five rounds. He was very decent and harmless, but our Troop Sergeant, George Haywood, had no great use for this very underdone subaltern. One day George sat on a truss of hay filling nose-bags, when he strolled up aimlessly, tapping his legging with his stick. George took no notice, so by way of being sociable he burbled : " Sergeant Haywood, do you know I'm a Regular ? " Without stopping in his work or looking up George replied dryly : " A regular what, sir ? " The lad beetled off round the corner to think it out.

There came a heavy fall of snow soon after our arrival at the brickfield. This drove the troops into billets and *estaminets*, where they cowered round fires and braziers trying to keep warm. Jim Fleming and I went for long walks in the snow to all the surrounding villages, and scraped acquaintance with landlords and landladies in numerous *estaminets*. There was a biggish forest within a mile of our village, on the far side from the coast. We were intrigued by strange tracks leading out of this and across the neighbouring fields. They were something quite new to us, and one day we discovered that they all converged on a small mound in a field just outside the village. Here stood three or four stacks of unthreshed wheat. From various signs in the vicinity of the stacks we came to the conclusion that the visitors were wild boar. They had pulled out sheaves of wheat, and made large burrows in all the stacks, where they could sleep undisturbed after eating their fill of wheat.

Jim and I held a council to decide what was to be done about the wild boar. We knew from observation that they did not emerge from the forest in daylight. We also observed that at that particular time a bright full moon rose about 8.30 p.m., and, shining on the snow, gave splendid visibility for a hundred yards about midnight. Accordingly we borrowed two rifles, took five rounds of ammunition each, and after cutting the tips off the bullets, loaded up and set out for the stacks when everybody in the village was fast asleep. Cautiously and silently we made our way into the field and lay down in the ditch in ambush about fifty yards from the nearest stack. We waited for upwards of an hour, but saw nothing, and were beginning to be famished with the cold. Still making no sound, we got up and advanced slowly to the stacks. No sign of life anywhere about. Then Jim bent down and looked into one of the holes where the sheaves had been pulled out. Immediately, with a loud snort, a boar rushed straight out and nearly knocked him down. I was standing on Jim's left when the animal jumped out, turned left, and then raced along at top speed to our right. He was travelling at a hot pace, and I realized that time was precious if we were to get in a shot while he was still in sight. I could not fire because Jim was in the way, but pulling himself together he raised his rifle and fired what must have been a random shot in the hurry and excitement. He missed, of course, but the boar turned almost about, and, realizing that he was about to pass on the other side of the stack, I ran round in time to see him dashing past some thirty or forty yards away, making straight for the forest. I raised my rifle and tried to aim, making allowance for his pace, but the moonlight was not by any means as clear as it seemed. However, in a couple of seconds I got a satisfactory aim, pressed the trigger, and had the satisfaction of seeing the boar turn a somersault in the air and then lie still. Jim came round to me with a whoop, and when we reached our quarry we found it to be a full-grown animal and still alive. A bullet in the head put it out of action. Then came the question of getting the carcass home. We decided to go back and rouse a labourer at our billet and get him to fetch along a handcart. He came with us and with some difficulty the three of us loaded and carted the dead boar into the village, where we dumped it down with the shoemaker, whom we knew to be the biggest rogue in the place. He promised to keep silent, and to skin and cut the carcass into joints in return for the skin and a piece of meat. Feeling very pleased with our night's work, we pulled the rifles through, returned them to where we had borrowed them, and went to bed.

Next day we distributed boar's meat to the four Troops, and took along a fine ham to the Sergeants' Mess. The cook roasted it and when it was served at dinner, old Hindenburg, our Sergeant-Major, seemed to enjoy it. And first-rate it was, too. Then Hindy put out a few feelers in an attempt to discover what the meat was and where it had come from. No answer being forthcoming, he grew quite wild, glared at Fleming and me, and threatened to give us away if it came to light that we had been poaching. The troops enjoyed the meal, too ; but, of course, their curiosity was aroused. Then one day Mr. Peat, again back as Troop Officer, asked me if I had shot any wild boar lately, and invited me to make an expedition one night with him. I pretended to have no knowledge of boar-shooting, and the matter faded out.

Some brainy person in the upper reaches of the Division hit on the scheme of running an inter-Troop football league as soon as the snow disappeared. This idea caught on. It was the first time anybody had shown any interest in the occupation of the men in billets. As a Troop contains forty men, and there were some hundred and twenty

Troops in a division, the scheme would mean pleasant jaunts to away matches and pleasant reunions at home fixtures, quite apart from the benefits accruing from training and the fostering of the Troop spirit. As it happened, our Troop could produce a fine eleven. We had with us men from three or four units who had played in their unit's first team. The league was run on the knock-out system. We ran away with our first couple of matches ; then came a severe test at home against the most fancied Troop of the Brigade, Sligo Taylor's Troop, 2nd Life Guards. The field was a quagmire, some of our team had to turn out wearing army boots, and not a soul from any other part of the Regiment came to give us a shout. Our opponents arrived with a horde of supporters armed with rattles, tin cans, and trumpets. No quarter was asked or given in the match and we finished winners by two goals to one.

Then the regiment woke up to the fact that it had a Troop well in the running for the Brigade championship, if not that of the Division. But luck is a funny thing. In the midst of our elation, it was discovered that one of our number had contracted measles, so we were all examined by the medical officer and placed in isolation for three weeks. That put the lid on our hopes, and the ensuing period of segregation was so miserable in the cold, lousy billets, that it does not bear thinking of.

The weather soon brightened up, and to our great surprise we were now honoured by a visit from our Regiment's band. Medals look well on bandsmen, and though they went no farther than our billets on the coast during their week's sojourn, each one was duly decorated with the British War and Victory Medals.

The regiment never ceased to send working parties up to the front during the whole of the winter. I accompanied two or three of these myself. They were dull affairs, because of the long dragging days, but there was always liable to be a little excitement on our night tasks. We must have put up enough wire on various parts of the front to enclose the Yellowstone National Park. An average task for one night for forty or fifty men was the erection of a hundred yards of African Apron. Creepy work it was too, especially before the advent of the corkscrew stakes. I take off my hat to the two Sappers of the Royal Engineers who always joined us on the site of our labours, appeared to come from nowhere and when work was done vanish to the same place. They did more work with bare hands than all of us put together.

An officer, not of our Squadron, and not over popular, went up one night in charge of a wiring party to a part of no-man's-land with a bad reputation, where work had to be carried on within hearing of the Germans. Unfortunately for him, he had with him on this occasion two tough fellows, Archie Goodall and Frank Askey. On drawing tools from the dump he warned the men that the work must proceed in silence owing to the proximity of the enemy. Eventually they reached the scene of the night's labour, distances were silently stepped out, material laid down, and with every man in his place doing his own bit of job, work began. Presently somebody in the darkness brushed the back of Archie Goodall's neck with a strand of barbed wire. Archie swore aloud. The officer, who happened to be at some distance from him, hissed : " Keep quiet, there ! " Archie, still swearing, paused a moment and blew back a piercing raspberry. The officer, now seeing red, set out for the point from where the raspberry had come, but Archie, being a wily bird, downed tools, and sensing a move of this sort, made his way to the spot where the officer had been standing before the fun began. Arrived here, he stumbled across a haversack, which he picked up, and on examination discovered to be an officer's. He whirled it a few times round his head, then let it fly away in the direction of the German lines. By this time the lieutenant was feeling his way back, so Archie set about returning to his original position. The former's temper, none to sweet at the best of times, was sorely tried that night. He nearly burst when he couldn't find his haversack, though I believe he would have preferred to find Archie. But he didn't.

Back at the brickfields weather was slowly improving, and the French Interpreters developed a habit of borrowing horses from the Troops, with the Squadron Leader's permission of course, and riding away to an Interpreters' binge in some town several miles away. They always brought the unfortunate horses back in a miserable state some time in the small hours. This was very much resented by the owners of the horses. We decided that next time our Troop was detailed to find a horse for an Interpreter we should give him a scallywag, then all get away and leave him to his fate. This particular horse would not leave the ranks and travel by himself, and in his obstinacy he resembled a mule. When the Sunday arrived along came the Interpreter to take over his mount. Our man had orders to lead out the horse into the road, hand it over, and then clear off quick. All our Troop had assembled behind the hedge of an adjoining field to watch the upshot. The Frenchman mounted, settled himself in the saddle, and with his groom mounted behind, prepared to move off. Our old long-faced friend was true to his colours and refused to budge. Whip and spurs were of no avail. Then the Interpreter dismounted and started to lead him. He went slowly a few yards, then stopped dead. The Interpreter set about him with his whip, lost his temper, swore at him in French, and finding him unmoved by that language, must have decided to try him with English. Anyhow he gave the unfortunate animal a terrific kick in the ribs, and white with rage screamed at him : " Come on now, will you ! You bloody liar ! No ? " Finally we saw a scene I'm sure none of us will ever forget. The Interpreter mounted, his groom moved up in front of him, took the reins of his master's horse over its head, and led the old broncho, with its head well stuck forward and still protesting, out of the village, while the Frenchman, a pathetic picture, sat on its back, dumb. He never came to our Troop for a horse again.

In February all working-parties were recalled and cavalry training began on the broad sands by the sea. This was in many ways a pathetic effort. We started off with the elements of equitation, like recruits in the riding-school. The Brigadier was due to inspect us, and as it was discovered that his pet fad was calling individuals to ride forward alone from out the ranks of the Troop, much time was devoted to this movement. We had gradually lost several of our original horses, and they had been replaced by remounts, reputed to be of American origin, but all of which were the queerest quadrupeds we had ever come across. These were without exception lanky, coarse-bred blacks, in whom the herd instinct seemed to be so strongly developed that they had a peculiar dread of being alone. When ridden, they were for the most part totally unresponsive to the usual aids. It was quite common to see a rider applying leg and spur with all his strength while the animal reined steadily back. They would also move forward straight ahead in spite of all efforts to turn them to the right or left, with their necks bent right round till their heads touched the rider's knee and they were actually looking backwards. I have also seen one sprint a hundred yards on its hind legs like an outsize ostrich.

Every morning the Troop-officer sat in front of his Troop and called the owners of these 'India-rubber pigs,' one at a time, to 'walk march,' but without the smallest result. They could not be made to budge. They also communicated this trick to the good old horses, and thus we came to a deadlock. Then one morning Lord Somers, second in command of the Squadron, and I dismounted, provided ourselves with good long sticks, and when a name was called and the order 'Walk march' given, applied the sticks for all we were worth to the rump of the animal concerned. This, when persevered in with plenty of elbow-grease, and accompanied by appropriate language, brought about a complete change. We soon reached a pitch where any one of these horses would dart forth spontaneously if either of us approached him from behind. At last the Brigadier arrived and proceeded with his little game. He was several days too late. I had to keep my place in the ranks, but Lord Somers was strolling about in rear of the Troop, and the General was surprised at the alacrity with which all our horses quitted the ranks.

Then followed Troop and Squadron drills and one or two schemes on the country roads and across the still waterlogged fields, where we were taught to capture villages by galloping round them from two sides at once.

There was seldom any break in the monotony of this childishness, but one day I was warned to go on a little errand which proved to be exciting and interesting. It seems some new batteries of artillery with their ammunition columns were then being formed in back areas. I had to parade after dinner and get along to Montreuil with thirty-six men, under Lieutenant Morrice, to detrain seventy-two mules at the railway station, and deliver them to an ammunition column just forming back at Buire le Sec. We duly arrived at the station and found our mules waiting for us in trucks, eight mules in each truck. There was no assistance from railway-staff, so handing over four horses to each man, we got on to the siding, and manhandling a sort of portable platform, succeeded in getting the mules all out into the deep mud. It now dawned on us that the serious side of our task was about to begin. At that moment each man in the party was holding either three mules, two mules, or four horses, and our immediate objective was to bring about a re-distribution so that finally each man would be riding one horse and leading two mules. With a little thought this will be seen to be no easy problem, especially as the horses resented the approach of the mules and kicked, squealed, and plunged to some purpose. After much swearing, and as night was falling, the little column was formed up, and Mr. Morrice leading and I riding in rear, we started on our ride of two or three hours in the darkness to Buire. The first half-hour saw some lively scenes, as half the mules wanted to get the journey over as quickly as possible, while their fellows wanted to stay in Montreuil. I rode up and down the column on old Herbert, dealing with lazy ones, crazy ones, and aisy ones, like Father O'Flynn in the song. A few here and there broke away, and I did some cowboy work rounding them up in the adjacent fields. Before we had been ten minutes outside the town, a mule passed me *ventre à terre* in the wrong direction. Here was a pretty problem. Should I report his departure and spend the night looking for him in the streets and lanes of Montreuil? The man who had been leading him had decided to hold his peace, so I did the same, and determined that no more mules should break back past me. After all, I thought, if we hand them over seventy-one instead of seventy-two they will not be far out. Eventually we reached the ammunition-column and handed our charges over. We were just moving off on the return journey when somebody came rushing after us shouting something about being a mule short. We rode on, we had had enough of mules for one day, and arrived back at the brickfields in the small hours.

It became more and more evident from day to day now that there was something in the wind. Efforts were made to get horses fit. Here was the only fault I had ever to find with George Haywood. He was machine-like in his ideas of justice and fairness. The daily ration for each horse was, say, nine pounds of corn. George religiously measured out the allotted amount for each horse, and never a grain more nor less, whatever the difference in size of the animals. Now my horse, Herbert, was the biggest and hungriest horse for miles around. Others in the Troop were half his size and had half his appetite. These little devils were as fat as butter, while poor Herbert grew slim and touchy on short rations. There was nothing for it but to make a private *cache* of my own in a corner of the brickfield, where I soon had a store of corn, and as George always made out the feeds himself, it was simple to add a couple of extra handfuls to Herbert's nose-bag. The hay ration I supplemented by paying a few extra visits daily to the stables and filling up Herbert's hay-net. Soon he was happy, and plump, and shining, and an object of delight to our Veterinary Officer, Captain Helis, who on inspections always admired him, said he was the best bred horse in the Regiment, and spoke of him as ' My old friend.'

XXIX

TOWARDS the end of March 1917, the Division left the coastal area, and marched up to the Arras sector to see if a job could be found for it in the impending battle. The weather was vile, with rain for long spells, intermixed with sleet, and piercing east winds fairly froze the marrow in our bones as we scampered about for a week or so in the bleak, hilly country round Wanquetin. Day after day we scampered all over the place, often walking and leading our horses for miles, during which exercise the arches of my feet broke down completely and I was almost on my knees. Night after night we pegged down and bivouacked on an open rain-swept hill-side, and all the time rations were short, so that we froze and starved and swore. What we carried out all these evolutions for, I, like old Kaspar in the poem, could never well make out. I would have reported sick early on with my feet, but we knew that eventually we might have a chance of going into action, and my pride would not allow me to take this course. So I just carried on in agony every time we came to a spell of walking.

On 9 April, Easter Sunday, we moved right up into the town of Arras after nightfall and stood about mounted in side-streets for half the night, drowsing in the saddle, while our hungry, tired horses became restless. I sat on Herbert in a narrow street with George Ford of the 'Skins' on my right. George's horse kept crunching a broken bottle under his hind hooves. All the time there was a terrific row going on just outside to the east and north of the town, and shells came falling into it in bunches. When it was well after midnight we moved back and out into a nearby field. Jock Morrison and I had a line of built-up ropes down and the Troop tied to them in a jiffy. I then sheered off to inspect some tents lying on one side of our field. These we found empty of human beings, but in one

was a store of food and drink. On lifting a flap and shining
a torch underneath I read the legend ' Black and White ' on
a case of whisky, and alongside it discovered a box of soup
squares. I won the soup squares and cleared off, giving the
whisky a wide berth. As day was breaking on the 10th,
George Haywood, who was very hungry and liverish, spotted
the line Jock and I had put down in the dark, and as it was not
too straight he had it pulled up and straightened. Everybody
was liverish that morning. No rations had turned up. There
was absolutely nothing to eat. Horses carried two days' corn
ration, so they just had a handful, while the men walked
about trying to get warm, or sat huddled in groups.

Then I got a dixie of water and made our soup. It
worked out at about four men to a pint throughout the
Troop, but its odour, which was delicious, must have been
torture to the rest of the Regiment who had absolutely nothing.

The same afternoon we went up again through Arras
and out past the suburb of Blagny. Here we crossed the
Blagny–Tilloy road which had been unused for three
years, and halted in a valley just beyond what must have
been the German front line a day or two before. Close to
where we settled down lay two German machine-gunners
on their backs, dead. One had been shot through the head,
his companion bayoneted through the chest. Their
machine-gun had gone, but beside them was a mountain of
empty cartridge-cases at least three feet high, which told
its own tale. These were stout fellows. Many English
dead lay about, mostly in shell-holes.

We tied our horses in bunches, and sat down anywhere
just waiting for orders. Night fell, and some of us
scrambled into holes and corners trying to sleep. The cold
was severe. Jock Morrison disappeared for a few minutes,
and came back wearing a cardigan. We were practically
standing to all night.

The morning broke bright but cold. It was my birthday,
11 April. We still had nothing to eat. The horses were on
their last handful of corn. Gypsy Smith's little black horse
had swollen gums and could not manage the corn. I saw
Gypsy take him along to a pool of water, fish out some
small, hard biscuits, which were the last of his own rations,

from a bag, soak them in the water, and attempt to feed them to his horse. Hard pressed as we ourselves were with hunger, it was hard to see the horses starving.

The sun rose gradually, and the morning passed in aimless inactivity. About midday three aeroplanes came out of the blue, heading straight for us. The one in front was British, the others Germans, hot on his tail. The Germans fired repeated blasts into him till he came down a few yards in front of us. Then they swung away to the east and were out of sight in a minute. Many of the 2nd Life Guards' horses were hit by the German machine-gun bullets. We had no reply ready. They could have returned and riddled us if they wished.

Some of us were of the opinion that the enemy airmen would report our presence to their artillery, and expected a lively time to follow. Eventually a few shells came over, but nothing much, and only small ones. The very first shell killed the Sergeant-Major, the Quarterbloke, and Old Bob, the Farrier, of 'K' Battery, R.H.A., who were a few yards along to our right.

The afternoon came, and still we stood there. A rumour reached us that our 8th Brigade had been ordered up to take Monchy, and that in all probability our turn would come soon. Still nothing happened. More rumours reached us to the effect that the Blues were now actually in Monchy, but that the attack had been costly enough to be counted a failure. We learned that in spite of all our training in cutting out villages from the flanks, the 8th Brigade had galloped straight at their objective. Their Brigadier-General was killed. We were sorry for him. We considered he had done the best a brave man could do. He must have realized what a hopeless task he had been set, and instead of sending his men forward he had led them. More than that no man could do.

Suddenly we were ordered to mount and get back out of it. Why, after dawdling about for so long, we should have set off now back at top speed, I could not understand. Our Troop formed the rear of the column. Just as we started, Joe Blake's pack-horse, old Badminton, who was stiff and weak, sank into the mud and in his efforts to extricate himself caused the pack to slip round. I fell back to help him, and by the time we had the old horse again under way, the column was swallowed up in the houses of Blagny, and Joe and I with our three horses were all alone and saying some harsh things about the war in general.

Now it began to snow, lightly at first, but within half an hour we were enveloped in a regular blizzard. We made for the race-course, where we were ordered to peg down for the time being. In the blinding snow we did all that could be done for the horses, tying them up in Troops as best we could, and covering them with blankets. There was now the prospect of spending the night on the bleak field, with just a ground-sheet. We put off our own settling down for the time being, and had a look round. Visibility just then was perhaps twenty yards.

Most of my comrades strolled, miserable, to the hedge on the nearest side of the course. On peering through this, we discovered, to our unspeakable joy, a fair-sized stack of unthreshed oats just on the other side. Brigade or Divisional Headquarters had, however, spotted it first, for it was found on closer investigation that a solitary red-cap was doing guard over it. We were not to be denied possession of this straw for our shelter and corn for our horses. We decided to try guile. It was proposed that John Lawrence should walk boldly through a gap in the hedge, go up to the stack, and pull out a sheaf under the military policeman's nose. He was then to run for all he was worth back through the gap, then act as the situation demanded. John acted his part as directed. The red-cap behaved as we had anticipated. At first he could hardly believe his eyes. Then he shouted after the retreating John, and, receiving no response, set off after him. Now we came into play on the stack, and in less than two minutes every man of us had an armful of sheaves and was hurrying back to our lines. Out came our jack-knives, and we cut the heads of corn into nosebags. The famished horses nearly mobbed us. There wasn't much for them, but it helped. Then we shared out the straw, taking care to give a helping to our Sergeant-Major and Quarterbloke, so that they would be tarred with the same brush as ourselves. John had no difficulty in shaking off his pursuer, who must have felt a fool when he returned to find his charge no longer there. I hope the poor lad didn't get into serious trouble.

We now found a wire fence to which we tied our ground-sheets, and, scooping out the snow, put in a good layer of straw. Ted Pettit had no pal, and tied his sheet on a strand rather too high. As soon as he scooped the snow away underneath, more blew in from outside. I shall never forget the sight of him standing watching all his efforts go to the devil, and turning the snow pink with his language. Ted loved his horse more than anything on earth. When the animal had finished a few ears of corn Ted had scrounged for it, he went and removed its nose-bag. He then put on his British Warm, and making a desperate effort to scoop out the snow, threw himself down in his bivvy in blank despair. He had not been more than a minute in this position when his horse broke loose, came across to Ted, and began to nibble the straw beneath his head. Ted saw red. He was in the act of getting up to slay his old friend, when some of us burst out laughing. This restored Ted's sanity. He put his arms round the old horse's neck, kissed it, and led it back to its place with as much straw as he could spare from his bivvy to keep it quiet.

Night and darkness fell quickly. We could not help thinking of the Blues, 10th Hussars, and Essex Yeomanry, but especially of our old friend the Blues, holding out in this weather in Monchy. I joined groundsheets with George Haywood and Jock Morrison and made quite a good bivvy. George Haywood was having trouble with his back again, and was much worse than he would admit. My feet were none too promising. Suddenly word was passed that a rum-issue had made an appearance. I went and fetched ours. This was something worth while. The rum for forty men was given me in an earthenware jar. When I got back I gave a good tot to George Haywood. To my surprise, the first sip made him sick and he would not drink the remainder. On tasting it myself I found it was about fifty-fifty creosote. Nobody could drink that mixture. There was nothing to be done except throw it away and get down to it.

The sentries had an awful night. Any horse who was still fit to do so broke loose and went foraging for himself. Herbert had a prowl round, pulled the straw from under Sergeant-Major Hindy's bivvy, and Hindy declared he also ate his haversack containing the Squadron roll and other documents. Anyhow, after that night Hindy never saw it again. It was under his head when he lay down.

The officers retired to sleep in the grandstand. 'B' Squadron Leader somehow got left outside. He had some straw from somewhere, and was troubled all night by visiting horses. Every time he found one near him he would squeal : " Sentry ! Sentry ! Come and tie up this horse ! " The unfortunate sentry had more horses to deal with than he could tie up in a week, so at length, exasperated by the endless calling, he threw all discretion to the winds and shouted back : " Get up and tie the b—— up yourself ! " The Captain said no more.

When at last morning came the snowing had ceased, the ground was covered with a couple of inches of white, and close by our bivouacs lay several horses dead and stiff. The poor devils had no means of counteracting the cold. Herbert spotted me and neighed and skipped about, thinking perhaps I was a conjurer who could get corn out of a hat. Fortunately forage and rations were now issued, and in a few hours' time the dead horses were buried and we felt alive again. All except George Haywood. He was in for a bad spell, but he stuck it bravely for some days longer.

That day we rode back to a desolate village called Simencourt, tied up our horses in the usual muddy field, and had our own quarters in bell-tents. And thus ended our share in the Battle of Arras. Our Machine-Gun Section, under Splash Hall, was lent to the Canadians at the beginning of the battle, remained behind for some weeks, and did good work.

The villagers remaining in Simencourt lived in a state of abject poverty. Jim Fleming and I made friends with a little family consisting of a woman and her two children, a boy and a girl, aged seven and nine years. They had no idea what had become of the father. Nobody seemed to worry about them. Goodness knows how they lived. We gave them, when we could manage it, a tin of jam or bully. We became greatly attached to them during our stay of a week or so, but never heard from them afterwards. We visited the house every evening out of sheer delight at spending an hour in their company. Both mother and children had certain characteristics which we had not met for ages, and with which in the ordinary course of our existence we were not in touch. It did us both untold good to find that the war had not levelled everybody down to the barbarous state with which we were in daily contact.

We did nothing here except wallow for a few days while the wretched weather continued. A man cleaning a revolver in a tent managed to shoot himself through the leg and at the same time wound four or five others, though none seriously. How these things happen nobody can explain, but happen they do. However, it's an ill wind that blows nobody any good. This little bunch went off with cheap 'Blighties.'

My arches were worse if anything, and George Haywood at last reported sick. He also was sent home, and I was now left in charge of the Troop, which I kept till May of the following year.

We were moved back from Simencourt to some villages south of Hesdin. Our Squadron billeted in a large farm in the grounds of a château and beside a forest. It was dark as usual when we got in, so I lay down for the rest of the night in a room in the château, fearing that my feet would at last compel me to go sick, but determined to hold on for dear life now that at last I had got charge of a Troop. Next morning we woke up to find the weather changed for the better. The sun was shining. I lay on some straw in a room with mural paintings, and groups of angels on the ceiling. But here occurred one of those strange things which have happened to me from time to time. On a ledge beside my shake-down I found a pair of steel spring arch-supports. I had never heard of such things, much less seen them, before. I guessed what they were for, put them in my boots, and found them a perfect fit. They were exactly what I required, and from that day forward I skipped about like a young goat. I said nothing about this find to anybody, and I never heard that anybody had lost them.

The beautiful weather continued. On the far side of the forest I discovered the hamlet of Rachinette, and, in company with old Brum Morris of my own regiment and some friends of the R.H.A. Battery, had some pleasant evenings there. Jim Fleming had his Troop in another village nearly three miles away. This made our meeting for the time being wellnigh impossible.

My spell as Troop-Sergeant was soon interrupted. One day George Beasneys rode into Hesdin alone on business. That same evening, well after dark, his horse returned without him. A subsequent search produced George lying by the roadside nursing an ankle which was badly sprained if not broken. He was sent down to Hospital, where he remained a month while I did his job as Quarter-bloke, and Sergeant Tommy Parker of the 'Skins' looked after my Troop. Later on, when George returned, he looked very down in the mouth. He complained that he was a certainty for England, but that the Senior Medical Officer at the base hospital, being a brother Buffalo or something, as well as an inveterate bridge-player, kept him in the hospital to make up a four every night. Eventually they grew to dislike each other, so George returned to the fold, and I to my Troop.

In George's absence I went up to the Somme as Quarter-bloke when the Brigade took over a part of the line known as 'The Birdcage' in front of Epehy. The Germans had only recently evacuated this area, and it was absolutely desolate. I had a strenuous time, working day and night, drawing and delivering rations and supplies. My drivers were good fellows, all Dragoons, and included Peter Swain, Nigger Stapley, Wally Brooker, and the inseparable Dapper Smith and Harry Pudney. Every night I met Jim Fleming in the outposts, where we had a tot of rum, exchanged scandal, and he did the honours, showing me the lay-out of his little patch of line.

The weather was splendid. The sun shone all the time, and the horses back at Tincourt, as well as those looking after them, had a real rest-cure. Back here in the wagon-lines, Drivers Dapper and Harry attempted to improve the shining hour by establishing a laundry. They discovered a

huge amount of soap which Beasneys had gone on collecting and had never issued. There was plenty of water in the
nearby Somme. The tail-boards of the G.S. wagons did
duty as scrubbing-boards, and they advertised widely that
they were prepared to collect, wash, dry, and deliver
laundry at the moderate rate of half a franc for a pair of
socks, underpants, or shirt. No reduction was made for a
full set, for which they charged a franc and a half. They
were soon inundated with work, and all day long they could
be seen scrubbing the troops' underwear and hanging it out
to dry on a maze of lines in the brilliant sunshine. At the
end of a week their takings were far beyond anything they
had dared to expect. In fact their success turned Dapper's
head. If he could get so rich in such a simple way and in
so short a time, he argued, why not make a bid to become a
real Rockefeller in a night? So against the advice of the
more cautious Harry, Dapper bought a Crown and Anchor
set and sallied forth one evening to skin the troops. Alas
for poor Dapper's dreams of easy wealth! Nothing would
go right for him. In two or three evenings he was completely cleaned out. And now he learned the truth of the
saying, ' Nothing succeeds like success,' for on returning to
his laundry-work, he found that now he was known to be
penniless, his former clients deserted him, preferring either
to do their washing themselves or to go lousy.

Our tour in the line finished, I was able to hand over to
Beasneys and take up my own work again in the Troop.
Another spate of training on a Brigade and Divisional
scale was carried out in the St. Riquier area, and then we
started out once more on our wanderings. Early in July
we found ourselves with our horses picketed and our men
in bivouac beside the little town of Acq, five miles north-
west of Arras. Here we lay in brilliant sunshine without a
care in the world, when on the morning of 12 July, Orange-
men's Day, I received a letter from my mother. Enclosed
I found, to my surprise, a few inches of orange ribbon.
Goodness knows why mother sent it. It did not appeal to
me at all. But I knew somebody who would be touched.
So I set out in search of him, and having found him,
solemnly presented him with the colour of his patron saint,

King Billy. He received it with joy, then disappeared for the remainder of the day.

It was getting dark that same evening, and I was thinking of retiring for the night, when I was startled by the sound of a shot behind me in the direction of the guard-room. Another shot followed immediately, so I set out to investigate. The hut in which Sergeant-Major Hindy and George Beasneys lived was close to the guard-room, and I soon discovered that a scuffle was in progress on the ground in front of the hut. The Sergeant of the Guard, Jock Boyles, assisted by somebody else, was holding the Orangeman down on his back, and trying to take from him a revolver which was now pointing up in the air. Just then the door of the hut opened and Hindy himself appeared on the threshold. Billy saw him, succeeded with a tremendous effort in firing another shot, and at the same time shouted to him : " Hello there, Hindenburg ! You're just the hoodlumbird I'm looking for ! " By this time poor Billy had been disarmed, and on being deposited in the guard-room and searched, further munitions to the extent of a bomb in each jacket pocket were found on him.

Little could my mother have guessed the damage that wretched little strip of ribbon might have caused. And how was I to guess that Billy would, on receiving it from me, relapse into a state of primitive Orangism, go away and get drunk, pack a loaded revolver and two bombs, and set out with the intention of exterminating a perfectly good Sergeant-Major, as Sergeant-Majors went ? I felt very guilty about the whole business. A better soldier than he, or a kinder fellow, did not exist. Everything he disliked he called a ' Hoodlumbird.' That was the worst one ever heard from him. He was duly tried for this escapade, awarded a term of imprisonment, and disappeared from among us to work out his sentence back at the base.

It was not long before we started off again on musical chairs, during which we moved farther north, finally settling for a while round about the town of St. Venant, then the Headquarters of the Portuguese Army. Here Jim Fleming and I had our two Troops in the same field, and when circumstances permitted had a very interesting time.

XXX

I HAVE never come across such a pretty little town as St. Venant. Viewed from the outside, with its walls, battlements, gates, and moat, it sent the mind wandering back to the picturesque days of the long-bow, before gun-powder and its allied products of the laboratory and foundry had appeared among us as civilizing factors. Jim Fleming and I, after gazing in rapture at its outward features, would not have been surprised had we entered the town and found it peopled by fifteenth-century folk. Once across the bridge, however, and within the gates, we met the usual war-time collection of troops, including Portuguese, and the inevitable frowsy *estaminets* with their watery beer and poisonous rum. The Australians had sojourned there, hence the inhabitants were aloof, whilst all commodities in shops were dear and of poor quality. Failing to locate a comfortable hostelry, we soon ceased to visit the town.

Our old billeting area, Ebblinghem, was only about twelve miles from St. Venant. I approached Jim Fleming with a view to paying the old place a visit, but as he had been home wounded during our stay in that area he was not keen. Jock Morrison offered to accompany me. We secured a pass from the Squadron Leader, and on the morning of 28 July 1917 set out to walk to Steenbecque, whence we proceeded to Ebblinghem by train. Our first visit was to the farm of one of Jock's old hosts, Jimmy Brisbart, where we received a cordial welcome, and sat down to lunch with the family. They were jolly decent people, pressed us to stay, but having a big round of calls to make in a short time we set off after lunch via the ' Rat and Cat ' for the village. Calling in on our way, we discovered the place chock-full of Australians. They were all half tipsy, and at first suspicious of us, as they took us for police. Eventually they thawed, but we had no wish to linger, as they appeared an uncouth crowd, loud-voiced, and foul-mouthed. I was rather puzzled about them, as I had previously met many of their countrymen up on the Somme and found them delightful fellows. These were for the most part without the free-and-easy, almost gentle manners of the Australians we knew. They resembled more than anything else Dublin corner-boys. I had an opportunity of discussing this sample of Aussies later on with somebody who was connected with them, and he informed me that many Irishmen, attracted by the pay of six shillings a day, had worked their passage to Australia and enlisted in the A.I.F.

Jock and I continued our pilgrimage down to the village, where we dropped into the old 'Maison Commune.' The flag-stones were shining, and we were greeted like long-lost brothers. André, having reached the age of eighteen, was away in the Engineers, and Jean was now the sole male representative of the family in the old place. The father had got worse and was now practically helpless. A stream of soldiers kept coming and going, and to my great disappointment I had no chance to say more than a few words to Anna. This completely spoiled my visit. There was nothing for it but to move along; and, as evening was approaching, pay our last call before getting back, on Mme. Dassonville. The good old lady had not changed in any way, was overjoyed at seeing us, and gave us a feed which put me, at any rate, in good humour again. I was given detailed accounts of all matters connected with the farm, and wished I could have had the chance to lend her a hand again.

Very much disillusioned, but full of good fare, Jock and I set out on our return to St. Venant just as darkness was falling. We had to walk the whole twelve miles, so we struck off on the road leading through Lynde and Morbecque. Our way led through the Australian billeting area. All along the roads were groups of drunken Aussies, who treated us to an assortment of jibes as we passed, and, in one or two cases, taking us for police, actually followed us. But Jock and I looked a pretty tough proposition, so they kept a respectful distance. We reached our lines about 2 a.m., and were on duty as usual next morning at reveille. That was the last of Ebblinghem as far as we were concerned.

It was now decided that the Squadron should hold a sports meeting in a neighbouring field. I was asked by the Squadron Leader to construct a jumping course for the mounted events. With a fatigue party I erected five jumps, a brushwood-and-wattle affair in each corner, and a stiff wall made of corn-sacks filled with earth in the middle. John Lawrence had just returned to us—from somewhere. During his absence his little mare, 'Molly,' had been given to Angus, a young Trooper of the Greys. Being a good jumper, Angus entered her for the jumping competition. But the luckless Angus had never ridden the mare over a jump, and had no idea what he was asking for. The sports passed off very nicely till it came to his turn to go round the jumping course. Molly cleared the four corner obstacles like a bird, then her rider had to take her straight down the middle of the field and negotiate the wall. She made for the jump like a streak of lightning. Angus seemed to have lost control. The mare misjudged the take-off, hit the jump almost with her chest, turned completely over in the air, and landed with her full weight on top of her rider. She struggled to her feet, but the man lay still. At that moment John Lawrence, who was standing close to me, shouted in a voice that could be heard all over the field : " Hurroo ! She's killed the hoodlumbird ! " Angus was carried away more dead than alive. We never saw him again. The sports fizzled out. Before long I wangled John's horse back to him, and he was prouder of her than ever.

It seemed that I was doomed to be a sort of Jack-of-all-trades throughout the war. I now had settled down to running my Troop just as dozens of other Troop Sergeants were doing all around me. Without any warning I was ordered to hand it over to somebody and go away on a month's bullet-and-bayonet course at the 1st Army School. How on earth had they selected me ? There were some thirty sergeants in the regiment, most of whom had never had a change of any sort for years. And what was the use of the course ? Even if I became a good bullet-and-bayonet instructor, I should never be allowed to give any instruction in that line when I returned. Nobody ever did.

All my grousing was of no avail, so one morning I reported to the 1st Army School back in the miserable village of Linghem, just behind Aire. Some three hundred Sergeants from the various units composing the 1st Army assembled with me. We were ushered into the lousiest billets I have ever seen. I was allotted to an empty barn, around whose walls were erected seven or eight tiers of wire-netting beds. Here were housed about a hundred poor devils in absolute squalor and discomfort. The whole barn walked with lice ; no delousing measures were ever taken ; and on waking up and looking round, at any time during the night, one could always see a dozen or more of one's fellows stripped naked and busy with lighted candles, doing all they could to reduce the numbers of vermin.

During this course the sun shone all day and every day. We began work with physical training of the ' O'Grady sez ' and ' Crows and Cranes ' variety. Then followed breakfast. It was served in another verminous, stinking barn. Then came the morning parade of the whole school, followed by the two-mile march to the ranges and bayonet courses. One of the instructors was what one would call in these days a ' pansy.' His uniform was foppish and ridiculous. So was all his behaviour. He saluted and bowed to all female inhabitants of the village, who must have thought him barmy. In his relations with us he tried to pose as a soldier and disciplinarian, but could not quite put it across. The school Sergeant-Major was a young lad, a mere schoolboy, of the Royal Scots, with a squeaking voice and underdone appearance. Our first morning parade nearly led to a scene, so much were we all amused. I found myself, together with a Sergeant of the 2nd Life Guards named Arthur, and another of the 19th Hussars, in a squad of twelve under the command of Sergeant Legros of the Canadian Black Watch. We were a happy squad, and our Sergeant Instructor a fine fellow.

Work on the ranges and bayonet courses was intensive

and interesting. It appears that a move was being made by the powers to bring back the rifle into favour with the men in the ranks. For the past two years the bomb had held pride of place. It was rumoured that many advantages had been lost on the Somme owing to the refusal of the troops to consider anything as a target if it happened to be outside bombing range. With the loss of interest in the rifle the rate of rapid-fire had diminished to nothing, and the bayonet tended to become an implement for chopping wood and mending fires.

From 8 a.m. to 1 p.m. we worked at high speed. There was a small grove beside the ranges, and here the Chief Instructor, a stout Major of the Connaught Rangers, sat all day mopping his face with a handkerchief, watching everything that went on, and bawling out at every instructor who happened to pass near him : " Ginger 'em up like hell ! " We reached the barn for dinner after our morning's work, and two-miles' march back, hungry and hot. The dinner was not fit for pigs. It is difficult to understand how we stood up to such hard work for twelve hours a day with such scandalous food and sleeping quarters. The afternoon was a repetition of the morning, and after a while there were night operations. As usual, the rifle interested me, and when it came to rapid shooting I was well ahead of the others. One instructor could fire twenty-five aimed shots in a minute. So could I after a week or so of practice.

There were lectures on theory, range-finding, use of ground, fire-control, indication of targets, and a dozen other things. I just did sufficient to keep up appearances, and for most of the course had no idea there was to be an examination at the end. This lasted two days, was a mixture of practice and theory, and when the results were published I found I had come second out of the three hundred. The Sergeant whose name headed the list belonged to the Artists' Rifles. I was quite pleased with this, and now looked forward to returning to old Herbert and my Troop. Imagine my dismay when the Company Commander informed me I was to remain behind at the school as instructor for the next course. My friend Arthur of the 2nd Life Guards was also retained.

For the next three weeks I had a squad of young Sergeants of the various London Battalions, and good lads they were. We were very happy together, though my spirit was elsewhere. Arthur and I now billeted in a private house, and had managed a clean-up. Food in the Sergeants' Mess was better, but that is all one can say for it. The Company Commander told me one day on parade that my squad was the best in the school. The next day he cursed me in front of all and sundry because my squad returned singing the popular verson of ' Colonel Bogey ' after night operations. On one or two Sundays I got permission and walked the eight miles to St. Venant, where I spent the day with Jim Fleming and Herbert.

My friend Arthur decided to borrow a bicycle and cycle the fifteen miles to Staple one Sunday to visit a village girl to whom he considered himself engaged. As it happened, it rained hard all day. Arthur returned like a drowned rat and in a frightful rage. He told me he walked straight into the girl's house on arriving in Staple, and had the shock of his life to find his photograph removed from its place on the piano and a picture of a French soldier there instead. The girl and her mother were rather flustered, and from what I gathered, the visit fell rather flat.

The course duly came to an end. The Commandant informed us that the school was going to be dissolved. We very nearly shouted : ' Hurrah ! ' The Portuguese, it seemed, were taking over the area. That was good news. If this change had not taken place I might have been there till the end of the war. I'm certain the regiment would not have worried about me.

Meanwhile the Regiment had moved away from St. Venant, and by cadging lifts in lorries and trudging a few miles I eventually cornered my Troop in a field near Pernes. Nobody was the least bit interested in where I had been, so I was asked no questions by anybody. My batman, Warren, had taken a fancy to old Herbert and had looked after him well. Mr. Peat was now our Troop Officer, and a better one nobody could wish for. Tommy Parker of the ' Skins ' was second Sergeant.

Again we began to lead a gipsy sort of life, wandering

around all over the place. While we were spending a few
days at Camblain Chatelain the order came from Regimental
Headquarters that I was to appear before the C.O. 'What
have I done now?' I asked myself. I was completely at a
loss. I reported and was marched in. The Commanding
Officer took no notice of me for a moment, but went on
writing. Then the Adjutant handed him a paper. He
looked at it, then at me, and barked: "You came second,
huh?" For the life of me I could not make out what he was
getting at. Again he barked: "You came second, huh?"
I gave it up and said nothing. "That's all," mumbled the
C.O. and I was immediately marched out and shooed off
back. For part of the way I was nonplussed as to what all
this could have been about. Then it suddenly dawned on
me that the great man had been congratulating me in his
own way on my success at the 1st Army School. That was
the end of the matter.

A second spell in the line in front of Epehy followed.
Again for some reason I was Quarterbloke, and worked
with my old Drill Sergeant, Tom Phillips, who was then
Regimental Q.M.S. We had an easy time, and our limbers
were in a field back at Villers Faucon. I knew my way
about, so the nightly jaunts with rations were easy. Tom
Phillips was a good man to work under. We were short of
nothing.

The line was not so quiet as on our last visit. There was
quite a lot of shelling of roads and tracks at night, so that
one of my drivers, a burglar in private life, became so
jumpy that I discovered he was paying another driver to
go up to the line at night in his place. I stopped this
practice, and almost the next night was sorry I had done so.
I happened to have to go up with the windy driver alone on
some special errand. We had a half limber and two horses.
The track ran for some way beneath a high bank. Just at
this point on our journey the enemy chose to send over a
feeler, and six shells burst in a bunch just above us. I shall
never forget the state into which this threw my driver. He
lost all control and whimpered like a whipped child. I felt
this would soon be too much for me and I would start
crying myself, so I dismounted him, bundled him, still

s

sobbing, into the half limber, and took charge of the horses myself.

One night the Leicesters were caught relieving in the outposts and both parties almost wiped out with trench-mortars. Shortly afterwards, when our regiment held the outposts, the Germans sent over a strong raiding-party. Fortunately for us, Gus Russell had his machine-gun in one of the posts, and being on the alert managed to do some good shooting. He caught the raiders from a flank and blotted the party out. They were all brought in later by our fellows. The officer in charge of the raid, a Prussian Captain over six feet tall, and dressed in immaculate uniform, including gloves, was laid out for some days on view in a dugout. I never went to see him, not being interested in dead men of any kind, but the dug-out was for a time a sort of Madame Tussaud's.

We were relieved from this sector in time to get ourselves and our horses in some sort of trim for the great part we were promised in the impending battle of Cambrai. Back we trekked through Peronne to our horses, and after the usual preliminaries the Division, in fact the whole of the Cavalry Corps, made its way up to the country behind Cambrai. We entered the village of Chuignolles, known to the troops as 'Chicken-'oles,' on about 18 November, and Mr. Peat and I put our horses in some tumbledown stables constructed long ago by the French. My Troop slept in a large empty hut close by. The weather was cold, but not unpleasant.

The Cambrai push was looked forward to as the opportunity for which the Cavalry had been waiting for years. The whole Corps was to be rushed through the German lines and then get to work on communications and all sorts of things beyond. The idea appealed to us, we didn't see why, profiting by our experience on the Somme in July 1916, it could not be done this time. I have a distinct recollection that the men were eager and hopeful. There was not an unfit horse or man in our Squadron at any rate. We had been told something of the scheme, and Mr. Peat and I knew exactly what we had to do. He was riding Tony, a sturdy little horse and a fine jumper, and of course I had old Herbert, whom nothing short of a tank could stop. In his wallets Mr. Peat carried two bottles of whisky, which we were to share out behind the German lines.

Here is a roll of our Troop at this time :

Troop Officer, Lieutenant J. H. Peat		1st Life Guards (late Middlesex Regt.)	
C. of H. Lloyd, R.		1st Life Guards	Troop Sergeant
21164 Sergeant Parker, T.		6th Dragoons	
2496 Corporal Morrison, J.		1st Life Guards	Bomber
19558	,, Warren, W.	1st Dragoon Guards	Hotchkiss Gun
3489	,, Deane, C.	1st Life Guards	
3647	,, Finlay, W.	,,	Gas, P.T.
3292 Trooper Bertwhistle, P.		,,	
3122	,, Blake, H.	,,	Hotchkiss Gun
21114	,, Cradden, J.	6th Dragoons	Bomber
3275	,, Carpenter, R.	1st Life Guards	Bomber (M.M.)
21091	,, Dowds, J.	6th Dragoons	Hotchkiss Gun
3245	,, Fisher, H.	1st Life Guards	
3535	,, Finn, G.	,,	Bomber, H.G. Pack
21151 S. Smith Ford, A.		6th Dragoons	Farrier
3405 Trooper Greatrex, F.		1st Life Guards	Sniper
3285	,, Hallsworth, F.	,,	Signaller
7873	,, Hutchinson, L.	2nd Dragoons	Stretcher-bearer
3446	,, Lavender, P.	1st Life Guards	Sniper
3119	,, Lowe, W.	,,	
3547	,, Lane, A.	,,	
3330	,, Maunder, R.	,,	
3364	,, Meenehan, W.	,,	Hotchkiss Gun
2500	,, Nisbet, E.	,,	Trumpeter
19618	,, Pigrum, E.	1st Dragoon Guards	
3398	,, Rutter, J.	1st Life Guards	Hotchkiss Gun
2597	,, Smith, W.	,,	Signaller
3270	,, Smith, E. C.	,,	Cook
3373	,, Savage, J.	,,	Hotchkiss Gun
3620	,, Wood, J.	,,	
3445	,, Warren, W.	,,	
3326	,, Wilson, J.	,,	
3828	,, Woodridge, A.	,,	
3680	,, Yates, G.	,,	

We were, for all sorts of reasons, below strength, but the Troop contained a good leaven of experienced soldiers, and we were all fit and well.

The preliminary bombardment at Cambrai began at

6.30 a.m. on 20 November 1917. The Cavalry Corps stood to at dawn. We stood to all day, waiting for an order that never came. Our tempers began to fray and were not improved when we heard that a Regiment of Canadian Cavalry had gone right through the German lines on its own. Nobody knew anything; no orders or explanation were forthcoming, so late in the evening we off-saddled and stood down. There could be only one reaction. The men put their horses snug, then slouched down into ' Chicken-'oles,' where they proceeded with all their might to get drunk.

XXXI

AFTER a week or so of futile mudlarking in the
Cambrai Sector we trekked back to the accompaniment of a snowstorm of some violence. A thick
layer of snow soon covered the whole country-side. Then a
severe frost set in and lasted for some weeks, during which
period more snow fell from time to time. One afternoon,
therefore, within a stone-throw of Christmas, the Regiment
trickled into a group of squalid villages behind Auxi-le-
Château. I had the Troop to myself, my Troop Officer
having come to grief in some way or other. Jim Fleming
found himself in a similar position. Jim was allotted a
village. I was quartered in another about a mile away from
him, where I shared the accommodation with Squadron
Headquarters and had my digs in the Sergeants' Mess.

The inhabitants were, for the most part, hostile. On
marching in, the billeting officer directed me to a huge
farm, spacious enough to provide cover for all my horses
and men. At least it looked like that at first glance.

We skidded into the farmyard on the slippery ground,
and were met inside the gate by the proprietor. He looked
an ugly customer. His greeting consisted in waving his
arms and howling withering imprecations at us in his
native patois. Such a reception was nothing new to us.
On these occasions, experience had taught us the best plan
was to smile at him, enquire politely after his father's health,
and all the time keep moving in. We carried out this
time-honoured plan, nearly flattening him out in the snow
as we did so, and made a bee-line for his barn.

Within it there was ample room for forty horses, but on
looking more closely, the interior was seen to be divided
into two portions of almost equal size by a stout cross-
beam about four feet from the ground. Possession is nine
points of the law, so we sent twenty horses into the access-

ible half without more ado. The old man stood by leering and jabbering. It was plain he hated the sight of us, and hoped we would give it up and move to other quarters.

The horses had to be put under cover at all costs. There was only one door to the barn, and if we persisted in stabling the whole forty there, we had to choose between breaking a second door into the barred half, and cutting a gap in the cross-beam. Suddenly I had an inspiration. Like all his kidney the old boy was a miser. I took a twenty-franc note from my pocket and slipped it to Tommy Parker, saying : " Show this to the old tyke and lead him away on the pretence of wanting to purchase something. Keep him away from here as long as you can." Tommy was an expert at a job of this kind. They were off in a second.

Out came a saw from the pioneer pack, and like lightning I cut a chunk about three feet long from the beam. I took care to saw it obliquely at both ends with a view to replacing it in position afterwards. In went the remaining horses. Plenty of mud was rubbed on the freshly sawn surfaces, all sawdust removed, and the piece of wood put back. Then we scattered, leaving the biggest fool we could find on stable guard.

On one side of the farmyard ran a long outbuilding full of evil-smelling straw. Here the men settled down for the time being. Another outhouse with a hearth at one end was appropriated as cook-house. Then somebody went to the well in search of water, but our hospitable landlord had already removed the chain and bucket. He never replaced them during our term of occupation.

While an attempt was being made at conjuring up some sort of a meal I strolled quietly back to the barn. Everything was peaceful and the horses snug. I had not been there five minutes when I noticed the farmer coming running, swearing like a man possessed. Evidently he had become aware of the disappearance of the surplus horses and feared the worst. I slipped round a corner before he saw me, and watched him. When he reached the doorstep and saw horses in both halves of the barn, he raised his arms to the sky and gave vent to a long howl. He paused a moment where he stood, then stepped gingerly inside and began feeling the cross-beam from end to end. Suddenly the detachable piece came away in his hands. He gazed at it spellbound for a moment. Then he dropped it like a hot brick, dashed away out into the road, and disappeared raising Cain up the village street.

We managed a meal of some sort, after which we returned to the barn to settle up the horses for the night. Everything was proceeding smoothly, when I suddenly remarked our host standing in the doorway again. He hopped in, and after him trooped in solemn procession the Squadron Leader, the Second in Command, and the French Interpreter. I was called forth and accused of cutting a chunk out of the beam. I asked indignantly : " What beam ? Oh, that ! Why, it must have been in that state for ages. Look at it. That doesn't look to me like a fresh cut." The two officers, who were exceeding weary, shared my opinion. The two Frenchmen did not ; but I brazened it out, and got away with it.

The farmer retired within his house, a beaten man. I never set eyes on him again. I made him a little present when I left, though. I had amassed two spare saddles, and I found a few boxes of a thousand rounds of ammunition, corroded and no longer serviceable. The whole cargo went down his well the morning we marched out. That was the only occasion on which I ' committed an offence against an inhabitant of the country in which I was serving.' Looked at in the cold light of to-day, it seems an act of considerable wickedness. However, *à la guerre comme à la guerre*.

A few days saw us fairly well fixed up and making the best of things. Within a week the Brigade took over a piece of the line on the extreme right, next to the French. A party consisting of about half the Squadron went up dismounted. Jim Fleming and I were left behind with half a Troop each and a full complement of horses.

The proximity of Christmas caused our thoughts to veer in the direction of festivities. Meanwhile my Troop had secured a good mess, complete with a kitchen and range, in an *estaminet*. The Sergeants' Mess was, as usual, at that epoch of the campaign, miserable but habitable. Jim Fleming and his men were in clover. A lady in his village, who had two sons at the front, and was one of those great Frenchwomen who helped to preserve any faith we had left in our allies and in humanity in general, had placed a fine empty house at his disposal. There were rooms galore and a spacious hall on the ground floor, in which she installed some tables end to end. To these she added chairs, crockery, and even went to the length of providing white table-cloths.

Christmas Eve was actually upon us before some genius woke up to the deplorable fact that we should have nothing to eat on Christmas day except rations. We knew there was to be an issue of turkey and Christmas pudding, supplied from the depot at home ; but these commodities had a sad knack of diminishing almost to vanishing point whilst *en route* via the official channels.

A collection was made. The officers contributed liberally, and everybody else gave what he could spare. The proceeds were handed to me, together with a G.S. wagon and four horses, and I was ordered to get away to Auxi-le-Château and buy what I could find. My old friends, Drivers Dapper Smith and Harry Pudney, were to accompany me. It was afternoon before we could set out ; the scene of our shopping activities lay ten miles distant, and it had begun to snow for all it was worth.

Darkness had fallen long before we reached the town. We had a nasty journey in the blizzard ; the going was particularly bad down the long, steep hill leading into Auxi. Here we had to walk and help the horses along, as well as manhandle the wagon now and then.

Within the little town everything was spotless in its mantle of snow. The lights from the numerous shops twinkled out at us through the thickly-falling snow-flakes. A more Christmassy-looking little place it would be hard to imagine.

I left Dapper and Harry in the shelter of a wall with the horses while I went further in to spy out the land. I soon came to the market square. Standing at one corner I found the most palatial butcher's shop I have seen. Perhaps its splendour was enhanced by the fairy-like surroundings in which it was set that evening. Anyway, there it was in front of me, all chock-full of joints of meat hanging from hooks in a blaze of light. A broad tier of stone steps led up to the entrance. I mounted these and entered. Within there was not a soul. Suddenly from out the back of the shop appeared a young woman. She was of middle height, very neatly dressed, and very comely. About her was that indescribable air of good breeding and womanliness which distinguishes the best women of France, and is seldom met among women of other countries. She greeted me with a charming smile, and in a jiffy I had bought four excellent legs of mutton. She got somebody to help me with them to my wagon ; then we wished each other the compliments of the season, and I took my leave with a wonderful feeling of contentment. I had actually conversed with a civilized woman who had treated me with a courtesy to which I had long been a stranger. My few minutes' conversation had completely restored my faith in myself and my fellow-men. The war had not driven everybody crazy.

Next I located a greengrocer's, and the remainder of my cash went out on vegetables and fruit. Here we bought some fine apples. Dapper was in the act of taking a bite out of one when into the shop tripped two girls. Immediately they saw us, one of them blabbed out in the accents of the Mile End Road : " Garn, give us a bite." Dapper paused in his efforts and gaped open-mouthed. Harry went all hot and bothered. I felt as if the floor was about to open and swallow me. Luckily we were ready to go, so we grabbed our purchases and bolted. The two flappers screamed out into the street after us, but we quickly turned a corner and heard no more of them. They were the first W.A.A.C.s we had encountered. Somehow we were not cheered by the meeting. The same thought was in the minds of all three of us : ' What the hell are those flappers doing out here ? '

The snow was pelting down harder than ever. We had a terrific job to negotiate the hill again. Right on top, at a cross-roads, stood an *estaminet*. Here we pulled in on the lee side, and leaving Harry with the horses, Dapper and I went in and ordered rum grog. Up it came, hot and strong. Then Dapper relieved Harry. The change-over was repeated once more, and with two stiff glasses of grog inside each of us, the remaining six miles or so of level going were a mere cake-walk.

Next morning the troops were early astir. A feeling of hushed expectancy was in the air. Nothing very inspiring in the way of rations turned up. That is where the Christmas shopping came in. I found myself acclaimed on all sides, and so charitably disposed were the troops that had I accepted but a small fraction of the drinks offered to me, I might have passed Christmas Day and the ensuing Boxing Day in a state of complete oblivion. Cooks were all excitement. Here at last was an opportunity for that long-suffering and grossly maligned body of men to show what they really could turn out in the way of a dinner.

The cooks surpassed all expectations. With midday came the best dinner we had had for years. It was the sort of feast whose ghost would haunt us on hungry days to come. Still, we were bent on living in the moment at hand, and letting the future take care of itself.

I received an invitation to dinner from both Troops. These I declined as it was impossible to be in both villages at once, and if I accepted one, the other Troop might feel slighted. I decided to have dinner in the Sergeants' Mess, then drop in on my own Troop for a drink and a sing-song immediately afterwards.

When I made an appearance everybody was full of good fare. The meal was voted by all a howling success. Now things were cleared away, drinks sent round, smokes lit up, and the Captain came in to wish us a Merry Christmas. We duly drank his health, proclaimed vigorously to the whole population of Picardy that he was 'a jolly good fellow,' and he took his departure. An ancient piano stood in a corner of the *estaminet*, and with its faltering support we roared the old songs and choruses lustily till four o'clock.

A message arrived from Jim Fleming's Troop saying I was expected to look in on them early in the evening, when they would be having their concert. Jim came down to

the Mess for tea with that twinkle in his eye I knew so well
and which announced to all the world that he was feeling
pleased with everything and everybody. After tea, horses
were attended to and he and I strolled together up the
mile of white road to the other village. The sing-song was
about to commence. We took our seats at the head of the
long table and proceeded to show the French bumkins
what British soldiers could do in the way of a song or two,
given the right atmosphere.

Unlike that of my own Troop, this particular sing-song
had a somewhat sad ending. For some reason or other the
supply of beer in that village had run out in the afternoon.
The troops hated wine, but money was plentiful, so before
Jim and I arrived on the scene each man had provided
himself with a bottle of benedictine. We immediately
foresaw dire results, but Christmas is Christmas, so we
kept our forebodings to ourselves. They now proceeded,
in intervals between songs, to drink the liqueur in generous
gulps from their enamel pint mugs. We warned them to
ease up, and slipped out quietly before very long to pay a
visit to Madame, Jim's landlady. She had made him
promise that we would call in during the evening.

How such a woman could have been produced in such
an environment will always remain a mystery. The village,
even in the most prosperous times of peace, could not
have been anything more than a centre of much squalor
and hard toil. In such surroundings she had lived her life.
We had met her sort before, the very salt of the earth,
refined, intelligent, calm, and kind, so we just marvelled
again and left it at that. If we had been her own sons she
could not have shown us more kindness. She made no
fuss or show. She was just her natural self. The ensuing
hour is one of the bright spots in my memory.

At about 9 p.m. we stood up and took our leave. Once
out in the roadway both our minds had but a single
thought : ' What about the lads and their benedictine ? '
We made straight for the billet. What a picture the scene
in the hall would have made ! There they were in their
places, just where they sat when we left them an hour ago.
Nearly every man gripped a bottle or a mug in his hand,

and every one was fast asleep where he sat. Some had fallen forward; others leaned backward; all were dead to the world.

This was a serious state of affairs on a winter night with snow on the ground and a sharp frost. Quickly we collected all their blankets, and with half of them made a bed in a corner. Then one by one we conveyed our unconscious friends and laid them down gently thereon. Not one opened an eye during the process. We then covered them over with the other blankets, and having collected the remains of the benedictine and extinguished all lights, left them to their dreams, if any.

Back we ambled to the Mess to report all correct to the Sergeant-Major. The moon shone brightly on the glistening snow. It was the sort of Christmas night our grandparents used to describe to us long ago. As we entered the village gusts of children's laughter reached us on the air. Then, on rounding a bend in the road, a glorious sight met our eyes. Twenty or thirty little boys and girls, with Ted Pettit at their head, were sliding in a long line back and forwards on the frozen pond. How old Ted was enjoying himself! The kiddies, too, were having the time of their lives. It seemed a sin to disturb them, but after a while we hauled Ted away from his playmates and took him along to the Mess for supper. After supper Ted and I insisted on seeing Jim 'home.'

A surprise awaited me when we got back. An order had come for me to go up at once into the line at Vermand. My departure was timed for 3 a.m. Obviously some Sergeant had become a casualty, and I was to take his place.

Sergeant-Major Hindenburg had retired for the night. It was now getting on for midnight. There did not seem to be much sense in my going to bed for three hours when the next night would in all probability find me looking over some parapet or other away up in the outpost line. Ted Pettit and Freddy Whittle saw things in the same light, so we dug out the man of the house and inquired if he had any champagne. He had.

We sat and sipped and talked all sorts of rubbish. Freddy's dislike of the Sergeant-Major vented itself in a

torrent of abuse. He had no picnic with old Hindenburg ;
indeed his patience had always been something to marvel
at. Now, the springs of his long pent-up hate loosened by
the action of the wine, he stood up and roared repeatedly :
" To hell with Hindenburg ! " Ted and I were endeavour-
ing to make him sit down, and he was still yelling his
war-cry at the top of his voice, when the door opened
softly and there stood Hindenburg in person on the
threshold. Freddy subsided, and Hindy without a word or
a sound turned and departed just as he came.

That definitely put an end to our Christmas celebrations.
Next morning Freddy lost his job as Sergeant-Major's
batman, and I set out for Arras, where I was to catch a
train of some sort and work my way up to the line.

XXXII

I CAN no longer recall anything concerning my journey, except that it seemed endless and I was half-frozen with the terrible cold. I reached the wagon-lines the following morning, where I discovered the Farrier, Snapper Knight, busy preparing the Christmas dinner, the materials for which had just reached him. I whiled away the time till dark, when I made my way forward with the rations.

My unit happened to be out in reserve. The troops lay in dug-outs and tin-huts in and around the grounds of a dilapidated château. Rumour had it that this property belonged to the Duke of Rutland. Everything was in such a state of desolation that I am sure nobody grudged it to His Grace. Absolutely nothing survived, except the ten-foot brick wall all round the garden, and that had several wide bites taken out of it here and there by shells. The 2nd Life Guards lay inside the wall ; we outside it. Snow covered everything to a depth of several inches, and the ground beneath was frozen hard.

The dug-outs occupied by the men were shallow, crumbling, and verminous. Remaking these would have been a profitable job in more respects than one. No attempt was made to organize working-parties or exercise of any kind which would set the men's blood in circulation. The intense cold forced them to spend long hours within these miserable holes.

The N.C.O.s, the usual old gang, Gus Horsman, Jerry Shepperd, Charlie Wilcox, Young Yarnell, Alec Macdonald, Bogey Giles, George Boylan, and myself, had for domicile a tin hut with wire-netting bunks all round, and a stove in the middle. There was somewhere a Sergant-Major, Old Bill, but he did not condescend to mix with us. Space was very limited, and the inactivity extremely painful. In our present capacity we seemed to be fulfilling no useful purpose whatever.

In the evening when the rum arrived, we mixed our
ration with condensed milk and water and warmed it on
the stove. This brew relaxed the tension somewhat and
relieved the dreadful boredom. We sat on our bunks
round the stove, and woke up gradually to the extent of
carrying on an intelligent conversation. Once or twice
we even rose to the heights of song. Old Gus was then
in his element, and the roof and sides of our abode vibrated
to the strains of ' Just a song at twilight.'

The men were considerably worse off below ground.
Their existence was no better than that of the rats who
shared it with them. Small wonder if they grew grumpy
and touchy the very first day. A soldier will carry on with
any sort of work, however strenuous or dirty, and nobody
who understands him will take any notice of grumbling as
he does so. He is perfectly happy at work ; the reaction
of his body to exertion is good for him, and he is aware of
this fact. A state of discontent brought on by a period
of helpless inaction is a serious matter. Much trouble here
and there in the war might have been avoided if only men
had been kept busily engaged in some intelligent, useful
occupation.

We had orders to stand to at dawn and sunset, just as in
the front line. The morning after my arrival I came as
near to being mixed up in a mutiny as anybody could wish.
One officer with our party was reputed to be brave and
resourceful in action, which he undoubtedly was, but he
seemed not to care a straw about the feelings or comfort
of the men, and even appeared to enjoy irritating them.

On this particular morning we turned out in the dark
and formed up as usual. It was intensely cold and raw.
One of the officer's favourite tricks when on duty was to
keep us waiting, and finally to come creeping up from
some unexpected direction to see if he could catch us in
loose formation. Long before he appeared we were frozen
to the bone. Men broke ranks and walked about ; some
even attempted a smothered smoke ; all were talking.
Suddenly out of the darkness, already slowly changing to
grey, came the officer's voice : " Put those cigarettes out !
Stand still ! Stop that talking, or I'll keep you standing

here till eight o'clock ! " From out the rabble, now getting back into ranks, one or two scarecrows lifted up their voices and shouted back to him some obscene words of advice. He was not expecting this. " Take those men's names ! " he screamed. " I heard what they said."

Nobody moved. One could feel a sort of electricity in the air. It only required somebody in the ranks to say another word, and pandemonium would have broken loose. Somebody, I believe it was old Gus, had the presence of mind to get the N.C.O.s together, march up to the Sergeant-Major, and report all present and correct. The Sergeant-Major took the report, passed it to the officer, and the men were ordered to stand down. No action of any kind followed. But it had been a near thing.

This prevailing spirit of discontent and mischief showed itself in other directions during those dreary days. A most excellent and popular officer, Major Tom Gurney, commanded the detachment of 2nd Life Guards. He was served in the capacity of Q.M.S. by an equally excellent and most conscientious N.C.O., Micky Sparrow. On the night before we moved up into the outposts the rations arrived in limbers as usual about 8 p.m. Micky Sparrow drew his limbers up to a hole in the garden wall, and dumping his supplies on our side of it, had them carried through to his own territory by hand. Amongst the load was a wooden box containing two gallon jars of rum. Micky took this lovingly from the limber with his own hands, and deposited it tenderly on the ground. He then turned his back on it for a fraction of a second to get something else from the wagon. When he turned round again the case of rum had vanished ! For a short spell Micky went stark raving mad. A hurried search of the ground in the immediate neighbourhood conducted with the aid of a flash-lamp revealed no traces of it. The precious liquor had been spirited away in the twinkling of an eye.

As is usual with disasters, the tidings reached Tom Gurney's ears within the space of a few minutes. Up he rushed to the limbers, swearing and shouting for the luckless Micky. A small crowd of spectators had collected by that time, and Tom was heard to roar in his excitement :

" If you don't find the stuff before morning, I'll have you stuck up against this ruddy wall and shot." This unprecedented smash and grab operation took people's breath away. There never had been anything in the history of the Brigade to approach it for the sensation it caused at the time. Suspicion fell on one or two groups of playboys in my Squadron, but without result. The rum was never recovered ; nor was the theft ever brought home to anybody. The grim secret was well kept by just three people —the two who actually stole it, and myself, who a little later and quite innocently became the third.

Within the château grounds stood a canteen of sorts, wherein one could purchase cigarettes, biscuits, and hot cocoa. It was not much frequented by our men. Frenchmen from the batteries of 75's immediately on our right swarmed there. The poor devils had no money, but their industry in making cigarette lighters out of cartridge cases was astonishing. They tried to turn an honest drink or smoke by selling and bartering these as well as rings and other trinkets.

Every day the Germans shelled the place, but none fell on us. Our successors were not so fortunate ; for the night after we moved up Fritz dropped one right into the canteen, wiping it out with everybody in it. We were lucky again. Small wonder that throughout the Brigade we were known as ' God's Own.'

On the fourth evening we paraded after sunset and made our way up into the outposts. The going was good on the dry, hard snow. It was pleasant to stretch one's legs again and to get clear of the pettifogging existence of the reserve line. Our way led for about two miles along a sunken road. It was the deepest road of the kind I have seen. A good way along we came to a quarry. Here the cooks dropped out and repaired to the cookhouse which was dug into one side of the large pit. Another half-mile or so and we reached a mine-crater, with barbed wire just beyond it. Here we climbed up two flights of steps on the right and found ourselves in a communication-trench. Three hundred yards along this, and we halted and got on with the relief.

Half an hour later I found myself with a hotchkiss gun

T

section and a few riflemen in one of the outposts about forty yards in front of the front line. I was also responsible for two small posts on either side of me with a Corporal and three or four men in each. My post was a deep, well-constructed affair with fire-step in front and on both sides. It was in three small compartments so as to localize the effects of a shell. Head cover was poor. It consisted of a biggish dug-out on the right front, and a tiny, one-man shelter on the left of the front fire-step. The latter I made my own ; the remainder fitted into the other.

Everybody was alert all night in the outposts, and the sentry who during the day stood on the fire-step, went out over the top as soon as it became dark. In front was a broad belt of wire, and the sentry's chief occupation was to keep his eyes glued on the wire and his ears alert for the snip of wire-cutters.

The whole of the ground was covered with snow. It was still freezing. Solid ice was thick over every part of the posts. We dared not mount our hotchkiss gun, nor could we leave our rifles on the fire-step for fear of the moving parts becoming frozen together. Never before had we experienced such Arctic conditions, but there was one great compensation—there was no mud.

Well, here we were for three days and nights. My right-hand man was Joe Tregilgas, as stout a fellow as one could wish for in the line, an excellent Corporal, but possessing one outstanding characteristic which I knew of old—he was an impulsive beggar. His first action on taking over was to ram a S O S rocket down his rifle-barrel and sling it over his shoulder. That gave me a turn straight away, but Joe was too good a fellow to fall out with, so I let him carry on. I lived in a state of anxiety all the time, in case he should accidentally touch the beastly S O S off. If he had done so, we should all have been blown sky-high in about two minutes.

Joe and I set about taking stock of things. We had signed for ten boxes of ammunition and twelve boxes of bombs, and trusted to the honesty of the outgoing tenants. Now when we located these stores beneath the fire-step, we found to our dismay that the whole lot, with the exception of two boxes of ammunition and two of bombs, was frozen up as hard as a rock and absolutely immovable. The ground round about might have been solid stone for all the impression one could make on it with a pick-axe. Here was a pretty situation if we were attacked. Raids on both sides took place frequently in the snow. The raiders dressed in white and were invisible at any distance against the white background. Never mind. The gun team had their boxes with them, and each man had two hundred rounds. We should be badly off for bombs; but we must just chance it and trust to luck again.

The first night was uneventful, except for the arrival in our midst of an issue of hot stew at midnight and tea towards morning. In the daytime we managed to get some sleep.

On the second night we were feeling quite at home in our cold storage. Soon after dark Joe and I were having a quiet chat at the back of the post when we noticed somebody creeping across in our direction from the line. It turned out to be an extremely young brand-new officer, whom we had never seen before. He introduced himself and informed us he had been sent out to inspect the post and especially to see the ammunition supply. Joe and I nearly chucked a fit when we heard this. "I want to see all the rifle-ammunition and all the bombs," he burbled. I had run up against this type before. I knew by the cut of his jib that he would not depart till he had seen, or believed he had seen, what he had been sent out to see.

With a politeness and style that would have made a West End shopwalker turn green with envy, I shepherded the babe to my tiny funk-hole and invited him to be seated inside. He had barely room to sit upright. I now dropped the sack which did duty as a door, and passed him in a candle-end which he lit and stuck on a ledge. A hurried whisper in Joe's ear, and our plan of action was arranged. "How many boxes of ammunition have you?" came from behind the sack. "Ten, sir," I replied. Joe took his station by the door; I knelt just inside. Five times Joe passed me in each box and five times I submitted to the bright young fellow inside for his scrutiny, then passed it back to Joe again. I had some trouble in persuading our visitor that the boxes must not be opened till the contents were needed. "But how am I to know what is in them?" he asked. With a superhuman effort I stifled an appropriate reply and said: "The seals are unbroken, so there can be no doubt about them."

"Are the bombs sealed too? How many have you got?"

"No, sir. We have twelve boxes."

"Good," he chuckled delightedly to himself, "then I shall be able to see each bomb?"

"Yes, sir."

The same trick was repeated with the bombs. I handed in the boxes open. He actually lifted each bomb from its place, fondled it awhile, and then replaced it. His inspection finished he bade us good night and departed highly satisfied. So were Joe and I. That young innocent would have raised old Harry if he had discovered how we were actually fixed.

Nothing cropped up to break the stillness and peace which reigned all round us, and on the following night we were relieved and went back slightly into support.

While in the front line and supports we worked by Squadrons. In reserve we concentrated into a Regiment again. There were three Sergeants in my Squadron party, George Boylan, Bogey Giles, and myself. The pukka Sergeant-Major was not up with us, so George, being the senior, proclaimed himself Sergeant-Major, and Bogey Giles went one better by either losing or breaking his false teeth. This necessitated Bogey's immediate departure down to Hospital for a new set. I now found myself the sole Sergeant for duty in the Squadron. My job for the next three or four days was a twenty-four hour one, a full night and day occupation.

In the daytime the Captain gave me a batch of thirty men and set me on to the draining of the communication-trench in preparation for a possible thaw. At night I had to see two hot rations of stew and tea distributed in the posts and line to our successors. These commodities were drawn from the cookhouse in the quarry by a carrying party, who bore them to the line in specially designed containers carried on the back like metal rucksacks. It was my business to see that all those in the line were supplied each time before I came back to the quarry. This was no child's play. The going was rough and slippery. Our stretch of front was comparatively long. More than once a carrier's heels went from under him on an icy slope and he measured his length on the ground. None of them was ever hurt, and no stew or tea ever lost. The packs were very strong and securely screwed down. Carriers were not employed on daytime duties.

The two cooks of my Squadron were, like myself, twenty-four-hour men. They cooked for the supports in the daytime and for the outposts at night. Great fellows they were. Hard cases both who, behind the line, dodged everything they possibly could, but when in or near it they invariably rose to the occasion and gave of their best. They were Sydney Cross and S. H. Shaw.

On our second night in support I returned to the cookhouse after the stew round absolutely dead beat. I flung myself down on a fairly dry patch of floor with an overpowering desire to get off my feet and legs for a while. I must have looked pretty well all in. Cross and Shaw noticed my condition. I saw them exchange glances and other signs. Then Cross produced from a cranny in the rocky wall a water-bottle full of rum, mixed some with hot water and sugar, and Shaw passed me the steaming mug. I sat up and sipped it slowly. It warmed me up inside and made a new man of me. I rolled myself up in a blanket and slept like a babe till the tea delivery.

When I got back I was given another tot in a mug of tea, and before slipping off for another short nap, I must have looked my curiosity, though nothing in the world would have induced me to express it in words. All the laws of hospitality were dead against such a step. I, personally, could not get a tot of rum beyond my ration for love or money. Shaw's face lit up into a broad grin. " Arrah go to sleep now and forget it," he said to me. " That's a drop of ould Micky Sparrah's, if ye'd like to know." So that was that.

The support line was a well-constructed, business-like affair. The trenches bore the hall-mark of German thoroughness, and were liberally sprinkled with forty-foot

dug-outs, all facing the wrong way round. I had survived
my spell of day-and-night work and had been relieved, I
forget how, or exactly when. George Boylan and I now
shared duties in this line. We both hated dug-outs; we
found they had a demoralizing effect, so we slept in a hole
in the parapet. It was just wide enough for two, and had
a covering of corrugated iron and turf. We were shelled
pretty frequently here, and it was heavy while it lasted.
One night in particular I remember we lay very still while
shell after shell falling just round the corner shook the
ground all round us and sprinkled our funk-hole with odds
and ends.

Then one night rain set in. The snow disappeared, and
with it all our tracks. We felt like rabbits in a freshly cut
corn-field; everything looked strange, and we had to
start all over again finding our way about the country-side
in the dark. It rained just long enough to convert the hard,
frosty going into slush.

Casualties occurred in the outposts and support line, and
I took part in a particularly vile raid. I want to forget all
that, anyway.

While in support, George and I went along nightly to
the Sergeant-Major, Old Bill, to report and receive orders.
He lived in solitary state in a cosy dugout nicely lined with
match-boarding and dug deep beneath the edge of a small
quarry. We usually arrived about 9 p.m. We had no
great liking for Old Bill. He was an austere person who
gave himself airs in our presence, and he had a tremendous
idea of his own importance. There is no doubt he was a
good soldier in his own particular way. When in 1918 he
reached the limit of age or service, he refused to go home.
He was killed in the line a month later.

He never neglected the elements of hospitality, and
always produced a mess-tin of hot rum and milk, which we
gratefully sipped, while listening, or pretending to listen
to him as he sat there expounding his principles. He was a
stickler for principles. According to him, nothing could
be more unprincipled than N.C.O.s who took advantage of
the opportunity conferred on them by their rank to appropriate more than their just ration of soldiers' rum. "In

fact," he would say, " I've actually known N.C.O.s who always carried a water-bottle full. Now that sort of thing didn't oughter happen among good soldiers." Of course we agreed, and cleared off at the first suitable lull after the rum and milk were finished.

A week or two passed and then we were ordered to stand by to hand over the sector to a relief on a certain evening. The rain seemed to save itself up specially for those occasions. It came down in sheets ; the relief was hours late ; we stood about in the open cursing and waiting. Old Bill's dug-out happened to be just behind where we stood. I heard my name called in an undertone, and on looking round saw George standing beckoning in the doorway. I slipped away unnoticed and found George all alone. The Sergeant-Major's equipment hung on a peg. " Just feel the old man's bottle," said George. I did. It was chock-full. Out came the stopper. Rum! Not another word was spoken between us. In record time the precious spirit was transferred fifty-fifty to our own bottles. Another second and we had rejoined the troops outside in the rain without being seen or missed. Old Bill lived up to his principles that night. There were many poor devils waiting outside in the downpour whose need was greater than his.

The night was well advanced when the relief was finally completed. Wet to the skin, cold, and hungry, we marched miles through the mud and rain till we reached a light railway. Here awaiting us were undersized trains, consisting of roofless wooden trucks which seemed too wide for the narrow-gauge track. They were covered all over inside with inches of slimy mud.

Each truck was filled to capacity and away we went. The American driver seemed to take us round sharp bends on one wheel. Most of us were too dead with fatigue to care what happened. A train behind us, full of people from another unit, actually left the rails, turned turtle, and killed a number of men.

We travelled all the rest of the night. Daybreak found us detraining at a sort of terminus where our horses awaited us. We mounted and rode back to billets.

XXXIII

WE were not left languishing for long in billets. About a week after our return, we paraded one morning in pitch darkness and the whole division started marching back again in the direction of the line. Away we rode up over the old familiar roads and through the desolate country of the Somme to Peronne, and from there to a hole at the back of God Speed, called Trefcon. Our destination was again the extreme right of the British line. I remember one day during our uneventful progress as I rode beside Jim Fleming I was suddenly overcome by a premonition that this was our last ride together. I communicated my thoughts to Jim, but that hard-headed Scot had no use for my ' blethers.' I was right, though. It was our last ride together.

There was no sign of human habitation at Trefcon. The horses were stabled in well-constructed huts round which the mud was a yard deep. In the roofs were a number circular holes made by bombs dropped from the air. Each hut was divided into three or four compartments by stout barriers of earth to localize the effects of bomb bursts and save some of the horses in case of a direct hit. The men not in the line were quartered in foul huts where it was impossible to get warm. These were surrounded by a deep trench to provide cover. They were a nuisance, as people kept falling into them in the dark. We were shelled and bombed frequently. Altogether it was a depressing area and our existence was again drab and pointless in the extreme.

After a couple of weeks of this sickening mudlark, I was suddenly sent on ten days' leave. It came as a godsend. Again I just missed the longer period of fourteen days which was introduced shortly after I returned. I had my horse saddled, and accompanied by somebody to bring him back, rode into Peronne. I took train in what remained of Peronne station, and that was the last I was to see of my good old horse, Herbert. He developed eye-trouble while I was away, was sent to the sick-lines, and must have been still there on 21 March when the Germans came over. From Peronne I travelled to Chaulnes, a busy junction in the midst of unspeakable desolation, thence to Boulogne, and so to Birmingham, where my family had now settled. I had a very important mission to carry out on the way. George Hindy confided in me that he was due for leave shortly and was going to get married. He entrusted to my care a letter for his future wife; it was too important to trust to the Army Postal Authorities, and I was to post it immediately on my arrival in London.

My leave passed quietly among my people in their new home. Again I had to buy riding-pants to make myself look presentable. At home they could not understand why I could not get to see my brother in the 2nd Dublin Fusiliers who formed part of the 5th Army just alongside us. Poor devil, he was already in the outposts with his machine-gun section, and there he remained till the great attack on 21 March. My leave soon passed. It was my third in three and a half years. Little did I guess how soon I was to be back in England again. In those days it seemed as if the war was destined to go on for ever. Long ago we had lost the ability to picture to ourselves what life would be like without it.

On my way back, while riding along a track between Peronne and Trefcon in the early morning, I was surprised to see a little boy of about eight or nine crawl out from a hole in the ground and set off up the track with a jug in his hand. On closer examination the hole proved to be the entrance to a cellar where a house must have once stood. I called out good morning to him and asked him where he was going. "Going to fetch the milk," he shouted back, and went on toddling up the road. Some poor devils of civilians with children were hanging on to the remains of their homes by the skin of their teeth. I often wondered where he could get milk in that place, and what was his fate in the terrible days of the German break-through.

I hardly had time to look round in Trefcon before I was packed off on a course of instruction to the 5th Army School at Pont Remy. Any port in a storm! It could not be any worse than Trefcon.

As the weather was particularly vile during most of the time, the course was rather uninteresting. The school was more comfortable than the 1st Army School, but far inferior to it in other respects. The very first morning on parade my Platoon Officer Instructor, a smart young Lieutenant, came up and greeted me with : " Hallo ! Glad to see one of the old regiment here. You belong to the First, don't you ? " " Yes, sir," I replied. " I don't suppose you'll remember me," he went on. " I joined the First Life Guards in nineteen-sixteen. I was in Corporal Roache's Troop at Knightsbridge." Jolly good ! A stout fellow ! Joined up in 1916 and here he was now, my Platoon Officer Instructor. A fat lot he could teach me ! But that was the price one had to pay for being a regular soldier.

However, we had some fun there. It was not in the nature of things to collect in one place a quantity of officers and men from an Army Corps which included the 16th Irish Division without an occasional lark. Our outstanding effort was a burlesque production of *Chu Chin Chow*. This was a very fine piece of work, and ran for three nights. A blood-and-thunder officer from the staff lectured us on the best methods of exterminating Germans. We had met this sort before. A wonderful fellow ! We could not help wondering how many Germans he had killed, and concluded pretty few.

The middle of March had come before the course fizzled out. In the meantime, all unknown to me, it had been decided to dismount the Household Cavalry and convert them into Machine-Gun Battalions. For this purpose they had been moved back round Abbeville, and I was able to walk from the school to billets in a straggling village. Many of the horses had gone already, and some of the older Dragoons were being sent home. The whole place was overshadowed by gloom. Not that we minded being machine-gunners or anything else. We had had a taste of most things in the campaign ; but parting with our horses

who were almost part of ourselves and who had shared
everything with us for three years was a heavy blow. We
had never been given a chance as cavalry. The opportunity occurred more than once, but it had been allowed to
slip, as at Cambrai, and we had been left in the lurch.
There was a certain amount of bitterness over this. But it
was too late now. Our riding days were over and done
with.

Almost immediately on rejoining I was detailed to proceed with the remaining horses to Marseilles, where they
were to be handed over to the Indian Cavalry Depot. This
meant that our old friends were bound eventually for the
Near East and would never see home again. There were
one hundred and eighty all told from the three Regiments.
Captain Matthay was in charge. Immediately he met me
he asked what had become of Herbert, and was very grieved
when I told him. I was the senior N.C.O. The others were
Martin of the 2nd and Nutty Webb of the Blues.

We paraded next morning at daybreak and I rode
Nesbit's old steed Albert to the station at Long. We were
a sad little cavalcade, the last remnants of three fine Regiments, riding barebacked in a straggling, heartless line,
along the desolate country road in the chill of dawn.

It was the morning of the fateful 21 March. Just as we
came near the station the sun was coming up out of the
mist. All at once the bombardment opened up away behind
us. So violent was it that even back at Long the air was
full of its din and the ground trembled beneath our feet.
We held our breath and listened. It was 'the day' which
we felt in our bones had been coming for weeks. It seemed
a foolish move to break up a Cavalry Division and send it
back from the very spot where the attack was delivered just
a bare week before it came. There can be no doubt that
as the Germans advanced in the open we would have been
useful both for mounted and dismounted work.

For a few moments our little party stood spellbound,
trying to imagine what it must have been like up above,
and yet thankful in a way to be out of the mess. For a mess
it was. Captain Matthay telephoned for orders, but was
told to proceed. Into each truck we put eight horses, two

trusses of hay, a sack of corn, and two soldiers. Inside half an hour we were steaming away for Marseilles. I remember everybody was very silent for the first day of the journey. There was also some difficulty with the horses. They kept falling down one by one in the trucks. The track was bumpy and the floors soon slippery. It was no joke sorting out eight plunging, kicking horses, one of whom was down, in the confined space and darkness of the beastly old truck. The journey lasted three days and three nights ; weather was fine and grew better as we travelled south. It was not too bad once the horses had got their sea-legs.

Arrived at Marseilles, a detachment of Indian Cavalry under a tall, black-bearded Sergeant-Major, was waiting on the siding. They took over in quick time. It was a cold-blooded business, and I got out of the way as fast as possible. I was recalled by a crash behind me on the siding. On looking round I saw little Sally in a heap on the cobblestones. It appears a young Indian had jumped on her back so suddenly that, stiff as she was, she lost her footing and fell. I looked round just in time to see poor old Sally standing with her head up in the air, looking the very picture of indignation. Immediately the Indian Sergeant-Major approached the young cavalryman, landed him a terrific kick, and cursed him violently for five minutes in his native tongue.

We then took up our kits and marched across the town to a rest camp pitched on terraces on a hill overlooking the Mediterranean. Here we had to wait till sufficient men could be collected going north to justify making up a train. The camp was pleasant ; we were shown every hospitality, and Captain Matthay was kind enough to raise some money for us and see that we had everything we needed for our comfort. Only an odd piece of news reached us now and then from the line, and that was not reassuring.

We were held up for a fortnight, and during that time we explored the town under the expert guidance of a gigantic sailor named 'Lofty' and his diminutive pal 'Titch' of the Middlesex.

It was a most pleasant sojourn, though when all was

quiet we could not help wondering what was happening to the Regiments up in the Somme area.

The journey back from Marseilles was monotonous in the extreme. We were turned out of the train in Rouen and shut up in rest billets. This pleasant caravanserai was surrounded by barbed wire; the sleeping quarters were verminous, and the neighbourhood bristled with Red-caps. Two or three days' rest here very nearly drove us to desperation; but in the end we were herded into a train and sent up north where we rejoined our units in camp at Étaples.

It was now the beginning of April. Immediately we split up into two groups. The N.C.O.s went along to the Machine-Gun School at Camiers for a six weeks' course. A large draft which included instructors, came out from home and instructed the men in camp. Most of the old Dragoons and our farriers were now sent home.

The Machine-Gun School lay just behind the sand-dunes east of the village of Camiers. We were quartered in bare huts, where we slept on the floor. The weather during the whole six weeks was magnificent. In a little copse behind our hut the singing of the nightingales kept us awake at night. We were a very happy, hardworking crowd, who laboured with a will for twelve hours a day, mostly doubling with guns, tripods, and boxes of ammunition through the deep sand. At the end of our little day we still had sufficient energy left to play terrific football matches in which the shining lights were Jack Johnson and Joe Green of the Blues, Mackintosh of the 2nd, and George Boylan and Jim Fleming of the 1st.

To the school staff our strength and energy were a marvel. Being on an average of small stature, a gun or tripod made a load for any of them, whereas we flipped the things about like walking-sticks. The instructors were excellent fellows, but very young. Once or twice we caused strained relations on parade by smiling at their efforts to treat us like recruits. Finally they grew wise and attempted no more to reform us. They were wonderful gunners and very proud of their school record time for running a hundred yards with gun and tripod, mounting gun, and firing one shot. I forget what their actual time was, but Jim Fleming and I resolved quietly to lower it for them before leaving the school. One morning towards the end of the course we obtained permission to make the attempt. Jim acted as No. 1 and I did No. 2. We took about two seconds off their record. Like good sportsmen, they were not peeved, but regarded it in the light of a compliment to their instruction.

Once a fortnight when George Beasneys came over from camp and paid us, Jim Fleming and I each drew a hundred francs. That evening we ate grilled steak and chips and drank a bottle of good wine. This wine was a brand we had not met before, and so good was it that our fortnight's supply of money never lasted us more than a week.

The course finished, back we marched to camp at Etaples and set about forming and equipping the new battalion. We were now the 1st Battalion Guards' Machine-Gun Regiment. I took over No. 4 Section of 'D' Company. In accordance with tradition the distribution of equipment began with No. 1 Section of 'A' Company, and by the time my turn came, I had to take just what was left. My Section did not have even sufficient tents to accommodate them all. I quite forget who my Section Officer was, but I must have had one of some sort.

One could not very well have chosen a worse site than that on which our camp was pitched. An important railway, with a bridge fifty yards from the end of our lines, ran along the east edge. Immediately across the line were two large general hospitals. Along to our left among the dunes was an extensive ammunition-dump ; and down towards the town lay a reinforcement camp, in and out of which large bodies of troops were continually moving. All these features made an ideal target for enemy planes. A German airman anywhere above the square mile of ground could not fail to hit something. They came along too, night after night. One evening about 10 p.m. we stood and gaped open-mouthed as hut after hut in the hospitals across the way was blown sky high. The huge red crosses were illuminated at night ; but apparently airmen don't care.

The evening of 19 May saw us finally and completely formed in our new unit. The last of the old stagers were bound for home next day. Hindy and Beasneys were going, and Snuffy Webb and Gus Horsman had come out to take their places. By way of a send-off, we gave a swell concert in the mess. The old songs were sung all over again and choruses roared vigorously. Bella Bently got up and sang 'If you were the only girl in the world,' and George Beasneys, being well primed, recited 'Kissing Cup' as he had never done before. It was a rousing evening. Jim Fleming and I sat together taking it all in, and helping now and then with a chorus.

At about 11 p.m. a warning came that enemy planes were on the move overhead, so the concert terminated, lights were extinguished, and we moved away to our tents. I still had no shelter, so Jim Fleming invited me to share a corner of his tent. I lay down with my feet just at the tent door. The other inmates besides Jim and me were George Boylan, Jock Boyles, and Waspe. In the tent on our left were Hindy, Beasneys, Snuffy Webb, and Gus Horsman. On our right was a store-tent wherein slept Trumpeter Godwin and a storeman. There were eleven persons altogether in the three tents.

All was quiet so far, and we were just comfortable in our blankets when old Beasneys came scratching round our tent and asking for a match. The drone of planes could be distinctly heard overhead, so somebody told him to run off to bed. But he must have got a match from somewhere, for the next instant he actually struck a light outside our tent. A fraction of a second later I heard the hiss of a falling bomb; there was a blinding flash, and then silence, except for a groan here and there among the wreckage of the tents. I felt nothing in the way of pain. I tried to stand up, but discovered I could not. My left leg was smashed. I then caught sight of my right hand as I lifted it up to my face. There was a large hole in the back of it. Still I felt nothing, and all around me there seemed to be no signs of movement. I shouted for someone to come and pull us out. Along came little John Cangley of the 'Skins.' He got hold of me, lugged me out on to the grass, tied me up as best he could in the darkness, and stuck close to me.

We were finally all taken and laid down in a large

marquee in pitch blackness. John Cangley still stuck to me, and I shall always be grateful to him for doing so. I could perceive that most of the inmates of the marquee must be dead, because nobody talked or made a sound beyond an occasional groan, and I was afraid of being left alone as I was bleeding a good deal. Two stretcher-bearers came in carrying a tall man, and the flash of a torch revealed the crowns on the sleeves of a great-coat thrown over him. " Who have you got there ? " said a voice from the pitch darkness. " Must be old George Hindy," replied the owner of the torch. " He's dead too." Then from the far end of the marquee came a feeble effort in a well-known voice : " Old George Hindy's not dead yet ! " And so it turned out. Hindy was hit through the lungs. He and I were the only ones left alive out of the eleven. Hundreds of others were killed in other parts of the camp.

Thus Fate played its last little game with us. It looked too as if every move had been worked out and timed to a nicety. There was no compensating element about the beastly business either. It was not as if we had suffered these awful casualties in the heat of action, where there was a chance of giving back as good as we received. We had just been blown to smithereens like a shoal of fish by a depth-charge.

The killed included some fine men. The eight N.C.O.s who perished in our two tents wore between them seventeen decorations, including two D.C.M.s, one Médaille Militaire, one Croix de Guerre Française, one Croix de Guerre Belge, one Meritorious Service Medal, and one King's South African Medal. Young Waspe and I were the only two in the batch who had collected nothing more than the 1914 Star.

Soon lights were lit in the marquee, the living sorted out from among the dead, and a convoy of ambulances (which Frank Askey had fetched on his own initiative) conveyed us across to the 24th General Hospital. Here stretcher-bearers of the R.A.M.C. took us from the ambulances to carry us inside the Hospital. Two jabbering dwarfs caught hold of my stretcher and lifted it a couple of feet off the ground. Then they dropped it with a crash, and one of them turning to me exclaimed : " Blimy ! What weight are you ? " I did not enlighten him, but I asked him with all the politeness I could command to be kind enough to carry me head first, on account of my broken leg. But they would not hear of anything of the kind. The little swine bent down and lifted me up again. As they did so, my feet, which stuck out beyond the edge of the stretcher, caught in the seat of the imp in front. My leg got a violent twist, and he knew it, but it made absolutely no impression on him. I was thankful they had not to carry me far.

Once inside we went in turn straight on to the operating table, and I remember nothing more till I woke up next morning in a bed in one of the wards. My leg lay in splints between sand-bags, and my hand was bound on to a splint. The ward contained about forty beds, whose occupants were for the most part arm and leg cases.

I still felt no pain of any sort, but I was terribly weak and dazed from loss of blood and shock. The ward was a large wooden hut, beautifully clean and airy. The surgeon, Captain Noonan, had his own quarters outside, but he lived in the ward and slept in a corner bed. At all hours of the day and night he was up to his eyes in work, either in the theatre or alongside some poor fellow's bed. A fine fellow, he had been a Battalion Surgeon, but having been badly wounded in action, he had been put on hospital work. The nursing staff comprised two sisters, Brodie and Jones, and a V.A.D., Miss Blood. All seemed to be equally efficient, and between them they divided the day and night into three shifts of eight hours. Working without a break, and passing from patient to patient, it was just possible to dress each man's wounds once in twenty-four hours. They had, of course, all sorts of interruptions in their work, and, as many of the wounds were frightfully serious, deaths in the ward were frequent. Three men died in the beds next to mine in the first forty-eight hours.

After a couple of days the dreadful shadow began to pass ; deaths occurred less often, and men began to buck up a little and talk among themselves. It was soon rumoured among us that our Battalion Headquarters was anxious lest any men might be sent home who were in any sort of condition to

u

rejoin the battalion within a few days. One morning before very long an officer came into our ward to see things for himself. Captain Noonan and a sister were dressing a patient, but the officer absolutely ignored them and proceeded to saunter along from bed to bed, looking as black as thunder, and asking each of us what was the nature of his injury. His round of inspection finished, he walked out just as he had come in. Captain Noonan looked very peeved, and turning to me he asked: " Was that one of your officers?" "Yes, sir," I answered. "Hm," remarked the surgeon. " I wonder whether he's a very shy man or just a very ignorant one?" I could easily have enlightened him, but deemed it best to hold my tongue.

We remained nine days in the 24th General Hospital. Then an offensive started, and all of us who were considered out of danger were packed off to England to make room for the fresh stream of wounded.

XXXIV

IT was with deep regret that we left the 24th General Hospital. Our train to Boulogne was made up of cattle-trucks, inside which iron frames were fitted on which stretchers could be fixed. Sister Jones saw us off at daybreak.

In my truck were all sorts of wounded, including a few Germans. The crossing was uneventful, and that same evening I was trundled into the receiving-ward of the 'nth' London General Hospital. Old George Hindy was somewhere in the convoy, though at the time I was not aware of it. We were quickly sorted out, and two orderlies took me upstairs in a narrow lift, where they gave my leg a nasty twist. They lost their way, and took me to a face ward, where the hideous sights beneath the green shaded lights gave me quite a turn. Then came another corkscrew journey down in the lift, and eventually I was washed and tucked away in a ward.

Next morning I thought I had woke up in the monkey-house at the zoo. One-armed and one-legged soldiers in blue sat eating breakfast round a table. They did so to the accompaniment of a continual jabber, contorting their faces into the most weird grimaces. They turned out to be Newfoundlanders, and very decent fellows they were, too, when one got used to their simian habits.

Then followed three solid months in bed. I slept and slept day and night, only waking up for meals and visits to the operating theatre. I never knew George Hindy was in the Hospital till I heard of his death. It appears he was taken down into the grounds one fine afternoon to a garden fête. The journey in the lift was too much for him. The piece of metal in his lung moved, hæmorrhage set in, and he died within half an hour. I was now the sole survivor of the little party of N.C.O.s who were in the two ill-fated tents on 19 May.

In June 1918, the 'nth' London General Hospital contained fifteen hundred patients, of whom some twelve hundred were officers, located in bungalows in the grounds. The 'Tommies' occupied wards in the building, none of which were on the ground floor. Thus, when a Tommy started to walk with crutches and wished to go out into the grounds, he had to choose between begging a harassed, disobliging orderly to take him down in the lift, or else chance the winding stone stairs. Time and again men fell downstairs, and in some cases that meant anything up to a fresh amputation.

Our blue hospital suits were foul things. They were flung at us when we got up from bed, without any regard for fitting. By exchanging garments it was sometimes possible to build up a respectable outfit.

First-rate concerts took place weekly. Half an hour before the commencement, officers came hobbling along, each carrying two cushions, one for himself, the other for a nurse. No place was left for the Tommies. Any who were brave enough to go had to scramble on to the window-ledges and radiators, or hang on by their tails from the rafters.

It seems a mistake to have had officer and men patients in the same hospital. We could not help being Tommies, any more than they could help being officers, but the contrast was too violently marked at every turn.

The surgeons were a remarkably fine body of men. No job was too insignificant, and none too delicate or complicated for them. Great, cheerful, kind-hearted, courageous men, they gave us all of their best, without favour and without stint. To them the humblest Tommy was just as important a patient as the most senior officer.

For a long time my right hand was in a frightful mess. I tried writing with my left, but made no progress, so I wrote no letters, and in the end lost touch with everybody.

Bogey Giles came across from Knightsbridge every Sunday to visit me. Mr. Peat came once or twice. The greatest surprise in the way of visits was supplied by the appearance one Sunday of Major Barry, whom I had not seen since our last spell at Ypres with the limbers, in May

1915. He remembered distinctly every man, and every horse too, of our little column. It was good to live the old days over again, and to realize that they held pleasant memories of difficult work well done, for him as well as for me.

In October 1918 I was able to walk fairly well, if wearily and painfully, with the aid of a stick, and though my hand was still in a bad way, I was bundled off to a Convalescent Home in St. John's Wood. This place was a palace compared with the Hospital. There was plenty of room and plenty of good food. The one fly in the ointment was the Matron, Miss Gwendoline Dixie. I soon found myself in the soup with her. As luck would have it, I was the senior N.C.O. in the Home. On my arrival she summoned me to her office in order to enlighten me as to what my duties were. They were legion. The good lady expected to be treated like a Company Commander.

During my three-months' stay I never once brought a fellow-patient up before her for any reason. Soon she felt neglected, and told me one day in a rage that my predecessor, a Sergeant-Major of the Grenadier Guards, had some 'prisoners' for her every morning. "*He* was a soldier," she informed me, and then nearly burst when I replied : " Poor chap ! "

The men detested her, and played silly practical jokes which did not improve her temper. The limit was reached when some idiot stole into her office one day and fixed a needle in her chair. Nothing was heard of the fate of that needle for weeks. She was as thin as a whippet, without the faintest suggestion of a curve in her whole carcass. She might very easily have sat on the chair several times and missed the needle altogether. Then, one day, she felt some discomfort, was X-rayed, the needle located, and an operation performed for its removal.

The Matron was dancing-mad. The patients played on this weakness by inventing invitations to dances at Knightsbridge and elsewhere. This ruse was rumbled at length, and her temper became more and more threadbare.

On the morning of 11 November 1918 I was crossing London in a taxi to have my leg X-rayed, when suddenly, somewhere in the wilds of Battersea, a great commotion started in the streets. We pulled up to inquire the cause of the outburst, and were informed that the Armistice had been signed. The news had a stunning effect on me. I could not make head or tail of it. I was back at the Home for dinner. The Matron rushed into the dining-room with a gale of wind in her cap, announced the glad tidings, and called on me to stand up and propose the King's health. As there was nothing stronger than water available or forthcoming, I refused, greatly to her annoyance.

I was glad when, one day in February 1919, a message came from the old 'nth' London General Hospital, saying an Army Educational scheme was about to be launched, and asking if I was prepared to accept employment at the Hospital centre. Needless to say, I jumped at the offer. The Matron was overjoyed at the prospect of getting rid of me.

Before leaving the Home I had a surprise. I had always impressed on the other patients that I would not tolerate any goings-on which might get the servants into a row. They were all jolly decent girls, especially Margaret, the senior. Before leaving I went below stairs to say good-bye to them. Margaret was not there. I had never spoken above half a dozen words to her, and might have cleared off without seeing her. I was making for the front door when Margaret suddenly appeared from nowhere, made straight at me, and, throwing all discretion to the winds, flung her arms round my neck and kissed me. Before I was aware what had happened she had disappeared down the stairs. I felt a bit confused, but at the same time touched and pleased. I felt that the line of conduct I had steadfastly pursued and enforced during my stay was completely justified.

Back at the old Hospital I found things humming. Two or three officers, university men and schoolmasters, had got together and were starting to build up an educational centre. They received me like a brother. Very soon I found myself up to my neck in both office and class-room. Our students were drawn from the hundreds of young men whose education had been interrupted by the war. Many wanted to matriculate. Others were anxious to take examinations of the various professional and commercial bodies. For my part, besides office work, which, as the only typist on the staff, fell largely to my share, I had classes in German, French, English, Mathematics, Geography, History, and Book-keeping. This period of hard work, from January 1919 to January 1921, was of untold benefit to me, so much so that I completely forgot my physical disabilities, almost forgot I was still in the Army.

Towards the end of 1919 I ceased to be a patient, though I continued to be employed at the Hospital Educational Centre. On donning khaki again I felt I had made a considerable step forward. I had to report immediately at Knightsbridge Barracks, and here I did business for the last time with my dear old friend, the Orderly Room Sergeant. He had grown stouter during his three years' holiday at Rouen, but he was still brisk and had lost nothing of the Gordon Selfridge manner. My visit resulted in my becoming supernumerary to the establishment of the Regiment, a sort of excrescence, who just wore the regimental badge and drew his pay weekly on a Friday.

The ensuing summer found me undergoing a course at the Army School of Education. I determined to treat the month as a holiday, so in company with a fellow-student of the Royal Horse Artillery I consumed much excellent beer and walked many miles over the pleasant surrounding country. Each student was supposed to specialize in some particular branch. I was by way of being a modern language expert. My friend of the Horse Gunners was completely neutral, so we both decided to make an intensive study of Social Science.

Our subsequent investigations into this absorbing subject afforded us much merriment. Our lecturer was the School Commandant, and I'm afraid we often side-tracked him rather barefacedly into discussing all sorts of things which concerned neither ourselves nor the School syllabus.

The modern language students took themselves and their job seriously, so I had a narrow escape. One of their leading lights was quartered in my hut. While on the Rhine he had purchased an ancient German Dictionary as big as a gravestone. Every evening he lugged out this gigantic tome, sat on his bed, and learned a new page of words before lights out. He was a Scot named MacWillie, which he pronounced MacWoolly, making it sound much more fitting.

The course finished, I returned to the Hospital with a good report, and feeling much better for my holiday, buckled into the job of typing myriads of applications for patients wishing to be interviewed by a Re-settlement Board. Many of the applicants seemed to do quite well out of it. Realizing that without a university degree my chances of getting into the teaching profession were very slim, I decided to ask for an interview myself, with a view to securing a four-years' course at a university. The interview took place at an hotel in the Strand. I was politely but firmly told that as a pre-war regular soldier I did not come within the scope of the re-settlement scheme.

A rumour now was floating around to the effect that the War Office was contemplating the formation of an Army Educational Corps, so I resolved to begin work at once on my own account for a degree at the University of London, with a view to transferring to the Corps if and when it was formed. It came into being about the end of 1920, and I applied at once. A medical board examined me and, not taking any notice of my hand and leg, passed me as A.1. When the list of appointments was published I was included in it with the rank of Sergeant. That was an Irishman's rise with a vengeance—from sergeant in the first regiment of the service in 1914 to sergeant in the very last in 1921. However, I was now a fixture in the Army. That meant bread and butter, and time in which to work for my degree. Having obtained that, and acquired a good reputation, I might perhaps hope for promotion in a couple of years.

My first appointment as Sergeant Instructor, Army Educational Corps, was to Millbank Barracks. On reporting for duty I found my predecessors in the act of clearing out. They comprised a Captain, a Lieutenant, a Sergeant, and a V.A.D. typist. They all professed to feel sorry for me, and predicted an early breakdown under pressure of work. However, day succeeded day, and not a shred of correspondence ever came into the office. The entire number of men for school never mustered more than ten. For an hour every afternoon I taught them the rudiments of Arithmetic and some spelling. I was able to devote the whole of my mornings to my studies in absolute comfort. But what a beano the old firm must have had!

Somewhere about the middle of 1921, the General commanding the London District recommended me strongly for a commission in the Corps. It was too late. Everything was now cut and dried, and I must just wait.

A young Staff-Captain paid me a visit in the autumn. It seemed the Welsh Guards at Chelsea Barracks wanted an Instructor. He enlarged upon the advantages of working with a battalion of Guards, and persuaded me my talents were being wasted at Millbank. Before leaving, he had succeeded in convincing me that Chelsea Barracks was a paradise and the Welsh Guards a community of angels, so I consented to fill the vacancy.

On a certain afternoon soon after this visit I reported for duty at Chelsea Barracks. On seeing me for the first time, the R.S.M. of the Welsh Guards promptly put me under open arrest for being improperly dressed. In the next half-hour I ran across him again two or three times and was promptly placed under open arrest on each occasion for something quite new and original to me. Rather a hospitable sort of cove, I thought. Being under open arrest meant also being confined to barracks.

By a stroke of good luck I was able to get a message away to the young Staff-Captain before the end of the afternoon, telling him what a promising start I had made. At 6 p.m. I walked out of the Barracks. Next morning I returned about 9 a.m. and got on with some work in the office. Nobody took the slightest notice of me, and henceforth the R.S.M. left me absolutely in peace.

The R.S.M. of the Welsh Guards wore the ribbons of the D.C.M. and M.M., and had proved himself a magnificent soldier in the war. When I knew him in 1922 he bore about the same resemblance to the average R.S.M. as Will

Hay does to the average schoolmaster. If he had thought
of going on the stage with a squad of recruits, and behaving
there as he did on the Barrack square, he would have been
famous and wealthy in a couple of weeks. He very nearly
turned my predecessor's hair white. The latter was a
Warrant Officer with little experience in the army. Just the
type the old R.S.M. loved. The R.S.M. would hide behind
a corner when he saw him coming, wait till he drew level
or had just gone past, then jump into the air and scream :
" Swing your arms there, that Warrant Officer ! Quick
time !   Left ! Right ! Left ! Right ! " And so he would
carry on till the poor devil bolted like a rabbit in through
the door of the Education Office. At other times the
R.S.M. would stand and glare at him through the office
window till he nearly drove him crazy.

After a strenuous year, which I would not have missed
for anything owing to the very decent treatment I always
received at the hands of the officers of the Welsh Guards,
and particularly from Mr. Robinson, the Education Officer,
I discovered that the Life Guards (1st and 2nd had now
been made into one regiment) at Regent's Park required an
Instructor. I applied, was transferred, and found to my
joy that Charlie Wright was R.S.M. of the new formation,
or malformation. Educational work here was child's play
after Chelsea.

The old Barracks were full of memories and associations.
Outwardly they were exactly as they had been back in 1912
when I last saw them. But the barrack-rooms housed a
brand-new generation of men, and in the stables were
horses which were complete strangers. In the same old
corner stood the canteen. It was as dead as a doornail,
though it was still possible to obtain beer in what remained
of it. Some four or five of the older Troopers, including
my two friends from the limber-column, Dumbrill and
Johnny Oram, were the only clients. They looked a forlorn
little group as they emerged from the old haunt every
morning when the trumpet sounded ' Stables,' the last
survivors of two dead regiments and of a regime that had
passed away for ever. With traditions clashing at every
turn, Charlie Wright had a difficult course to steer. Any

other R.S.M. might have caused serious chaos, and himself come a cropper in the process.

I was now very comfortable and was making good progress towards my degree at the university. Everything went smoothly, till in the summer of 1923 an officer made an inspection of all Educational Corps activities in the London District. He called one afternoon to make the acquaintance of our Commanding Officer, who was, of course, not in Barracks at that time. He was short and stoutish, rather like the figure of Napoleon at Madame Tussaud's. His uniform was lumpy in the region of the abdomen and about the calves. He wore field-boots, spurs with plenty of chain, and a tremendous cavalry sword whose hilt chafed him under the arm-pit, while the shoe of the scabbard dragged on the ground. To me he looked like a stout pink cabbage with two shifty eyes and lashed round the middle to a slender prop. He bade me conduct him to the Orderly Room. The place was empty save for Charlie Wright. Never having seen a soldier of Charlie's stamp, he advanced into the room, halted with a loud banging of heels, and mistaking Charlie for the C.O., gave him a pukka parade-ground salute. Charlie gravely returned the compliment, and then said with a twinkle in his eye which evoked an answering twinkle in mine : " You mustn't do that, sir, I'm the Sergeant-Major." The officer was embarrassed and looked ugly.

That October the Life Guards went to Windsor, and I was left behind as Instructor with the Blues. With them I was exceedingly happy, till in November 1923 I received orders to be ready to proceed to India, as my name stood at the head of the foreign service roster. I tried hard to find some reason for this sudden jerk, and could discover none except that wretched salute somebody gave Charlie Wright. However, by a series of wangles, I dodged my trip to the East both that trooping-season and the next.

The Life Guards returned from Windsor in 1925, and I passed my final degree examination with second-class honours in German the same June. I had been promoted to Warrant Officer, and was quite happy with my old friends, when the orders for India came again in November.

Charlie Wright and I talked the situation over, and decided that it would be madness to throw away all my work and let myself be buried alive in India for the next five or six years. His opinion was that I should obtain a post in a school outside, then quit the Army for good. Within a month I had secured an appointment as modern language master at a secondary school. A fortnight later I left the service, a free man. On the day of my discharge orders reached the regiment for my despatch to the Depot of the A.E.C. for preparation for my move out to India. They went back by the next post, together with the shattering information that I had just become a civilian.

Realizing that I was on the threshold of a brand-new career which would call for all my energies and abilities if I was to make good in it, I banished from my mind all regrets at quitting the service. During the best years of my life I had given to it the best that was in me, and received precious little in return. I would gladly go through it all again for the sake of the good times spent in company of the great fellows of all ranks who were my comrades.

Index

317